Til far og mor

Contents

Series Editor's Preface

In *The Missionary, the Catechist, and the Hunter: Foucault, Protestantism, and Colonialism,* Christina Petterson examines the role that religion plays in the Danish colonization of Greenland. She examines the mechanism by which the Danish spread Lutheranism among the indigenous (Inuit) population, paying special attention to inequalities of class, race and gender. Central to this process were Catechists, non-ordained assistants to missionaries, who were trained and educated by them, and helped spread Christianity. Petterson uses critical categories in her analysis of religion namely Foucault's concepts of governmentality and pastoral power. This enables her to demonstrate how the process of colonization is not simply economic or political but it entrails a process of subjectification where the identity of indigenous population is transformed. The book is an excellent example of critical research on religion and thus fits well into the series.

Warren S. Goldstein, Ph.D.
Center for Critical Research on Religion
www.criticaltheoryofreligion.org

Acknowledgements

This project began as a doctoral thesis in what was then the Department of Media, Music and Cultural Studies at Macquarie University in Sydney, Australia. It was completed as a book in Germany, where I lived and worked as a postdoctoral fellow at the *Graduirten-kolleg 'Geschlecht als Wissens-kategorie'* at Humboldt University in Berlin. I would like to thank series editor Warren S. Goldstein and Production Editor Michael J. Mozina for their hard work and valuable assistance in the publication of the book.

The research took shape in Australia, Europe, and in the Arctic, and in each place, I incurred many professional, personal, and material debts. First, I would like to thank my supervisors, Goldie Osuri, Anthony Lambert, and especially Anne Cranny-Francis. My deep gratitude also goes out to my assessors, Lyn McCredden (Deakin University, Australia), Søren Thuesen (Copenhagen University, Denmark), and Lars Jensen (Roskilde University, Denmark) for their enormous encouragement and constructive criticism. I am also grateful for the support, interest, and generosity of the staff and my fellow students in the Department of Media, Music and Cultural Studies, in particular Nicole Matthews, Jon Seltin, Maria Giannacopoulos, Elaine Kelly, Elaine Laforteza, Holly Randell-Moon, Gretchen Riordan, Nikki Sullivan, Jessica Cadwallader, and, from the Department of Anthropology, Lisa Wynn.

During my visits to Greenland, I enjoyed the kind hospitality of *Ilisimatursarfik* (the University of Greenland). Colleagues who had a direct influence on my work through conversations, discussions, feedback on papers, and so on, include Birgit Kleist Pedersen, Karen Langgård, Birgitte Jakobsen, Jette Rygaard, Gitte Tròndheim, Inge Seiding, Kathrine and Thorkild Kjærgaard, and Mariekathrine Poppel, as well as my former students, who all took a great interest in my work. The Greenlandic Archives, and archivists Niels Frandsen and Ole Christiansen, helped enormously by providing access to manuscripts, extended hours, and plenty of coffee. I would also like to extend a warm thank-you to Finn Lynge for his encouragement and kindness.

The Department of Arctic Studies at Copenhagen University provided me with hospitality in a highly authentic setting during my stays in Denmark, including generous access to a truly remarkable library housed in old warehouses on the very dock where the whaling ships from Greenland once offloaded their precious cargos.

Colleagues and friends in Greenland and Denmark helped me by scanning articles, dissertations, and book excerpts. For this assistance, I am particularly indebted to Søren Holst, Hans-Jørgen Wallin Weihe, Birgit Kleist Pedersen,

Flemming A. J. Nielsen, Inge Seiding, Kennet Petersen, Katrine Kjærgaard, Bolette Olsen, and Lise Uhrskov (for her long-distance archive checks). Then there were those who took the time to answer my emails, in particular Matt Chrulew, Henrik Wilhjelm, Birgitte Sonne, Mette Rønsager, and the staff at the Department of Arctic Studies.

I would also like to express my deep gratitude to a number of people who demonstrated confidence in my academic abilities and provided me in so many different ways with the opportunity and support to pursue my research: Lone Fatum, Kirsten Thisted, Lars Jensen, Jorunn Økland, Jacqueline Lo, Stefanie von Schnurbein, and Christina von Braun.

Finally, on a more personal level, there were all those patient people who simply listened: my family and friends in Denmark; my family and friends in Australia; Gillian Townsley; and, above all, Roland.

Berlin
July 11, 2013

Notes on Previously Published Material

Parts of chapter 1 have been published as 'Colonialism and Orthodoxy in Greenland' in *Postcolonial Studies* 15/1 (2012): 69–86

Parts of chapters 2 and 3 have been published as 'Colonial Subjectification: Foucault, Christianity and Governmentality' in *Cultural Studies Review* 18/2: *Secular Discomforts: Religion and Cultural Studies*: 89–108.

Chapter 4, section 1 (1. *Writing, Gender and Abstraction*) also appears in *Acts of Empire. The Acts of the Apostles and Imperial Ideology,* Taiwan: 2012.

Parts of chapter 5 have been published as 'Colonialism, Anthropology and Exceptionalism' in Lars Jensen and Kristín Loftsdóttir (eds.) *Whiteness and Postcolonialism in the Nordic Region: Exceptionalism, Migrant Others and National Identities,* London: Ashgate: 29–42.

Introduction

In Nuuk, the capital of Greenland, a statue of Hans Egede looks out over the ocean from atop a small hill. Egede was the Norwegian-Danish minister and missionary credited with bringing Christianity to Greenland in 1721. To his left, facing the sea, is *Kolonihavnen*, the colonial harbour in the historic district of Nuuk. Here, ships would arrive laden with supplies, and leave with the precious commodities, such as sealskins, whalebone, and whale blubber in such high demand in eighteenth-century Europe. Today, *Kolonihavnen* no longer operates as a harbour, and the National Museum of Greenland occupies the nearby old warehouses. Hans Egede's own yellow house from 1728 still stands in this district, a rare stone dwelling among all the wooden houses of blue, red, yellow and green. Today the Greenlandic government uses it as venue for receptions. Behind the statue, at the foot of the hill, is a big red wooden cathedral, *Vor Frelser kirke* (Our Saviour Church). The building adjacent to the church, today the bishop's residence, was the site of Greenland's first catechist college. It was here that indigenous catechists,[1] who came to play such a crucial cultural and political role in modern Greenland, were educated. On the other side of the cathedral is the grey wooden house that in the mid-nineteenth century was the home of the Inspector of Southern Greenland, the highest civil authority in the colony. Apart from the Inspector, the building also housed the first printing press and the first newspaper, *Atuagagdliutit* which was produced so that the Greenlanders would be entertained by reading stories about themselves and others. Today, the building is home to the Danish High Commissioner to Greenland. A short walk away, near the new city centre, is *Brættet*, the market where hunters and fishermen sell their catch.

This short walk takes in a number of significant places and institutions that I will analyse and discuss in the following pages, and it illustrates the interconnectedness of institutions and powers that we usually regard as discrete and unconnected. The mystification of neoliberalism and its economic system, capitalism, maintains that there is no connection between the civil authorities, the church, and the hunters. I will assume, however, that this logic attempts to obscure the systemic and symbolic levels of practices and ideologies, to cover them over with a smooth, unblemished surface. In this book, I will probe

1 A catechist is a non-ordained assistant to a minister who helps teach catechism, the basic and systematic exposition of the truths of the Christian faith. In Greenland, catechists were hired early on from the indigenous population to assist in instructing Greenlanders.

beneath this surface and cast light on the links between the Inspector, the church, and the hunters' market, and their effect on Greenlandic society.

My focus will be on the connections between Christianity and colonialism, highlighting the role of Lutheranism and its assumptions of race and gender in the colonial project. I will argue that the missionary was in charge of more than just such superficial elements of Christianity as converting 'pagans' and conducting services; he also introduced a social morality, framed within a patriarchal social order, that, thereby creating subjects from and according to this morality. This deeper and subjectifying function of Christianity will be brought to the fore in the analyses, and I will show how it slips into the background once its task is complete. This is where the printing press and the hunter's market then enter the story. The initial stages of colonialism focused on disrupting the hunting practices of the indigenous society while honing them to ensure maximum productivity, and then paving the way for different modes of interaction, exchange, and practice; in effect, this was the same process simultaneously visited upon the peasant population of Europe, namely, so-called primitive accumulation.

The implementation of these different modes of interaction, exchange, and practice took place in the course of the nineteenth century, when a substantial number of Greenlandic men born to Danish fathers take centre stage as indigenous catechists. The practice of recruiting catechists from the local population had already been in place for more than a century; what changed in the mid-nineteenth century was the establishment of catechist colleges to educate primarily those 'mixed' Greenlandic men of reputable heritage. The introduction of education coincided with the establishment of the printing press, which I will argue recast the Greenlandic society *in writing*. As part of their education, the men learned to express themselves in writing, which as a technique of abstraction and objectification profoundly affected the way in which they viewed the world and their fellow Greenlanders. One result of this process was the hunter, who became the quintessential Greenlandic identity and served as *the* connection between nature and indigeneity. The ideological force of this stereotypical image cannot be underestimated; it is still present today, and bedevils indigenous politics as well as 'Western' conceptions of indigenous peoples. What follows is, by way of introduction, an example.

Approaching Christianity and Colonialism

The feature film *Heart of Light* premiered in 1997, and was marketed as the first Greenlandic movie ever made; it was filmed in Greenland with Greenlandic actors speaking Greenlandic, and one of the two scriptwriters was a Greenlandic playwright. The film was well received by critics, and selected for the prestigious Sundance Film Festival in 1999. At the 12th Nordic Film Festival in Nuuk, a German film distributor enthusiastically proclaimed that the movie portrayed the "authentic" Greenland. However, the younger Greenlandic generation was not impressed. They felt that the movie did not express *their* understanding of the "authentic" Greenland (Rygaard and Pedersen 2003, 176). The younger generation simply could not see any points of identification with their own lives, either in the film's 'present' or in its 'past.'

If a similar analysis had been carried out with an audience from an older Greenlandic generation, the reaction would presumably have been different. The students who participated in Rygaard and Pedersen's project would all have grown up under the Greenlandic Home Rule Government, implemented in 1979. However, the older generation (including scriptwriter Hans Anton Lynge), were raised during the 1950s and 1960s, and schooled in Danish values and Denmark's valuation of the Greenlandic past; they would have seen this movie as an active reclamation of that past. The film's representation of the present, so unrecognisable to the younger audience, would perhaps have been quite in line with the memories and impressions of the older generation and its political disillusionment with the Danish Commonwealth. This very disillusionment is conveyed through the lead character, Rasmus, and his journey though the depths of despair before he begins to reclaim his pride. Through flashbacks, we come to understand that as a boy in the late 1940s, Rasmus was part of a generation that witnessed the Danish industrialisation of Greenland. We follow a man who goes from emasculated and pathetic to 're-masculated' and proud. We are invited to join a Greenlandic man in his 50s on a long journey home.

While I do not want to deny the liberating potential of the film, or its importance for articulating collective traumas arising from colonial violence, I would nonetheless suggest that it conceals some fundamental issues relating to power and representation in a colonial context—issues that remain unresolved. In an analysis of the film in chapter six, I speak of Rasmus as a social *bricolage*. Born into the Greenlandic elite, he is nevertheless drunk and unemployed when we first encounter him in the film; yet he emerges at the end as a proud hunter. He thus represents, at various stages, different classes in Greenland: the bourgeoisie, the socio-economic underclass, and then, of course, the hunter.

Another group of students, this one composed of Danish university students, also saw the film and loved it—except for one small detail. The event that sets in motion the narrative of the film is the suicide of Rasmus's son Niisi after he shoots and kills two other young people at a party. A funeral service for the young people is held in a church, where the minister gives a sermon and the congregation sings a Greenlandic hymn. The Danish students found this very odd in a film that presents itself as Greenlandic. Kirsten Thisted, who taught the class, noted that Christianity was for the students almost synonymous with Danish imperialism, and the Greenlanders themselves would most certainly regard this as a foreign element (2003, 32–33).

The reactions to the film indicate two important developments that I trace in this study. First there is the implementation of pastoral power, that particular way of governing by means of subjectification, with roots in the pastoral care of Judaism and Christianity, identified by French philosopher Michel Foucault. I trace the entrenchment of pastoral power in Greenlandic society and its outcomes, which are *not* religious, thus showcasing the point of departure in Louis Althusser's essay on marriage (1997, 231), that "the more the Church is entrenched in the state, and the more deeply it finds itself engaged in the state-controlled administration of souls, the less it needs religion." I will argue that the missionaries inculcated an understanding of self that was conditioned by the Lutheran social structure and its regimes of subjectification.

The other development I trace in this study is what I call *the ontological status of the hunter*, by which I mean the abstracted hunter identity that grew out of the various literary projects generated by the recording and publication in the mid-nineteenth century of Greenlandic oral traditions. I argue that the introduction of alphabetic writing, and the education of segments of Greenland's population according to Western standards of rationality and self-perception, generated an abstracted understanding of the world of hunting and 'nature,' and estrangement from it. This is signalled in the following quotation by catechist Niels Lynge in 1911 (in Wilhjelm 2008, 510): "The one who lives as a hunter, thinks like a hunter and the one who lives as a catechist, thinks like a catechist".[2] The quotation is the result of the racial politics and social administration of the Danish colonial power, and its fostering of a group of Greenlanders, the catechists, who were to become part of the ruling class of later Greenlandic society. This particular argument is not new, and has been made both in relation to Greenland and other instances of colonialism.[3]

2 Unless otherwise stated, all translations from the Danish are my own.

3 The establishment of a mixed-race elite was convincingly argued in relation to Greenland by anthropologist Hans-Erik Rasmussen (1982, 1983, 1986a, 1986b, 1986c) and in relation to colonialism in general by students of Spanish colonialism (Arias 2009; Beverley 2009) and French colonialism (Jennings 2004; Peterson and Brown 1985; White 1999).

Where the present work differs is in its goal to emphasise the role of the missionaries in the colonial project; I aim to explore the links between the mission and the colonial administration without treating them as discrete groups, a common approach of missionary studies[4] and many colonial analyses.[5] Most works dealing with colonialism see the mission and the colonial administration as discrete groups, with few exploring the systemic links between them.[6] An example of this approach may be inferred from the following excerpt from the introduction to the anthology *Converting Colonialism: Visions and Realities in Mission History, 1706–1914,* edited by Dana Lee Robert:

> Forced to operate within a political framework of European expansionism that lay outside their power to control, missionaries and early converts variously attempted to co-opt aspects of colonialism deemed compatible with missionary goals, and to change what seemed prejudicial to gospel values.
>
> 2008, 3

It is presumed from the outset that the missionaries and the early converts stand outside (yet within) colonialism, and *approach* it either positively

4 For studies of missions that attempt to undermine the relation between Christianity and colonialism, see Marion Grau (2011), John D. Blanco (2009), and Joel W. Martin and Mark A. Nicholas (2010).

5 Exceptions to this approach come from the field of anthropology, with the Comaroffs' *Of Revelation and Revolution* providing the study *sine qua non* of the socializing role of missionaries in the colonial field. See Jean Comaroff and John Comaroff (1991, 1997), Rita Smith Kipp (1990), Peter van der Veer (2001), and of course Vicente Rafael (1988), which is a historical/anthropological study. The theoretical sophistication of the work of the Comaroffs, however, does not extend to, for example, the studies of Kipp or van der Veer. This lack of theoretical engagement leaves important complexities such as race, class, and gender unexamined. A similar critique may be made of Carla Gardina Pestana's 2009 historical study, *Protestant Empire: Religion and the Making of the British Atlantic World.*

6 There are, however, several dissertations which address Christianity's disciplinary role in colonialism in Canada. See Chad M. Waucaush, "Becoming Christian, Remaining Ojibwe: The Emergence of Native American Protestant Christianity in the Great Lakes, 1820–1900" (Michigan State University, 2009); Eric Porter, "The Anglican Church and Native Education: Residential Schools and Assimilation" (University of Toronto, 1981); Tannis Peikoff, "Anglican Missionaries and Governing the Self: An Encounter with Aboriginal Peoples in Western Canada, 1820–1865" (University of Manitoba, 2002). See also John S. Milloy (1999) and the 2001 report by Rev. Kevin D. Annett, "Hidden From History: The Canadian Holocaust—The Untold Story of the Genocide of Aboriginal Peoples by Church and State in Canada—A Summary of an Ongoing, Independent Inquiry into Canadian Native 'Residential Schools' and their Legacy."

(co-opt it) or negatively (change it) from an external value system. I find this distinction problematic because it holds the individual missionary responsible and accountable while ignoring the deeper systemic relations between Christianity, race, class, and domination.[7]

A useful way to avoid this trap is through the use of Foucault's analysis of governmentality—the encounter between technologies of domination with technologies of self—developed in a complex genealogy in his lectures at *Collège de France* in 1977–78 (2007). I apply this theoretical framework to analyse the training of the catechists and their relationship to writing, thus using Foucault to critique separations of colonial and missionary agency. I also argue that the subjectification strategies used to create civil subjects are necessarily Protestant. By approaching governmentality and its relationship to pastoral power as a critique of secularisation theories, I thus draw out the particular Lutheran Protestant inflection of Danish colonialism and its civilising project. One of the most successful outcomes of this project is the ontological status of the hunter, which became cemented as the quintessential Greenlandic figure and led to reactions such as those of the Danish students, who see Christianity as an unauthentic element of Greenlandic life. However, unlike Ann Fienup-Riordan and others who see Eskimo-as-Hunter as a Western stereotype of Arctic indigenous people(1995, 5), I argue that this stereotype is the result of a long process of identity and class struggles *within* the Greenlandic community, albeit instigated by the colonial administration and its modes of pastoral subjectification techniques. It is this paradoxical process I address in the present study.

Motivation

The incentive for this research relates to John Beverley's observation in a different (Spanish) colonial context, namely that:

> Seeing the *criollos*, and the new mixed or *mestizo* population, as the main cultural actors in the formation of a properly 'national' culture was (and

7 The systemic relation between Christianity and race is central to two important studies: J. Kameron Carter's *Race: A Theological Account* (2008) and Willie James Jennings's *The Christian Imagination: Theology and the Origins of Race* (2010). Both of these studies are theoretically informed and theologically committed studies of the relation between race and theology within a specific African-American theological, historical, and cultural context. While my study does deploy racial analysis, and critically analyses the function of race within a Christian colonial context, my aim is neither to provide a genealogy of racism in Christian theology, nor to seek a way beyond it. Race is, along with gender, an important tool in generating a class of Greenlanders, but it is not an end of this study.

> is) at the expense of the exclusion or marginalisation of the population that were actually colonised ...
>
> BEVERLEY 2009, p. 541; emphasis in original

With few exceptions, most studies on Greenlandic perspectives of Danish colonial practices have focused on Greenland's elite, which consisted mainly—but not exclusively—of Greenlanders from marriages between Danish men and Greenlandic women.[8] Within literary studies, this is partly due to the tremendous success of postcolonial theory and its focus on hybridity, a feature particularly evident in the prolific work of literary scholar Kirsten Thisted (see, for example, 2002, 2003, 2004b, 2006a, 2006b), and to a certain extent in the work of linguist Karen Langgård (2004, 2008a). It is also partly due to the fact that the cultural elite is the most visible group, socially and historically. As it had access early on to higher education, this group also left behind written works and journals. This visibility has also had a significant impact on historical research, where the focus tends to be overwhelmingly on educated men, especially catechists, as in the works of Arctic scholar Søren Thuesen and theologian Henrik Wilhjelm. Mette Rønsager's thesis (2006) on the West-Greenlandic midwives remains, to some extent, within this group of studies by focusing on the elite/'mixed' group,[9] but it also moves beyond it by focusing on women, who are not usually visible actors.[10]

While the present research owes much to the analyses, archival excavations, and translations in these studies, it nevertheless focuses more on the *processes* conditioned by the colonial encounter.[11] Having worked through the material, I find it fascinating to observe how the colonial administration, Danish research, and current Greenlandic politics all systematically exclude from their

8 Not all children of Danish-Greenlandic relationships were, however, part of the elite. I shall return to this point in chapter five.

9 Rønsager notes that Greenlandic women from the group of "primary producers," i.e. hunters and fishermen, were trained as midwives in Greenland, while 'mixed women from the elite were trained and educated in Denmark from the mid-1830s (2006, 4).

10 An important exception is the current and intriguing work of archivist and PhD candidate Inge Høst Seiding and her thesis on colonial marriages and marital relations between Greenlandic women and European men. Seiding's case studies are based on extensive archival research and cut across all social strataifications.

11 In the Greenlandic context, I thus follow in the footsteps of anthropologist Hans-Erik Rasmussen (1982, 1983, 1986a, 1986b, 1986c) and anthropologists Thomas Kring Lauridsen and Kasper Lytthans (1983). In the broader colonial context, I follow anthropological scholars such as Jean and John Comaroff (1991, 1997) and Ann Laura Stoler (1995, 2002, 2009).

spheres of concern those men who are *not* hunters or catechists, thus ignoring a large number of disenfranchised men, or marginalising them as an isolated social problem. This exclusion takes place without any analysis of some of the mechanisms that generated this group in the first place.[12] This is one of the objectives of the present work; I draw attention to these men by highlighting the differentiation processes within the colonial society and pointing to how colonial politics privileged a few acceptable identities while excluding others.

I should also clarify what this work is not: It is not a study of the Greenlandic appropriation or subversion of Christianity, nor is it an analysis of the status of the Greenlandic religion alongside, behind, or within Christianity.[13] It *is* a study into how Lutheran Protestant Christianity changed Greenlanders' understanding of self and society—in other words, the subjectification techniques of Lutheran Protestantism, and their effect on Greenlandic society. Furthermore, although I draw upon several disciplines, including anthropology, sociology, history, and literature, this study is neither an anthropological/sociological study about Greenlanders and their society, nor a historical/literary analysis. My objective is to identify the Danish implementation of power and the social rearrangements brought about to ensure that this implementation took place in the most profitable way. To this end, I use these various tools in an interdisciplinary fashion because all these disciplines played an important part in shaping the Danish scholarly images of Greenland and its colonial history. Thus a reassessment of this colonial history, which puts Protestant assumptions of colonisation in the foreground, necessarily entails a sustained argument with the various processes of learning.

---

12 An exception is the work of sociologist Mariekathrine Poppel (2005a, 2005b) on masculinity and violence.

13 Christianity plays an important role in Greenland. In her 2009 thesis, Kathrine Kjærgaard argues that in the course of a couple of decades, the missionaries succeeded through various means (images, sounds, rituals, words, and architecture) to disseminate the view among Greenlanders that not only the Greenlandic people, but also their country was part of God's creation. According to Kjærgaard, this resulted in the conquering of Greenlanders' imagination and innermost feelings by the great biblical storyline, "with themselves as participants" (2009, 26). An example of this is the Greenlandic Christmas hymn Guuterput qutsinnermiu (Our God in the Highest), written ca. 1907 by Rasmus Berthelsen, a prominent member of the Greenlandic intelligentsia. The hymn is a rewriting of Gloria in Excelsis, the song of the angels announcing the birth of Christ in Luke 2:14. In Berthelsen's exquisite composition, the Greenlandic congregation takes the place of the angels and sings the announcement to the shepherds. Berthelsen thus brings the congregation into the biblical story, and pronounces the birth of Christ in Greenlandic. See Petterson (2008).

Lastly, and most importantly: How does this study situate itself within the field of indigenous studies, indigenous research, and indigenous politics? In Australia, it has become good etiquette to begin a ceremony or the public reading of a paper by acknowledging the traditional owners of the land. Macquarie University, for example, says on its website that the university is situated on Darug land.[14] However, as indigenous activists from the Aboriginal Tent Embassy in Canberra point out, this is a convenient way of not recognising indigenous *sovereignty*:[15] "Everywhere in society the Government is telling you that it acknowledges you as the TRADITIONAL OWNERS, that's because it doesn't want to acknowledge you as the rightful lawful sovereign title holder of your land."[16] This distinction between the legal and the purely ceremonial ownership of Australia, and what it actually means for the place of indigenous Australians within Australian society, is an example of the eye-opening arguments that impacted me directly in the course of writing my thesis on Greenland in Australia. It was here that my attention was drawn to the commodification of privileged indigenous identities, which can suffocate or severely limit the possibilities for indigenous activism. While some have commented on my seemingly bizarre geographical context—the two locations are almost directly opposite each other on the globe—it gave me the privilege of distance and a new context for understanding the complexities of colonial societies, the limits of postcolonial analysis, and the machinations of capitalism and its seemingly endless ability to expand and reproduce itself. The work of Aileen Moreton-Robinson, who speaks of postcoloni*zing* rather than postcolonial to denote "the active, the current and the continuing nature of the colonizing relationship that positions [Indigenous people] as belonging but not belonging" (2003, 38), was quite a revelation in regards to an indigenous perspective on the actual possibilities for postcolonial theory. In addition, the act of processing the work of activist film director Warwick Thornton[17] and artists Richard Bell and Gordon Hookey on the commodification of aboriginal art and spirituality have had a significant impact on shaping the argument of this book.

---

14 http://mq.edu.au/about/profile/welcometocountry.html, accessed 19 April 2012.

15 Indigenous sovereignty in Australia is a large topic. See Pratt (2003) and Moreton-Robinson (2004, 2007). The Internet is an important source for indigenous activism. See http://treatyrepublic.net/ and http://www.kooriweb.org/, both accessed 19 April 2012.

16 https://www.facebook.com/pages/Aboriginal-Tent-Embassy/210730945611610 from 19 April 2012, accessed 19 April 2012.

17 I am referring of course to Thornton's stunning 2009 feature film *Samson and Delilah* and his 2002 short film *Mimi*. Both films forcefully address the relation between white people and aboriginal art.

I believe that there are several ways of showing solidarity with indigenous people and the social problems generated by colonialism. Danish-Greenlandic colonial history, with its unequal power relations, has had a powerful and deep-seated history of effects. I have chosen to emphasise how such power structures were cultivated, managed, and appropriated. This means that I have consciously chosen not to focus on resistance and subversion, but this does *not* mean that I find such an approach insignificant or unimportant. My focus is based on the observation that such work is being carried out as part of the postcolonial agenda, while the kind of analysis I have embarked on has seemed less attractive, but remains, in my opinion, equally important. What this research ultimately seeks to accomplish is contribute to the dismantling of the Danish colonial attitude by drawing out the processes of its construction. An important step in this direction is the task of turning a critical eye to the part, not usually recognized, that Christianity played in the construction of colonial Greenlandic culture.

Theoretical Framework

As mentioned above, this book's theoretical framework is informed by Foucault's concept of governmentality, a term he uses to designate the art of governing associated with liberalism, as distinct from the command-and-law structure of sovereignty. What is different in governmentality from the commands of law and sovereignty is the concern with management, or conducting (in Foucault's words), of individuals who are shaped, or subjectified, according to a set of beliefs (2000d, 2007). This focus on individuals thus allows for theorising the relationship between technologies of self and technologies of domination.

Italian philosopher Giorgio Agamben (1998, 5) has critiqued Foucault for lack of clarity when it comes to the intersection between techniques of domination and technologies of the self. One of the likely causes of this lack of clarity is the tendency in the reception of Foucault's work to bypass pastoral power and its techniques, which holds an extremely pivotal position within Foucault's conceptualisation of governmentality. I shall argue this at some length in chapter two. The Greenlandic colonial context provides an excellent field for working through some of these issues because it allows for the tracing of specific subjectification techniques and the limits imposed on the subjected. Conversely, governmentality provides a way of theorising agency in a colonial context, and the restrictions this context entails, particularly the techniques of domination and how they were directed at—and appropriated by—certain groups within the population.[18]

18 I should note that Foucault does not in any way include the colonies in his genealogy of governmentality.

Within governmentality, the concept of pastoral power plays a central role. Pastoral power is, according to Foucault (2007, 164–165), a technique of power derived from Christianity, which targets the individual, subordinating him or her to another individual (the pastor) by means of monitoring and guiding. This technique developed from the medieval period and carried through into the political rationalities of governmentality. Importantly, Foucault distinguishes between pastoral power's ecclesiastical institutionalisation, which has diminished since the eighteenth century, and pastoral power's function, which has transcended the institutional framework. I expand on this idea of pastoral power and its political efficacy in the first three chapters by fleshing out Protestant techniques of pastoral power to supplement the predominantly Roman-Catholic focus in Foucault's work. Protestant pastoral power, or more precisely Lutheran pastoral power, has different subjectification techniques of self and domination, which I elaborate in order to analyse the workings of the Lutheran missionaries in Greenland.

The particular technology of self on which I focus here is writing. Owing to the prevalent position of Scripture in Protestant theology and missionary activities, reading and writing occupied a central position in the development of a Greenlandic intelligentsia. To theorise writing and its connection to truth and abstraction, I use German cultural theorist Christina von Braun's work on *logos* and the production of nature. Von Braun argues that writing—that is, linear writing—made it possible to move beyond mortality and the limitations it poses. In fact, writing made eternity and eternal life possible by offering a sense of permanence. Writing created, so to speak, two concepts of reality. On the one hand, there is the reality that is visible and that we can grasp through our senses; on the other hand, writing created a reality that transcended this material mode of reality, conveying the hope of another existence, one not subject to transitoriness. This otherworldly reality is not accessible to the senses, but is nevertheless constructed and demonstrated through writing. Thinking is removed from material reality and takes on an existence of its own, a process von Braun traces from the beginning of writing. I am particularly intrigued by her argument concerning writing as the vehicle for abstraction, because this gives new meaning to the introduction of phonetic writing to societies that did not previously have writing, as defined in Eurocentric terms, as a prime medium.

I use a combination of Foucault and von Braun to trace the implementation of writing and its connections to abstraction and notions of self and other in colonial Greenland. Writing and education was one of the primary ways in which the Danish colonial administration created differences within the population. This took place at the catechist colleges in Godthåb (present-day Nuuk) and Jakobshavn (present-day Ilulissat), starting in the mid-nineteenth century. While all Greenlanders in the conversion process learned how to read, and to some extent write, only a fraction of the men were actually trained to express themselves and their surroundings in writing, and thus develop a different sense of self. The men selected for further education were predominantly from 'mixed' families. These processes of subjectification were thus carried out within a framework that was already both gendered and racialised.

Writing thus meant the possibility to *represent,* and this is what I explore in relation to the ontological status of the hunter. However, I am also interested in how this status is replicated in the secondary literature. I have consciously attempted to *avoid* basing my analyses on pre-contact Greenlandic ways of life, religion, hunting habits, and so on, because these are already represented through writing, already shaped, as it were, through the lens of post/colonial history. I realise that this is not an original point, but carrying out the actual analysis of effects without referring to a 'before' has been quite challenging. Whether I succeed in this endeavour, or still reconstruct or carry assumptions of a 'before' within my analysis, I can no longer tell. It is nonetheless an important methodological point of my analysis, and one I was inspired to by anthropologists Jean and John Comaroffs' (1991, 1997) work on missionaries and colonialism in South Africa.

Another methodological clarification is that my approach should be seen as more inductive than deductive. I do not have a theoretical chapter from which I then proceed. Instead, I begin in the middle of things, and bring out points and analyses that I then draw together at the end. The theoretical discussions on gender, writing, pastoral power, and so on, are interspersed throughout the text. This means that some issues may not gain complete coherence until a later stage of analysis. However, a few guideposts might be in order.

In this book, I want to make three basic points. First, I want to reconsider the distinction between colonial powers and missionaries by showing that the mechanisms which produce the abstraction and idealisation of the hunter figure are connected to writing and scripture. Second, I want to show the culturally invasive effects of Danish colonialism in Greenland, and how the colonial administration managed to set certain parameters within which Greenlanders could act. Third, I will trace the subjectification process of a specific group of people, namely the catechists. I do so to show how the missionaries intervened in Greenlandic society, and to illustrate the effects of this intervention. The missionaries' objective was to foster a rational and controlled masculinity that removed the Greenlandic catechists from their social contexts and cultural background. I will examine how the Greenlandic catechists deal with such a process, and argue that the abstraction and idealisation of the hunter is a significant part of this process that can be seen in cultural productions of the present.

Background

The historical and geographical context is the former Danish colony of Greenland,[19] colonised in the early eighteenth century. Colonisation was intended to lend financial support to the Lutheran mission to the Catholic Norsemen who had settled in Greenland around the eleventh century, but had not been heard from since the fifteenth. Indeed, when the missionary Hans Egede and his family arrived in the eighteenth century, there were no Norsemen to be found, only the indigenous population today known as Inuit,[20] who then became the target of the mission.

The actual physical colonisation, or occupation, took place in the first 60 years along the West Coast, the most accessible given ocean currents and ice formations. The next territorial expansions did not take place until around 1900 (Viemose 1976, 26). In contrast, the restructuring of the indigenous economy and the reshaping society was an ongoing process from the very beginning, but gathered significant momentum after the 1750s and the consolidation of trade and the colonial economy.[21] As part of Denmark's negotiations in the 1950s to join NATO, Greenland's status as a colony ended and it became part of the Danish Commonwealth.[22] In the course of the

19 Greenland, or as its people call it, Kalaallit Nunaat (land of the Kalaallit) is the large (about two million square kilometres) island off the coast of North America. Its current population is about 60,000. Two-thirds of the island is in the Arctic Circle, and only the coast is currently inhabitable. The only non-coastal township is Narsaq, in southern Greenland.

20 While Greenland (Kalaallit Nunaat), its people (Kalaallit), and language (Kalaallisut) all form the national entity, "Inuit" designates the overall language group of the peoples inhabiting the Arctic regions of North America, Greenland, and Russia.

21 Trade in the early years was particularly hard, due to the difficulty of raising capital. The most significant ventures include the first trading company, the Bergen Greenland Company (1721–27); merchant Jakob Severin's company (1734–45); the General Trading Company (1747–74), and finally The Royal Greenland Trading Company (KGH), in 1774. See Sveistrup (1943) and Gad (1969, 56–103, 271–317, 379–406, 518–580) for more details.

22 The incorporation of Greenland into the Danish Commonwealth required a change to the Danish constitution to bring Greenland under Danish law and extend the protection of citizens' rights to Greenlanders. According to Danish law, a change to the Constitution must be approved by a referendum. Astonishingly, however, the important decision to include Greenland in the Danish Commonwealth was not considered sufficiently important to warrant a constitutional change in its own right. Instead, the decision was included in the proposed constitutional change to the law for succession to the throne (Olsen 2005, 41).

extensive social upheavals in 1960s and 1970s (discussed in chapter six), the Greenlandic elite gathered significant momentum, and on 1 May 1979, Greenland was granted home-rule government, which meant control over domestic affairs. In 2008, after prolonged negotiations with Denmark and a referendum in Greenland, the status of home rule was changed to self-government, effective 21 June 2009. Today, Greenland is still economically dependent on Denmark through an annual grant (*bloktilskud*) worth the equivalent of just under €500 million. The journey towards so-called economic independence will presumably involve mining of the many valuable minerals, including uranium and gemstones, and tapping the oil resources in Greenland that have become accessible as a result of global warming and the receding ice cap.

My focus in the present work shifts back and forth between various periods in the colonial history and a more general analysis of how the missionaries implemented their own ideological systems. From the semi-systematised, racialised missionary politics of the eighteenth century through the intensification of control, exploitation, and institutionalisation in the nineteenth, and the fragmentation and governmentalisation of the Greenlandic people in the twentieth, I trace how the colonial administration and the missionaries made Christian subjects of Greenlandic men.

I have chosen to analyse the role of the men for a number of reasons connected to the theme of displacement. Colonialism meant a pervasive dismantling of the Greenlandic household. In this process, men became the targets of colonial administration and practice. First, the colonial administration seized control of production, and then the colonial presence disrupted the sexual economy of the Greenlandic society. I aim to show how Greenlandic men, targeted as a viable labour force, were drawn into a system of control and surveillance and, in effect, displaced as masters of the house at these two levels.

At a socio-economic level, the Danish king seized control of trade, particularly through the establishment of colonies up and down Greenland's west coast, which increasingly shut down trading options with the Dutch and English, with whom Greenlanders had long been trading. Eventually the Danish state took exclusive control of trade in a monopoly that lasted until the 1950s. Through a number of administrative manoeuvres, Greenlanders came to trade less with each other and more with Danes, thus creating a level of individual interaction very different from the socially oriented trading patterns of Greenlanders prior to colonisation. The shifts in the patterns of consumption, which also included ammunition and such highly addictive goods as coffee, sugar, and tobacco, further developed networks of control and subjection.

The denigration and dismissal of Greenlanders' worldviews, and their replacement by Protestant Christianity—under the strict supervision of the missionaries—furthered this subjection.

At a material and economic level, Greenlandic men were physically displaced by European men within the family structure as a result of intermarriage and sexual relations between European men and Greenlandic women. In November 1766, Missionary Henric Christopher Glahn noted in his diary that

> the Greenlandic women do not need to be urged twice to enter into marriage with the Danes. Girls, who are so proud that they scorn the most dignified Greenlander, will not hesitate in entering into matrimony with the worst and lowliest sailor, although there is great difference in their circumstances. I know not the reason for it, although beads and pretty hair-ribbons perhaps assist towards this.
>
> 1921, 63

If European status was a valuable commodity, as this quotation implies and as Ann Laura Stoler asserts (1995, 48–49) in a different context, then it was a commodity available to women through sexual relations. In contrast, men had access to European status only if they had a European father and thus were employed by the colonial apparatus. The opportunities for men and women within the colonial system were therefore quite different. These opportunities were consolidated in the *Instruction of 1782*, a document that officially outlines the racial politics of the colonial government. The *Instruction* reveals the direct procedures through which the Danish administration attempted to regulate population growth and racial composition in Greenland. These measures were, effectively, precautions taken to control interactions between Greenlandic women and Danish men, in effect sculpting the population and creating a new group of Greenlanders.

Within this group of 'new' Greenlanders, I am interested in the catechists. As mentioned above, both Arctic scholar Søren Thuesen and theologian Henrik Wilhjelm have worked with this group of men in some detail. While I rely significantly on Thuesen's work, there is one assumption we nevertheless do not share, and which constitutes a main line of my argument in this book.

Thuesen argues that in choosing a position with no social prestige, the catechists managed to move beyond the ethnic (and economic) divisions established by the colonial administration. By situating themselves as a group that saw themselves as Greenlanders, but lived and worked as Danes, they thus problematised both ethnic categories. Thuesen continues:

> The catechists worked within the church, which precisely is the institution in Greenland that first broke away from differential treatment based on ethnic criteria, and furthermore had enlightenment, knowledge and education as its kernel.
>
> 2007, 13

This is a very important point since it concerns one of the major issues in the present work. It may very well be that the church was the first to employ Greenlanders, but in doing so it *actually drew the Greenlanders into a system of difference and hierarchy based on race.*

I will argue this point extensively in chapter one in relation to the missionary Niels Hveyssel, and his treatment of the catechists he employed. Moreover, the church used enlightenment, knowledge, and education as means of introducing a set of social and moral norms to which Greenlanders had to conform. The knowledge of the church was firmly and directly connected to a social structure that had to be implemented in order to contain the Protestant spirit, which apparently can thrive only in cultured and sophisticated surroundings. This line of argument will be advanced in chapter three, "The Lutheran Pastorate in Theory and Practice." The production and transformation of a racialised 'nature' entailed in this process is both a central argument of this work and a direct challenge to Thuesen's claim. Indeed, rather than disturbing ethnic categories and thereby being outside them, as Thuesen argues, I propose that the catechists in fact played a crucial role in *upholding* these categories.

Frederik Berthelsen, to whom I shall return in the first chapter, is a good example of Danish-Greenlandic categories. Frederik was the second son of Berthel Laersen and his wife, Susanna. Laersen came to Greenland in 1739 from the *Vajsenhuset* orphanage in Copenhagen to serve as a catechist in the mission. He married Susanna, a Greenlandic woman from the Moravian mission,[23]

---

23 The Moravian Brethren, also known as the *Unitas Fratrum* or the *Herrnhuter Brüdergemeine*, was in the eighteenth century a radical pietist movement from the Oberlausitz in present-day Germany. The founder, Count Nicolaus Ludwig von Zinzendorf, had family connections with the Danish court, and through these was granted permission to send missionaries to Greenland. The Moravian Brethren arrived in Greenland in 1733, left in 1900–01, and were significant competitors for the souls of Greenlanders. Moravian theology was characterised by an individual conversion experience, a heavy emphasis on emotions, and a strong personal relation to Jesus Christ. Finally, the physical blood and wounds of Christ were very central to Moravian theology. Their presence in eighteenth-century Europe was barely tolerated because they were regarded as a threat to the social order. By the late nineteenth century, they were seen as successful and professional missionaries, and today their membership stands at close to one million.

in 1744. Together they had three sons and two daughters (Ostermann 1945, 191–195). This makes Frederik (and his siblings) a *blanding* (plural: *blandinger*), the term used by the Danish colonial administration to denote the legitimate child of a Danish father and Greenlandic mother. It quickly became practice to employ the sons from these 'mixed' marriages initially in the mission and then in The Royal Greenlandic Trade, also known as 'the Trade.'[24] The daughters married other sons from 'mixed' marriages. Frederik Berthelsen, following in his father's footsteps, was employed as a catechist, and several of his own sons also became catechists.

An analysis of merchant accounts in chapter one indicates that Frederik Berthelsen's consumption habits were noticeably different from those of other Greenlandic catechists and of his brother, Joseph. Furthermore, Berthelsen's stance in the case of the 'Habakuk heresy,' also discussed in chapter one, is in line with the Danish missionary Hveyssel and thus the broader Danish Protestant position. Lastly, Hveyssel, who argues on Berthelsen's behalf for European rations[25] and a salary increase, privileges Berthelsen above his peers. The first two points relate to Berthelsen's lifestyle as conditioned by a colonial structure: First, his consumption habits were conditioned by his pay. Second, he would not have been able to maintain such a lifestyle had he received the same pay as other catechists. Furthermore, the importance of his support for Hveyssel was contingent on his position as a head catechist. His employment meant a significant income, which financed a certain lifestyle.[26] It also made him important enough for his opinion to matter.

Hveyssel's privileging of Berthelsen is part of the concrete colonial structure, a manifestation of a larger colonial mindset relating to gender and race. In Danish colonial politics, masculinity is split along racial lines, which in turn determine education and employment within the Greenlandic colonial context. Thus from early on, the colonial administration established a system of opportunity and exclusion based on race, a system that became formalised in

---

24 The Trade, or KGH, *Det Kongelige Grønlandske Handelskompagni*, was the state-organised trading company that held the monopoly on trade between Greenland and Denmark from its inception in 1774 to the mid-twentieth century.

25 Danish employees received a salary that consisted mainly of credit and rations of pork, grain, butter, and sugar. These rations were regarded as European and unsuitable for Greenlandic consumption.

26 In his article "Lønarbejdere som overklasse," Ole Marquardt (1998) demonstrates how the men who were fully employed on a permanent basis by the mission or the Trade constituted an upper class in nineteenth-century Greenland because their salary significantly—perhaps even excessively—exceeded what Greenlanders could earn as hunters and casual labourers.

the *Instruction of 1782* and which I will analyse in chapter five, "The Ontological Status of the Hunter or the Production of Nature."

Synopsis of Chapters

In chapter one, I follow one of the Danish patriarchs in his official capacity as missionary. Four years after Hveyssel came to Greenland in 1784, he became embroiled in the Habakuk heresy, which was the first unauthorised Greenlandic appropriation of Christianity. The Habakuk movement lasted a couple of years and its demise is usually credited to the intervention and control of head catechist Frederik Berthelsen. I explore Hveyssel's reports to the missionary college outlining the turn of events, not to reconstruct historical events (which has already been done elsewhere), but to examine and highlight the assumptions of gender, superstition, self-mastery, rationality, and race underlying the correspondence. In other words, I trace how Hveyssel represents himself as master of the Greenlanders, especially the catechists who worked with him, and how he differentiates and makes preferences along racial lines.

This forms the basis for the discussion of governmentality and pastoral power in the second chapter, where I develop my theoretical and methodological framework of governmentality, pastoral power, and colonialism. I engage in detail with pastoral power, and expand the historical background to situate Lutheran Protestantism within Foucault's genealogy. Following on the historical currents discussed in chapter one, I focus on some of the more doctrinal elements in Lutheran social philosophy. I highlight the concept of *natural law*, since I see this as one of the central mechanisms through which Protestantism presents itself as rational against what it labelled 'superstition'—pagan as well as Roman Catholic. While Foucault emphasises the confession as the site of (Roman Catholic) subjectification, I emphasise the practice of *catechism*, the daily repetition of central Christian doctrines, as the main locus for Lutheran subjectification. Because catechism is the duty of the father, I focus on the family, a central feature of Lutheran social philosophy and an important point of application of power in modernity. The family was a crucial feature in sculpting the Greenlandic social profile, not only because of the incorporation of the Danish father within its sphere, but also because the concept of family itself shifted from larger networks to the smaller nuclear family structure of the West.

The analyses of two first chapters come together in chapter three, where I place Hveyssel's representation within what I call the "Lutheran pastorate," which is the Protestant power structure in its Danish context, including its modes of subjectification and control. I outline some of the historical currents, which have established the Lutheran pastorate and its hierarchies.

The first three chapters thus establish the colonial context, and are followed by detailed analyses in the next two chapters. At this point, the overt Lutheran nature of pastoral power recedes into the background. In chapters four and five, I analyse how writing as a technology of self dovetails with the disciplining strategies of the colonial administration. That it is at all possible to speak of a technology of self indicates that we have moved further along into the levels of colonial control. The colonial administration at this point is persistent in promoting a certain group of Greenlanders, thus institutionalising what up to now had been the semi-informal practice of selecting the legitimate Greenlandic sons of Danish fathers for particularly prominent positions. This is the underlying theme of chapters four and five. In chapter four, my points of departure are the recording of oral traditions in the mid-nineteenth century, how writing transforms these traditions, and how these recordings provide ways of objectifying Greenlanders. I also examine Thuesen's work on the journals that the catechists were required to keep, and I discuss the literary production of the catechists in the nineteenth and twentieth centuries, chiefly disseminated in the newspaper *Atuagagdliutit*. Following Thuesen, I argue that through writing (in general, as an every-day practice), the catechists begin to construct their surroundings as 'nature,' and I move on to focus on the hunter as the foil to a catechist identity.

Chapter five looks at what I have called *"the ontological status of the hunter,"* which is the hunter-identity constructed by the catechists. In this chapter, I trace the emergence of this identity as part of a process of distinction. I first analyse the *Instruction of 1782* and its racial parameters for social stratification. I then extend the argument from the previous chapter to argue that writing facilitated this process of distinction by producing the hunter and nature as a part of the self-construction of the catechist. A significant point is that the catechists, while moving beyond the hunter lifestyle, nevertheless rely on the hunter for a sense of ethnic identity. This process of simultaneous adaptation and differentiation is part of the catechists' process of defining themselves as a distinct group.

Chapter six, "Rewritten Pasts and Scripts for the Future: Heart of Light," moves into present times and looks at the current effects of the politics of the colonial administration as discussed in the first five chapters. First, I analyse the ontological status of the hunter in the 1997 feature film *Heart of Light*. In my introductory remarks, I mentioned that the film conceals fundamental issues relating to power and representation in a colonial context, and leaves them unresolved. After having worked though issues of race, class, gender, and writing in the course of this book, the problems of representation and access to power become more apparent. I therefore discuss these problems in relation to the film. From there, I move on to analysing the film as a national allegory, using Fredric Jameson's theorisations on national allegory to explore the relation between the local and the global in the film. Finally, I move on to a broader discussion of indigeneity (in comparison with Australia) and discuss the place of hunting in conceptualisations of indigenous peoples within global politics and whaling policies.

I return now to the stroll around *Kolonihavnen*, beneath the statue of Hans Egede. We have passed the meat-market, the red church, Hans Egede's yellow house, the grey house that was the home of the Inspector of Southern Greenland and the printing press, and finally the red catechist college. I will argue that these institutions set the coordinates within which we speak about indigenous cultures, societies, and economies. Thus, even agents who believe themselves to be speaking on behalf of indigenous peoples are in danger of reproducing colonial stereotypes and of operating within the coordinates established by colonialism. My agenda in this book is to identify these colonial coordinates so as to question the conditions under which we speak about indigenous representation and rights.

CHAPTER 1

Setting the Scene

The Practice of Orthodoxy in Colonial Greenland

In 1788, the missionary of Sukkertoppen district,[1] Niels Hveyssel, sent a report to the Missionary Department in Copenhagen regarding a certain matter. Hveyssel described how Habakuk, a Greenlandic convert, had brought his maid Alhed on a reindeer-hunting expedition. This, Hveyssel wrote, sent Habakuk's wife, Mary Magdalene, into throes of jealousy.[2] Mary Magdalene then convinced Habakuk and Alhed that a long-dead couple had contacted her and revealed information about her fellow Greenlanders, both living and dead. This she solemnly wrote down and gave to Habakuk to deliver to Hveyssel, who reports that on receiving the message, he admonished Habakuk to behave himself. Hveyssel's admonitions apparently had little effect; the movement grew and attracted followers from all over and beyond the district – hunters as well as catechists. This came to be known as the 'Habakuk heresy' or 'Habakuk movement,' and it lasted until the early 1790s. In a sense, it became the archetype of all Greenlandic charismatic movements and their followers.[3]

It is tricky to begin with this episode because we have no accurate description of the movement or the actual heresy itself. What we do have are three reports from missionary Hveyssel, and five versions of the Greenlandic oral traditions. It is impossible to say what actually happened, not just because of the highly selective information in Hveyssel's reports, but also because of the

1 A missionary district consisted of a colony, which served as the administrative centre, and surrounding areas and smaller settlements. Colonies were established on good hunting grounds. Kangerdlugssuatsiaq, the fjord where the Habakuk movement congregated, was in the Sukkertoppen district, north of the colony, but almost inaccessible in winter and spring. The colony of Sukkertoppen was first placed at Gammel Sukkertoppen (Kangâmiut), but was moved south to Sukkertoppen (Manitsôq) in 1781 to concentrate efforts on whaling (Gad 1976, 375).

2 The names Habakuk and Mary Magdalene were given the couple at their baptism to replace their original 'heathen' names. Such new names were almost always taken from the bible, or in the case of the men, from the Danish kings Frederik and Christian. In this particular case, Habakuk (usually spelled "Habakkuk") is the title of one of the 12 books of the Hebrew Bible named after the 12 Minor Prophets. Mary Magdalene is named after the female disciple of Jesus who, according to canonical tradition, was the first witness to the resurrection of Jesus.

3 The Greenlandic verb *aapakorpeq*, which means "having heretical opinions," is constructed from the name "Habakuk" (Kleivan 1999, 49).

different emphasis of the Greenlandic sources. Of course there have been compilations of the various sources into a coherent narrative, but as I will show below, these are highly problematic and, perhaps unwittingly, they reproduce the colonial (and Lutheran orthodox) ideology expressed in Hveyssel's reports. I want instead to try and distil this colonial ideology, not only from Hveyssel's reports, but also in the interpretations of the so-called Habakuk movement. In other words, I want to understand the problem that lies beneath the veneer of orthodoxy and heresy.

I begin with these reports because they provide important insights into the discourses of gender and race assumed by Danish missionaries in the late eighteenth century, as well as an understanding of how those missionaries see themselves in the process of society-building. Hveyssel's reports to the Missionary Department present us with his ideals of rationality and his understandings of power and gender. Hveyssel's reports also show how he imagines a proper society should be ordered with respect to the roles of women, Greenlanders, and, above all, Danish men. Moreover, Hveyssel's reports reveal that he distinguishes among the catechists in his employment; he clearly privileges Frederik Berthelsen and his brother Joseph, both of whom he regards as different from the others. It is important to note here that Frederik and Joseph were the sons of the former missionary in the district, a Danish man named Berthel Larsen. They were, in the terminology of the colonial administration, *blandinger* – as noted above, the Danish word for people of 'mixed race'.[4]

The fact that I begin with the reports constitutes, as noted earlier, an important methodological point. It means that I am interested in what the reports can tell us about configurations of gender and race as they are expressed in the source material, not in reconstructing the history of the movement. The reason I use this source material rather than, for example, missionary diaries is because the accusations of heresy and dissent in the Habakuk material bring out assumptions of mastery and orthodoxy much more strongly than the every-day material. In other words, these reports bring out what is at stake when the social order is perceived as threatened.

So, I will present Hveyssel's representation of the events surrounding the Habakuk movement largely as he discussed them in his reports to the

4 The terms used to denote miscegenation are problematic, loaded, and potentially offensive because they presuppose ideas of racial purity. While *blanding* rests on a presumption of racial purity, it also has a host of social restrictions, to which I return in chapter four. For a comprehensive discussion, see Robert J.C. Young's study, *Colonial Desire: Hybridity in Theory, Culture and Race* (1995). See also Ann Laura Stoler's analysis of race and miscegenation (1995, 2002).

Missionary Department. From there, I set off in two related but distinct trajectories in the following chapters. The first is that of mastery, by which I mean to signify a system of domination based on gender, class, and race, which mutually enforce each other.[5] The strength of the concept is its openness to 'intermasculine' issues, which provides us with an analytical concept that can highlight the struggles between competing masculinities, something that a term such as patriarchy does not convey. Mastery entails an intensification of a certain masculine ideal, namely, one which privileges a disembodied rationality in complete harmony with the laws laid down in nature through creation. This ideal has been shaped and nurtured since Plato and subsumed into western thought, and it reaches its culmination in the works of Hegel in the nineteenth century – a process which Genevieve Lloyd maps out in *Men of Reason*.[6] This line of thought would have been part of the self-understanding of the colonisers, and part of their civilising and soteriological discourse, as imbibed through the Lutheran framework of which they were a part. I am thereby attempting to construct that which 'goes without saying'.[7]

How does Hveyssel construct his masculine self and rational beliefs in his reports back to the Missionary Department? To address this, I will trace the social setting he presupposes, analysing the assumptions and discourses of gender and race contained in these reports, and set them within a larger context of Danish colonial politics of gender relations. I am particularly interested in the connections he makes and the binaries he constructs between rationality and emotions, self-control and enslavement, as well as men and women, since these connections show the social and cultural contingency of gender relations. This will enable me to show: (i) how Hveyssel sees himself in relation to the catechists, and (ii) how a sense of hierarchy and paternalism was endemic to the relations between Danes and Greenlanders, and how this was manifested in these particular working relations. While the systematic construction and institutional implementation of this Western masculinity

5 The late Val Plumwood also used mastery to signify "not a masculine identity pure and simple, but the multiple, complex cultural identity of the master formed in the context of class, race species and gender domination… " (1993, 5).

6 Lloyd's mapping in *Men of Reason* (1993) is with respect to gender. For analyses that deal with mastery, philosophy, and race see Charles Mill's manifesto *The Racial Contract* (1997) and Joseph Pugliese's study of Hegel's *The Philosophy of History* (1994). For an examination of the underlying class assumptions in ancient Greek philosophy and literature, see Peter Rose's study of, among others, Homer and Plato (1992).

7 In Ann Laura Stoler's study into the archives of the Netherlands Indies, she sets out to chart that which is "not written," distinguishing it from that which is "unwritten" because it goes without saying or because it could not yet be articulated or because it could not be said (2009, 3).

does not commence until the nineteenth century, I think we can discern its inception here in the late-eighteenth century, particularly in the way Hveyssel constructs men and women within his narrative. He promotes a rational and self-controlled masculinity that can step back from a situation and assess its mechanisms. Hveyssel also sees Frederik Berthelsen as exhibiting this kind of self-control and analytic skill in the face of what he perceives as the Greenlanders' more emotional and uncontrollable reactions.

While the first trajectory focuses on the relationship between Hveyssel and the Greenlandic men under his tutelage, the second follows Hveyssel's reactions to Mary Magdalene. I analyse how Mary Magdalene's behaviour and teaching, which draws on otherworldly sources for its validation, is perceived as a direct threat to Hveyssel's authority and to the social order he is attempting to implement. I will closely analyse the social order that Hveyssel represents, as well as its background in Lutheran social thought. The construction of a society according to Lutheran social thought involves a simultaneous subjectification of individuals to this social structure. There is thus a connection, or an encounter, between the disciplined self and the social. This is why Hveyssel can see Mary Magdalene's behaviour as socially disruptive, even though he attempts to couch it in theological terms. The elements introduced here form important parts of the discussion in the next two chapters, which look at the Lutheran pastorate and governmentality.

Before I move on to a summary of the reports and their interpretations, which will serve as a backdrop for my own interpretations, I will briefly draw attention to the Greenlandic Habakuk traditions, which will not be part of the present analysis,[8] and which consist of oral traditions that began to be transcribed in the mid – to late nineteenth century. There are a number of versions, including one told by the artist Jens Kreutzman that was the first to be transcribed as part of a nationalisation process that sought to remember and preserve Greenlandic traditions. This process was initiated in the 1850s by the Danish Inspector Heinrich Rink, and will be discussed in chapter four. Another version was told to Knud Rasmussen by Old Sidse, whose grandmother was part of the community around Habakuk and Mary Magdalene. In the Rink collection, there is also a version told by Frederik Berthlesen's son, Iver Berthelsen.[9]

---

8 For a discussion of the Danish and Greenlandic sources and their content, see Lidegaard (1986). For an interpretation of the Danish and Greenlandic sources according to their historical context and gender ideals, see Petterson (2009).

9 There is also a version in the 1955 novel *Taseralik* by Otto Rosing, another as told by Jens Kreutzmann's son, Kristoffer, and still another by Jens Kreutzmann himself (Söderberg 1974, 72–73; Thisted 1997b, 19).

There are notable differences between the Greenlandic and Danish traditions: The former narrate events within the community and emphasise Habakuk as the chief antagonist, while the latter relate the problems from the mission's point of view and depict Mary Magdalene as the main perpetrator (Lidegaard 1986, 205). And while the Danish tradition sees the Moravian (emotive) influence in the district as a highly significant part of the disturbance, the Greenlandic traditions do not mention this at all (Söderberg 1974, 76). While the Greenlandic traditions differ among themselves as to who decisively put an end to the movement (some sources emphasise Frederik Berthelsen's role while others cite a collective dissatisfaction), they do, however, agree with the Danish traditions in their opinion of the movement as an aberration, something which must be fought. I have chosen not to include the Greenlandic sources because my interest in the material has less to do with the Habakuk movement per se and more about what the texts reveal about the ideologies of gender and race exhibited by Danes in their interactions with Greenlanders. Hence, the Danish sources have my more immediate interest.

Mary Magdalene and Habakuk: A Heresy Takes Place

There are three central reports from Hveyssel's hand on the Habakuk heresy. In the first, dated 1788,[10] he briefly notes Habakuk's reindeer-hunting expedition with his maid, and the wife's jealous reaction – according to Hveyssel's interpretation. After receiving Mary Magdalene's revelations, Hveyssel admonishes Habakuk, who was the bearer of the message, to behave himself, but he does not address Mary Magdalene herself at this stage.

Hveyssel's admonitions have little effect; he is informed after some time that Habakuk's wife preaches a doctrine with three points: (i) the deceased couple have commanded her to "spread" details about the faults of her neighbours; (ii) the dead have told her that they have received no new dwelling, but are in a "cheerless condition"; and (iii) the man who remarries after the death of his first wife only "borrows" the second, in that he will be reunited with the first in the afterlife. Hveyssel interprets the command to spread details about the shortcoming of the neighbours as simple gossip, and the claim that the deceased have no home as a sort of Roman Catholic purgatory. He does not comment on her third point, but notes for the record that he forbids her to lie,

10 *Rigsarkivet* (Danish National Archives): *Missionskollegiet og Direktionen for Vajsenhuset: Indkomne sager den grønlandske mission vedk.* 1786–88, folder 1788, no. 15: Hveyssel's report to the Missionary Department, 30 June 1788, point 5.

"disproves" her claims through references to the New Testament, and reminds her to obey the word of God. All of these exhortations take place in writing.

The next report, dated 14 August 1789,[11] is much more extensive. Here Hveyssel presents Mary Magdalene's preaching as a result of charismatic opportunism. Around the district, Greenlanders have heard hymns and bells, and seen a great host of dead souls floating in the air. Hveyssel notes that the Danes have heard nothing of these hymns and bells, although he admits he has vaguely heard "something." According to Hveyssel, Mary used the Greenlanders' visions as proof of the truth of her own teachings:

> As soon as it was heard for the first time in Kangerdlugssuatsiaq, Habakuk's wife, Mary Magdalene, about whom I reported last year, pretended to have secret conversations with the dead, who let her know that Judgement Day was at hand; that God was angry with their disbelief – since two years ago they had contradicted her when she claimed to have received similar revelations – and their godlessness, which mainly was that they had neglected the good Moravian customs, which the late Mr Laersen had implemented.
>
> 1789a, point 3[12]

For Hveyssel, Mary Magdalene uses the visions that others have had as proof of her own, placing herself in a privileged position as the interpreter of these events. She claims, he says, that God sent these apparitions of the dead to Greenlanders so that they might believe what Mary says, for they previously had not believed her: "And so that the Greenlanders now could believe her words, God had sent a great host of dead people, so that they could hear and see for themselves"(Hveyssel 1789a, point 3). According to Hveyssel, Mary is using the Greenlanders' visions to enact her own reformation among them, a reformation which included a return to Moravian customs. Whereas in the previous year, Hveyssel described the situation as dogmatic aberrations of a Roman Catholic nature, he now sees it as Moravian tendencies. In this way, Hveyssel makes Mary a part of, or a spokeswoman for, a larger competing Christian movement that this time is more visible and menacing.[13] Hveyssel is

11 *Rigsarkivet* (Danish National Archives): *Missionskollegiet og Direktionen for Vajsenhuset: Indkomne sager den grønlandske mission vedk.* 1789–91, folder 1789, nr. 23: Hveyssel's report to the Missionary Department, 14 August 1789, point 3.

12 All translations from the Danish archival material are my own.

13 As noted in the introduction, the Moravian Brethren arrived in Greenland by Royal appointment in 1733, ostensibly to assist the Egede mission in Godthåb (present-day

extremely frustrated. In his attempts to argue with the Greenlanders and refute her teachings, they refuse to listen:

> She has imprinted this notion in them, that should I or any other contradict her pretences, they mustn't answer, but immediately leave so as not to be corrupted by this ungodly speech. When something is said to them in admonishment, they should only answer: *κujanak* (God's will be done). They loyally follow her will, and when they can avoid contradiction in no other way, they begin singing one hymn after another.
>
> 1789a, point 3

Another problem is Elijah, another Greenlander, who says he has had similar revelations. While these are not nearly as "outrageous" as Mary's, the situation is still highly problematic for Hveyssel because Elijah's revelations lend legitimacy to those of the "wench."[14] Much to his dismay, even some of the catechists have turned to Mary. I will explore this turn of events in the next section; here I will just note that in this particular part of Hveyssel's report (on the dissent of the catechists),[15] he varies his terminology about Mary. Whereas it is usually wench, "here it becomes" "seductress," "prophetess," and "imposter." These terms give the impression that Hveyssel does not let himself be either seduced or tricked, and that the catechists, against their better judgement, have allowed themselves to be carried away by her revelations. The sexual connotations are particularly interesting and will be discussed below. Towards the Greenlanders, he uses a different tactic, namely a stream of written communications that constantly refer to the catechism as well as the New

---

Nuuk), although it is more likely that they were given approval to provide competition for Egede (Bredsdorff 2003, 71), which they certainly did. In their 170 years of missionary work in Greenland, they established six missionary stations: Neuherrnhut, Lichtenfels and Lichtenau in the eighteenth century, and Friederichsthal, Uummannaq and Illorpaat in the nineteenth century (Lidegaard 1993, 91).

14 A critical report in Copenhagen by Otho Fabricius points out that Hveyssel's own vague admission that he heard something in 1789 would have strengthened the Greenlanders' delusions (*Rigsarkivet* [Danish National Archives]: *Missionskollegiet og Direktionen for Vajsenhuset: Indkomne sager den grønlandske mission vedk.* 1789–91, folder 1789: Otho Fabricius's report on Kolonien Sukkertoppen to the Missionary Department, 12 June 1790). However, it unclear whether Hveyssel told the Greenlanders that he had heard something, or shared that information only in his report.

15 *Rigsarkivet* (Danish National Archives): *Missionskollegiet og Direktionen for Vajsenhuset: Indkomne sager den grønlandske mission vedk.* 1789–91, folder 1789, no. 23: Hveyssel's report to the Missionary Department, 14 August 1789, point 4.

Testament as expressions of the word of God, through which he tries to disprove her revelations.

A final serious issue is that of murder. Hveyssel notes in his report that Titus, one of the catechists who had joined the movement, had in some way facilitated the murder of his own mother because Mary Magdalene (according to Hveyssel) had accused her of being a witch. Titus

> was previously a tolerable catechist, now so much worse, since not only did he himself lay hands upon his old [unintelligible word] mother, because the wench accused her of witchcraft, but even talked his countrymen into beating her, indeed – in spite of my warnings – forced her through his evil behaviour to leave,[16] that is, if he hasn't thrown her into the sea himself. He, along with several others, has actually killed another woman who recently arrived from Holsteinsborg, and thrown her in the sea following Mary Magdalene's orders.
>
> 1789a, point 4

Another catechist, Sem, has likewise allegedly driven his mother away for the same reason. Hveyssel assures the Missionary Department that he will not take them back as catechists. He then continues with more mundane matters, such as his dwelling, his teeth (falling out from scurvy), and the financial accounts. He does, however, manage to get another letter, dated 27 August 1789 (1789b) on the ship to Copenhagen. Here he notes that Mary Magdalene is attracting a growing number of followers from surrounding districts. He continues:

> What harm will this not do to the mission, since all teaching and reasonable church services will be brought to an end according to this devilish person's evil intent? And I with my warnings and admonitions am unable to do anything about it. Even the Royal Trade and whaling must suffer because of this. I have notified the coming Inspector of these matters and requested that he assist me with force and punish the wench and her most prominent adherents. I await his response.
>
> 1789b

In his next report, in 1790,[17] he relates that things have apparently calmed down, so much so that some of the movement's adherents – he explicitly

16 Hveyssel presumably means caused her to kill herself.

17 *Rigsarkivet* (Danish National Archives): *Missionskollegiet og Direktionen for Vajsenhuset: Indkomne sager den grønlandske mission vedk.* 1789–91, folder 1790, no. 23: Hveyssel's report to the Missionary Department, 30 June 1790, point 1.

mentions Elijah – have admitted their fraud, expressed serious regret, and promised to improve:

> Habakuk and his wife are the only ones who will not let themselves be brought to repent, but this is much less significant, since they are abandoned by all the Greenlanders, even his own brothers. The violent behaviour of the man [Habakuk] towards the Greenlanders was really what caused them to open their eyes and pull away from him.
>
> 1790, point 1

Hveyssel is relieved that the issue has been resolved without force, but still feels that the perpetrators behind the killings should be "corporally punished" to set an example, and he will ask the Inspector to do this. He continues:

> Habakuk, who apart from being the person responsible for all this evil along with his wife, has in the way of the pagans taken a second wife, whom I cannot persuade him to leave, and has this winter bred a stillborn child with her. To him I have declared that I, from here on, will regard him as a pagan, not come to him or those who stay with him, and not baptise their children if they continue their deceptions and evil ways.
>
> 1790, point 1

These are the main points of Hveyssel's reports on the matter.[18] Anyone wanting a full historical exposition of what actually happened – to the extent that this is at all possible – will find Hveyssel's information sketchy. For this reason, the two comprehensive attempts to reconstruct the history of the movement (Gad 1976, 375–396; Lidegaard 1986)[19] also rely on the Greenlandic traditions mentioned above. I present these two reconstructions here, after my description of the source material, in order to show the extent of rewriting required to get a coherent narrative from the reports.

---

18 Hveyssel does mention Habakuk again in his report of 4 June 1791, in which he notes that the last families have left the couple, and that he has again admonished Habakuk to send away his maid Alhed, whom he has taken as a second wife. As a result, Alhed turns up at the mission, pregnant, and Hveyssel sends her to one of the settlements under the jurisdiction of the catechist Micka, who was to keep an eye on her. There she gave birth to a child who was alive at the time Hveyssel was writing. She then married a Greenlander, Eleazer, which greatly relieved Hveyssel.

19 There are a number of shorter discussions of the movement (see, e.g., Kleivan 1999; Thuesen 1988).

Mads Lidegaard (1986) understands the movement as an encounter between two religious traditions. Lidegaard's study is very descriptive, and uses both Greenlandic and Danish sources to reconstruct the historical sequence of events of the movement in order to foreground a group of people not usually visible in Danish colonial histories, namely, the local population. Lidegaard attempts to envision the population in the encounter between the old 'hunter religion' and the new Christian religion as embodied in the main characters. He carefully brings all these factors together for an eventful and dramatic narrative. From this template – the movement as an encounter between two religions – he analyses the specific elements of the movement. For example, in one of the oral accounts (Old Sidse)[20] of the community's life, where people could shift from laughter to crying in a matter of moments – and did so, daily – he determines that the tears in the congregation are Moravian, and the laughter, Eskimoan (209). This emphasis of the hunter religion is consistent with Lidegaard's view of Mary's part in the movement as a pious Christian attempting to draw the dissenting community back to the Christian faith. According to Lidegaard, Mary is the real and legitimate leader, while Habakuk is the opportunist who makes the most of the situation but ends up ruining everything.

Finn Gad (1976), on the other hand, largely follows Hveyssel's narrative, albeit with a sense of smug retrospect based on what he believes is his much firmer grasp of history than Hveyssel. Gad sees the movement as the expression of a conflict between Moravian customs and the Lutheran mission (380), personified in the university-educated rationalist Hveyssel confronting the revivalist emotions of Moravian influence (*herrnhutisk vækkelses-føleri*, 377). In line with his previous dismissal of Greenlandic traditions, Gad does not see the movement as a return to pre-Christian customs (391), but exclusively as an expression of fanaticism and collective psychosis. It more or less began, he argues, with Mary Magdalene's attempt to hold on to her husband through visions, after which she whipped herself into an ecstatic frenzy that captivated the sensitive nature of Greenlanders (379, 385). The movement died when the leaders literally could not deliver: Habakuk was in control of the harvest from the hunt, but gave nothing in return, while Mary prophesied endlessly about the end of the world, without it ever coming. When the community's material well-being finally hit rock bottom – all of the winter reserves had been consumed and all the ammunition had been spent firing salutes at every opportunity – support for the couple crumbled (390).

---

20 The account by Old Sidse, whose grandmother was a young girl in the Habakuk congregation, was recorded by Knud Rasmussen and published in 1921.

While Lidegaard makes use of the Greenlandic source material throughout his reconstruction, Gad puts it aside, using it only to fill in the blanks, especially when it comes to the end of the movement, which both researchers feel needs to be fleshed out in more detail than supplied by Hveyssel. Both, however, use the Danish traditions as their basic source. The priority assigned to the Danish reports in the reconstructions indicates that these are seen as more trustworthy than the Greenlandic ones.

Staffan Söderberg's dissertation (1974) on prophetism and the religious encounter between Danish and Greenlandic religious traditions follows a different line of questioning. Söderberg takes a more phenomenological approach, and analyses the role of the prophet in three prophetic movements in Danish-Greenlandic colonial history, with special focus on the Habakuk movement. He distinguishes between the Danish and the Greenlandic sources, but sees the Greenlandic tradition as an interpretation of the events from a Greenlandic point of view, which through its different perspective points to the inherent Lutheran bias in the Danish tradition (and, one might add, the interpretations of Lidegaard and Gad). Söderberg especially notes the constant references to the Moravian Brethren in the Danish material, but the notable absence of these in the Greenlandic sources. The Danish viewpoint thus sees the Habakuk movement as caused by the competing German mission, and this relegates characters like Mary Magdalene and Habakuk to being products of the missionary conflict rather than part of a specific Greenlandic agenda (40–41).

While Söderberg's primary interest is not a historical explanation, he nevertheless places his interpretation within a reconstructed context. Söderberg interprets Mary Magdalene's religious experiences as being in line with the role of the Greenlandic shaman, the *angakkoq*. He thus considers the prophetic movements as Greenlandic interpretations of the meeting between their ancestral traditions and the new Christianity whereby the prophet, in this case Mary, is a transitional figure between the shaman and the minister. Söderberg does not regard the prophetic movements themselves as arising out of resistance to colonisation and the Danes, and points out that the conflict does not arise until the authoritative interpreter (Hveyssel) dismisses the legitimacy of the movement and the authenticity of its prophet.

I find Söderberg's treatment of the sources far more interesting analytically than the discussions of Lidegaard and Gad. Söderberg's analysis opens up the possibility that the Danish and Greenlandic sources refer to different *discursive* events and not just to different *perceptions* of the same event. If so, it should be possible to move beyond the conventional ways of reading the sources, and consider alternative understandings of the traditions and the events to which they refer. This will take me beyond the compulsion or insistence that all the texts refer to the same event, which I propose *reduces* – or rather *excludes* – what the sources could otherwise tell us about historical conditions and configurations of gender and race. This will be the main line in my own interpretation in this book, which is why I focus exclusively on the Danish material to bring out how Danish traditions reveal assumptions of race and gender, rather than using them as sources to reconstruct the history of the Habakuk movement.

Racialised and Gendered Heresies

Hveyssel's reports present us with good indications of the understandings of gender at the time. This makes it possible, for example, to discern how Hveyssel understands his own position vis-à-vis his Greenlandic catechists. There are in the report a number of Danish men who are missionaries (Berthel Laersen and Hveyssel) or merchants (Kragsfeldt) or the Inspector (Olrik and his successor, Lund), as well as a number of Greenlandic men who are catechists (Micka, Christian, Isaak, Titus and Sem), and Habakuk and Elijah. Further, there are two Greenlandic women: Alhed, the maid whom Habakuk takes as his second wife, and Mary Magdalene.[21] But there is no trace of Danish women.[22] In addition, there is the category of *blandinger*, namely, the two men Frederik and Joseph Berthelsen, legitimate sons of a Danish father and Greenlandic mother, who hold a special status in Hveyssel's regard. In the following section, I examine how some of these people and some of these groups

21 In his report of 1787, Hveyssel notes that "I did not employ any readers last winter because experience has taught me that they were fickle. In spite of this, I would readily have employed a woman for Ikkerasik, since I was short of usable men, but none were to be had." Readers could thus be male or female, and were hired to read aloud from the bible or other edifying literature. While this is not immediately relevant to the case here, it does show that women could also find employment in the clerical realm, albeit at the lowest level. Other examples of casual work for Greenlandic women included maid, seamstress, and rower of the large *umiaqs*, an important means of transport. Payment for this casual labour was made in tobacco, sewing needles, or clothing. Another important job for women was that of midwife. In the early nineteenth century, midwifery took off as a woman's job, and was in fact the first occupation for which institutionalised training was available to Greenlandic women. Mette Rønsager's thesis (2006) analyses in detail the emergence of midwifery as an institution, the cultural struggles in the training and education of midwives, and the social processes of selection and education of the women.

22 Not even in the background, in that Hveyssel's mother-in-law was Greenlandic (Ostermann 1921, 145).

are constructed and positioned in Hveyssel's reports, with the following questions in mind: What connections does Hveyssel make between the various groups in terms of orthodoxy and heresy, and to what extent does race and gender play a role? How does he use the Greenlanders to bolster his own authority?

Masculinities in the Making

In this book, I argue that while the foil for the conceptualisation of the rational masculinity of the missionaries was the savagery and folly of the Greenlanders, for the Greenlandic catechists of the nineteenth century, the image of the hunter became the primary 'other' against which they constructed themselves as rational men. While I elaborate my theoretical approach within gender studies below, I want here to locate my argument within sociologist Tim Edwards's provisional three-phase model of critical studies of masculinity (echoing the three waves of feminism). Edwards describes the first wave as the sex-role paradigm developed in the 1970s, which emphasises "the socially constructed nature of masculinity" (2006, 2), the accompanying socialisation processes and social control, as well as the damaging effects of these constraints on men's development. This was followed by the second (political) empirically-driven phase in the 1980s, which criticised the singular and Western understanding of the first phase, and thus focused more on power and the relationship between a hegemonic masculinity (white, Western, heterosexual, and middle class) and subordinated or marginalised masculinities. Finally, the third wave of masculinity studies is influenced by poststructuralist theory and focuses on questions of normativity, performativity and sexuality. The emphasis here is on "artifice, flux and contingency" (3), and Edwards draws out representation and its connections to change and continuity in contemporary and historical masculinities as particularly important. While the second and third waves might not seem that different in their emphasis on masculinity as a social and cultural construction, Edwards nevertheless highlights a "lack of integration" between the two strands. Not only do they focus on different topics, but they also do not deploy – or even acknowledge – each other's work. Edwards refers to this as an opposing interface between broadly speaking *sociological* masculinity studies (second wave) and *cultural* masculinity studies (third wave) (3–4).

Given the emphasis in the present study on the emergence of a rational masculinity in a colonial context, one would perhaps situate this work within the second phase of masculinity studies and its emphasis on power relations between hegemonic and subordinate masculinities. This is what Greenlandic sociologist Mariekathrine Poppel does in her study on masculinity issues and

Greenlandic society (Poppel 2005a, 2005b),[23] relying on the work of Raewyn (formerly Robert) Connell. However, I consider Connell's analyses to be yet another example of Edwards's claim that "[t]he formation of a growing analysis of whiteness, and the even more incipient development of studies of non-Western masculinities, has yet to form anything remotely approaching an analysis of race, ethnicity and masculinity" (2006, 5). The profound reluctance of white academics working with masculinity theory to address the relationship between masculinity, race and ethnicity is, despite assertions to the contrary, likewise noticeable in Connell's research. Edwards notes that Connell repeatedly raises race as a crucial factor in her system of hegemonic and subordinate masculinities, but never addresses the issue beyond a token mention.

In the few places that non-European masculinities are mentioned in Connell's influential study (2005, 30–34), these other masculinities do not act as a foil against which Western masculinity is *produced*, but more as a backdrop to how western masculinity may be *understood*. It is precisely here, as well as in the exceedingly brief treatment of colonial encounters (186–87), with this seemingly static notion of Western masculinity over the masculinities of other cultures, that Connell therefore seems to fall prey to the very gender essentialism she is trying to avoid. Coupled with the elusiveness of "globalisation," and the colonial and racial violence that this euphemism attempts to conceal, her compartmentalised analyses of masculinity are very narrow. Her contribution to *Theory and Society*'s special edition on masculinities in 1993, "The Big Picture: Masculinities in Recent World History," suffers from the same problems despite the promising title. In that text, Connell's narrow analysis is coupled with a condemnation of the ethnocentrism inherent in the discourse of masculinity (600). While I do not disagree with this diagnosis, I nevertheless find it startling, since I regard Connell's influential book, *Masculinities*, as being a significant factor – maybe even *the* significant factor – in shaping the ethnocentrism of academic discourses of masculinity.

I place this present work within the third phase of masculinity studies, in that I am interested in the concrete *constructions* of masculinities in the colonial context. Thus, the present chapter is an analysis of how Hveyssel constructs his self-representation in the face of Greenlandic folly and savagery. In the following chapters, I examine how the catechists construct the hunter as the foil against which they depict their own masculinity. I therefore do not analyse pre-colonial Greenlandic religion[24] or hunting as a pre-colonial

23 I return to Mariekathrine Poppel's research in chapter six.

24 See in particular Birgitte Sonne (1983, 1986, 1999, 2000), Kleivan and Sonne (1985), Robert Petersen (1990, 1996).

manhood type,[25] but focus on how they are represented and function within constructions of Western masculinity.

A Matter between Men

In this section, I explore how Hveyssel represents the various men in the report, as well as the hierarchies within which they are placed. Mary Magdalene and the Greenlandic catechists thus become the foil for Hveyssel's self-representation as the Western rational male, as seems to be the case with the mission as a whole. In the missionary diaries, the religious struggles in Greenland were from the outset configured as battles between men of God and Greenlandic superstition. There are multiple references in the diaries of the earliest missionaries to the Greenlandic shamans (singular: *angakkoq;* plural: *angakkut*), who were designated witch-masters, as well as the witches (*illitsoq/illitsut*) and their "superstitions." The *angakkut*, however, were the primary target of the missionaries, and stories of the power struggles between missionaries and the *angakkut* are pervasive in all the early diaries.[26] Hans Egede relates this early case in his diary:

25 See, e.g., Poppel (2005a, 2005b).

26 In his foreword to Paul Egede's journal entitled "To Judicious Christian Readers," Hans Egede notes that he found it necessary to publish this journal by his son because it contains more "detailed information on their superstitions and their capacity and desire to accept the Christian faith" than the reader would find in his own journal. Indeed, compared to Hans Egede's journal, this one is literally teeming with references to *angakkut*. The reasons for this may be many, but I would point to three. First, Paul Egede himself mentions that the area itself, Disco Bay, is where "the Devil has its Greenlandic academy; there is an abundance of *angakkut*" (Egede and Egede 1939, 41). Second, and this resonates with Hans Egede's introduction, this particular journal by Paul Egede is much more theologically-oriented than that of his father. Hans Egede's diary is full of references to many different matters, especially problems with the trade, as well as his difficulties with the language. Some of these issues are not problems for Paul Egede; he knows the language, his reputation preceded him, and, according to his own assessment, his arrival was anticipated. Trade had been taken over by the merchant Jakob Severin, and it seems that it was less the missionary's task to oversee trade than was the case with Hans Egede. With fewer references to other matters in Paul Egede's text, the sections dealing with "witchcraft" and "superstitions" thus seem all the more pervasive. Finally, the journal seems to have undergone an editing process with an eye towards public consumption. In the introduction to Paul Egede's *Continuation of Hans Egede's Relations*, Ostermann mentions that there is in the Royal Library a manuscript entitled "Intelligence on the Greenlandic Mission, Its State and Continuation," written in the shape of a journal from 1734 to 1737 by Paul Egede. Due to the fact that the handwriting and orthography are different, and that several words and sentences have been left out, Ostermann declares it a copy, pointing out that it is

The 26th [January 1723], some Greenlanders approach us and announce that one of their experienced trick-artists had arrived at our neighbour's, and would carry out his trickery there this evening. Therefore we should come and see him. I said that I had seen it before, and that their trick is a lie and of no value, to which one of them replied that I was *Mickeckau* [useless] and could do no such things, since the man in question in his tricks had been transported to heaven. He saw no trace of me there, but he did see a dog eating away at an old wench and a girl carrying a *Kablunach* [stranger, usually a Dane] head in her hand, and whatever other fables he had been relating. When I answered that that was pure lies and concocted, they asked me to come over there this evening, so that I could experience it. For pleasure I went along with the bookkeeper and the master [of the skilled workmen]. There the trick-artist proceeded after lights out with his monkey games in the same manner as described earlier. When it finally came to an end, we said that everything which had gone on was all lies and shenanigans, since we understood and knew very well how they managed, which they denied, but couldn't contradict, since in all matters we convinced them of their swindling behaviour. They told us several other fables and swindles, which they in seriousness wanted to make us believe: that when the moon is gone and does not shine, he is in the ocean or on earth and takes seal and other animals up to the heavens to eat etc.

1925, 63

---

largely identical to the printed journal (he notes the aberrations in the footnotes). Ostermann (1939, vi) then states that the aberrations "mainly concern the Moravian Brethren and their relations. The mention of these Moravians is presumably erased from the printed version because of the dominant state of mind at the time, which was favourably inclined towards the Moravians." We don't know if this means that the journal was censored by the king, the university, or Hans Egede. However, the printed version contains very few references to the Moravian mission (see Egede and Egede 1939, 22, 75–76), and thus leaves the impression of its insignificance in the overall scheme of things. So there seems to be a market for literature on "witchcraft" and "superstitions" – or at least the desire to create a market for this kind of literature. This is supported by the following comment by Paul Egede towards the end of the journal: "Following orders from the praiseworthy Missionary Department, I have been more comprehensive in this journal of mine than in the previous. However, I have left out the travels and trips, where nothing noteworthy has taken place; nor have I written anything about our ordinary Danish church service and sermon, choir and catechisation for the people in the colony, as they really don't concern the mission" (Egede and Egede 1939, 110).

This constructed opposition between superstition/folly and reason is a crucial element in the power struggle between the Danish missionaries and the Greenlanders, and may also be seen to operate in Hveyssel's account. The Egede quotation, from two years into the mission, shows the competition for truth – or rather, as Foucault calls it (2002, 131), the struggle over who defines the regime of truth – which is:

> The types of discourse it accepts and makes function as true; the mechanisms and instances that enable one to distinguish true and false statements; the means by which each is sanctioned; the techniques and procedures accorded value in the acquisition of truth; the status of those who are charged with saying what counts as true.

In the quotation from Hans Egede, we are less informed of what counts as true because it is assumed that the reader shares his presuppositions. Egede spatialises folly so that what counts as untrue is located in the neighbour's home, at a walking distance from the dwelling of the Danes, where we may assume that truth resides. Note the argumentative tone in which the narrative is cast: "we understood," "they couldn't contradict," "we convinced them," and then the lies and utter follies that they wanted Egede and his companions to believe. Egede clearly regards the "monkey games" as deception and folly. He is thus speaking within a Protestant Christian discourse, a position that he regards as being the truth. From this discursive position, he passes judgement on what is true and untrue. Claiming the truth is most certainly an exercise of power, a position to which the missionaries will not yield. I have given this example merely to indicate the struggle over the right to pronounce what is true and what is not.

While the missionaries and their aggressive truth-politics had laid claim to speaking the truth from the outset, the Greenlanders had no such absolute and exclusive claims.[27] This locates the struggle on the terrain chosen and defined

27 Paul Egede's approach to Greenlandic lore is to dismiss anything that he has not heard of before in the older Norse traditions. This attitude seems to have annoyed the Greenlanders. In the following example, a man has been telling Egede about a people called *Erkiglit* who have snouts and arrows, and another people called *Iglokut* (halves) because they are as though they had been split down the middle and jump about on one leg. Egede's response is that he believes a little bit of the first because he has read in the work of Norwegian historian and playwright, Ludvig Holberg a similar description of Norsemen, and thus believes that this myth reached Greenland via the Norse settlers. However, he believes nothing at all of the second because it is so ridiculous that it could only be believed by children and fools: "To this he swore and said, 'we believe everything you say, but you

by the missionaries, who in time succeeded in persuading Greenlanders of their version of the truth. This persuasion took place through instruction and admonitions, rules and sanctions, but above all through reading and writing, since, by Protestant logic, the truth is in the text. The Greenlanders were converted to Christianity; they became Christian subjects to the Danish demands for the truth, which they learned to appropriate for themselves through the written word. As Foucault notes (2002, 131), "truth is a thing of this world," and in Greenland, truth was connected to writing. Hence, writing became an instrument of truth and power. The intersection between truth, power, and writing is also evident in Hveyssel's approach to the Habakuk affair, where Hveyssel writes endless letters, assuming that their truth content and mode of expression is self-evident.

The struggle for truth includes attempts to install a new set of norms of manhood in Greenlandic society, where the rational, controlled male with all his scholastic abilities becomes the paragon of masculinity over Greenlandic men, who were demonised as superstitious, irrational, and had to learn how to conform to a rational and Lutheran understanding of mastery and masculinity. I will explore this opposition in more detail in the coming chapters. Here it will serve as the means to examine the representation of men in Hveyssel's reports.

In his reports, Hveyssel constantly draws attention to his attempts to restore his power and establish control over the situation. This is especially the case in the report of 1789; he intersperses descriptions of the complete folly of Mary Magdalene's teachings, and the blindness and stupidity of her Greenlandic followers, with constant references to his own attempts at refutation through oral and written admonitions, scriptural proof, and pointing out the contradictions in her prophecies. In this way, he is discursively defining himself as the champion of reason against this foolishness.

Apart from himself, Hveyssel mentions a number of Greenlandic men: Habakuk, Elijah and the catechists. All the Greenlandic men are represented as being "out of place," in that nearly all of the "national catechists" (Greenland-born men trained as catechists, as opposed to catechists from Denmark) initially choose to support Mary Magdalene. Hence, they are purportedly *not*

---

won't believe anything we say and always contradict us'. To this I answered again that I did not require that they believe the incredible but left it up to him and others to contradict me, because it is only fools who take on all chatter without even contemplating whether it could be plausible or not – I knew very well that with them it is a custom to be amazed over everything they hear even though they quite easily could tell that it was the biggest lie, but then in order not to contradict the narrator, they approve of it so as not to be thought impolite" (Egede and Egede 1939, 86).

conforming to their assigned place in the "proper" order. Hveyssel sees this chaos as a result of Habakuk, the husband whose duty it is to bring his wife under control, not taking *his* duty seriously. However, it is *Hveyssel's* inability to deal with the matter that is noted in Copenhagen. Fabricius's report on the colony Sukkertoppen from 1790[28] notes:

> Hveyssel does not seem to be a grown match for the wiles of this woman, since any other missionary would have done better in restricting this fanatic from the beginning and it is indeed bad that he has even given the case his support by thinking that he himself at some time had heard the same music in the air as the Greenlanders.
>
> OTHO FABRICIUS 1790, point 3

It seems that the small detail of Hveyssel vaguely having heard the bells is a matter of concern in Copenhagen. The Missionary Department regards Hveyssel's "witness" as supporting Mary's claims. It is impossible to know Hveyssel's reasons for acknowledging the sound of the bells. A possible interpretation is that he is being tactical, and is attempting to defeat Mary on her own turf by inserting himself between the bells and her teachings. By acknowledging the bells, it becomes possible for Hveyssel to dismiss their significance and thus offer an authoritative truth about the bells to defeat Mary's use of them as 'proof' of the 'truth' of her own false revelations. In order to sever any connection between the two events – the bells and Mary Magdalene's teachings – it would be necessary for someone to hear the bells and to refute the teachings, as Hveyssel did. This tactic also shows up in Hveyssel's view of resistance to the movement as a matter of self-restraint:

> Frederik Berthelsen had, not far from there, let himself be blinded when he was with me in springtime at Iĸĸamiut. There he believed he had heard the melody of a hymn; I therefore allowed him – upon his request – during the summer to travel to Nappasoĸ, for fear that he would become more engrossed in the pretended revelations. In the meantime, I discovered some exaggerated absurdities, concerning which I wrote him, and thus put a final end to his doubts.
>
> HVEYSSEL 1788–89, point 4, item 3

28 *Rigsarkivet* (Danish National Archives): *Missionskollegiet og Direktionen for Vajsenhuset: Indkomne sager den grønlandske mission vedk. 1789–91*, folder 1789: Otho Fabricius's report on Kolonien Sukkertoppen to the Missionary Department, 12 June 1790, point 3.

Frederik Berthelsen had faltered, allowing himself for a brief moment to be blinded. However, he realised his error in judgement and, out of fear of becoming drawn in, requested leave. This ability to step back, evaluate, and act is the epitome of reason as developed in the Western philosophical tradition.[29] This brief note from Hveyssel, included in a report on another catechist, Micka, shows how Frederik Berthelsen demonstrates this rational self, and is surpassed only by Hveyssel, who heard something but did not assign it any real importance.

While neither Frederik Berthelsen nor Hveyssel are enraptured by Mary, Hveyssel says the other catechists have shown themselves less resistant to her charisma. In particular, Joseph Berthelsen, Frederik's brother, has been taken in (from stupidity rather than evil, Hveyssel reasons), and even acts as Mary's scribe, although he does admit that she is unreasonable (1789 report). In the report from the following year, when matters have settled down, Hveyssel gives Joseph this recommendation:

> The brother Joseph Berthelsen has with exaggerated stubbornness resisted us in these fanatical affairs, rejected all my admonitions and, directly against my prohibition, stayed with Habakuk in Kangerdlugssuatsiaq and strengthened the Greenlanders in their digressions and evil. For this reason he has not received anything at the Department's expense. Although he has now left their bad company and, as he claims, burned all the papers on which he had written all the alleged revelations of the wench and her followers, I have decided not to take him back into service in this district. If it pleases the Department in light of his poor father's long service to [unintelligible word] him, I would support this, but wish that he be placed somewhere else than here, where he has strengthened the deviants in their mad antics.
>
> HVEYSSEL 1790, point 3

Hveyssel is thoroughly displeased with Joseph Berthelsen, a former favourite who not only deserted the missionary, but stubbornly insisted on remaining with Habakuk. Hveyssel sees Joseph's actions as exacerbating the situation, encouraging the Greenlanders to dissent even further, when he should have been doing the opposite. Furthermore, by acting as Mary's scribe, Joseph is using his writing skills to support the movement instead of fighting it. Even though Joseph has repented, Hveyssel does not want anything more to do with

29 See also Louis Dupré's rendition in *The Enlightenment and the Intellectual Foundations of Modern Culture* (2004, esp. 45–77), and Charles Taylor's *Sources of the Self* (1989).

him and appeals for an alternative placement for Joseph. Hveyssel is very displeased with what he sees as Joseph's blatant disregard for his admonitions and prohibitions – and punishes him.

Before all this trouble began, Hveyssel had insisted on both Berthelsen brothers receiving European rations; according to merchant receipts, they did receive such supplies in 1787.[30] In addition to these rations, which included butter, bread, beef, and malt, they were given a certain amount of credit at the trade station. It is not explicitly stated how much money Frederik Berthelsen had to his name, but in 1785–86 he purchased goods for 35 rigsdaler, a considerable sum at the time. Thuesen (2007, 214) notes that Frederik was the head catechist, which probably accounts for his higher wage. Joseph's annual wage was 25 rigsdaler, less than Frederik but well beyond what the national catechists received. In the accounts listed, the national catechists purchased goods for three to five rigsdaler. However, the purchases of the two brothers are quite different. Where Joseph's habits were close to those of the national catechists, Frederik's were much closer to those of Hveyssel. While Joseph bought ammunition, tobacco, and odds and ends amounting to seven items in 1785–86, Frederik bought 39 items, including stockings, coffee, syrup, a blade, and Hungary water (perfume).[31] This extensive shopping list could be an indication of a sense of belonging, where Frederik saw himself as more European than his fellow catechists *and* was encouraged in this view by the missionary. His brother Joseph, on the other hand, was much closer to the self-understanding of the national catechists. This is very interesting since the Berthelsen family is, as Thuesen (2007, 211) notes, an early example of the soon-to-be-implemented missionary policy of recruiting catechists from the 'mixed' families (Thuesen 2007, 211).[32] It is therefore remarkable to see the contrast between the brothers in how they identify themselves at this early stage.

---

30 According to the accounts (see reference in next note), Frederik Berthelsen was already on half-rations in 1785–86. In a report from 1786, Hveyssel thanks the Missionary Department for allotting Joseph half-rations and a raise. (*Rigsarkivet* [Danish National Archives]: *Missionskollegiet og Direktionen for Vajsenhuset: Indkomne sager den grønlandske mission vedk.* 1786–88, folder 1786, no. 14: Hveyssel's report to the Missionary Department, 7 September 1786, point 4.)

31 *Rigsarkivet* (Danish National Archives): *Missionskollegiet og Direktionen for Vajsenhuset: Indkomne sager den grønlandske mission vedk.* 1786–88, folder 1786, no. 14: Merchant Lund's account from 1785–86.

32 In the aforementioned report by Otho Fabricius (*Rigsarkivet* [Danish National Archives]: *Missionskollegiet og Direktionen for Vajsenhuset: Indkomne sager den grønlandske mission vedk.* 1789–91, folder 1789: Otho Fabricius's report on Kolonien Sukkertoppen to the Missionary Department, 12 June 1790, point 3), Fabricius recommends the use of national

The final group of men in Hveyssel's reports are the national catechists. Hveyssel is quite obviously distressed about the "dissent" of the catechists, whose reactions to Mary Magdalene and himself he recounts in the report from 1789. Hveyssel lists five national catechists whom the mission employed to teach and preach to their fellow Greenlanders. The idea of establishing colleges to educate Greenlandic men who could then be placed in outposts and settlements, and thus act as the extended arm of the mission, was first proposed by Hans Egede in 1725 (Thuesen 2007, 49) and institutionalised in 1847 and 1848, when the two colleges were built in Godthåb (Nuuk) and Jakobshavn (Ilulissat).[33] However, the practice of recruiting indigenous men to assist the missionaries began much earlier. The first national catechist was Frederik Christian, who worked from 1729 (H. Egede 1925, 228; Gad 1969, 191) until his death in the smallpox epidemic of 1733–34. Danish catechists were also a significant part of the missionary staff and were recruited from among orphans in Denmark and schooled and disciplined at Vajsenhuset, a boarding house for orphans in Copenhagen, which was established in 1727 (Lauridsen and Lytthans 1983, 71). The motivation for recruiting Greenlandic catechists was partly a desire for cheaper labour, but also a cultural convenience; Greenlanders knew the language and could more readily relate to the daily practices of their fellow Greenlanders, their hunting habits, and the severe conditions of the land, according to one missionary Rasch in 1758 (Lauridsen and Lytthans 1983, 241), a point which the head of the Missionary Department, Otho Fabricius would repeat and implement in 1790 (see note 58).

In their thesis on labour and colonisation, anthropologists Lauridsen and Lytthans point to the consistent frustration with the national catechists' understanding of labour, which differed considerably from the expectations of the missionaries.[34] The major concern was the "wild and untamed" nature of the

catechists instead of men from Denmark for several reasons. The primary reason is financial gain, but the matter of language is also significant, since Greenlandic posed a significant challenge to the Danish missionaries. He further urges that national catechists be recruited from among the sons of Danish fathers, and that the smartest and most eager to learn be sought out.

33 I shall return to the important and comprehensive studies concerning this period by Thuesen (2007) and Wilhjelm (1997, 2001, 2008).

34 The work by Thomas Kring Lauridsen and Kaspar Lytthans, based on detailed archival studies of missionary correspondence from the selected period (1740–1765), is an analysis of the mission to Greenland as a socialisation process. Influenced by Foucault's *Discipline and Punish*, they carry out a micro-analysis of how socialisation took place and what it contained, tracing the actions of the Danes on the Greenlanders. They analyse how the missionaries placed themselves in a position of authority and control via various tactics,

Greenlanders and their neglect of their catechist duties when the weather was clear for hunting (1983, 243). These complaints were quite consistent and it became clear to the Danish missionaries that it was necessary not only to educate Greenlandic men, but also to discipline them so they would conform to a certain understanding of and relationship to labour (244). Greenlandic men, it was said, had to be taught that their salary was not a gift but a wage earned through work. The missionaries attempted to instil this understanding of work through admonitions, surveillance, and pay (247), but the many complaints over instability and laziness show that it was not as easy as the missionaries first envisioned. One reason for this was the inferiority of this kind of work – what Lauridsen and Lytthans call "spiritual labour" (223) – in the eyes of Greenlanders and of the Danish working class.

While the spiritual labours of the *angakkut* were well integrated within a Greenlandic worldview, and directed towards every-day concerns such as hunting and sustenance, the preaching of the missionaries did not seem to relate to anything important (Lauridsen and Lytthans 1983, 224). This is why the implementation of a different authority, namely, the rational man, necessarily meant a recasting of the entire Greenlandic society in a fundamentally new mould, issues that are elaborated in the following chapters. But this was a slow and comprehensive process that only began to take serious shape in the mid-nineteenth century. The attempts by missionaries to educate and discipline Greenlanders would in time result in the fostering of a rational masculinity, which had the double convenience of saving on labour costs while implementing indirect rule.

As has been pointed out by Gad, Thuesen, and Wilhjelm, the national catechists were caught in a double bind when it came to hunting and provisions. While Danish catechists were paid partly in wages (about 50 rigsdaler a year each) and partly in rations, the Greenlandic catechists were paid less than 10

---

and thus restricted the conditions for Greenlandic self-sufficiency (Lauridsen and Lytthans 1983, 183). Thuesen critiques Lauridsen and Lytthans for staging the conflict as one between two different but equal parties, and because their interpretation cannot explain the emergence of mediating interpretative systems among the catechists and the group of *blandinger* engaged in both systems. I cannot recognise Thuesen's figuration of their argument; it seems clear to me that Lauridsen and Lytthans emphasise that there is an inequality in structural power, but that the Greenlanders were not powerless in their negotiation of it. This acknowledgement of Greenlandic agency opens up space for future Greenlandic adaptations of Danish power and its avenues. However, these developments are well beyond the chronological scope of their work. Thuesen does acknowledge that the analysis by Lauridsen and Lytthans concerns the initial confrontations and thus describes events that came 100 years before what Thuesen discusses (2007, 61).

rigsdaler a year each, and expected to provide for themselves and their families (Lauridsen and Lytthans 1983, 254). The colonial administrators were adamant that Greenlanders should not become accustomed to Danish/European food, but should supply their own through hunting. This was part of the larger agenda of the merchants, who did not want the Greenlanders to turn away from their hunting practices, on which the Trade relied for profit.[35]

Turning to the catechists at Sukkertoppen, my readings of the archival material relating to this particular colony have been focussed on the employment of its catechists, especially from the years 1786–91. From this material, it is clear that Hveyssel understood the Berthelsen brothers as constituting a different group, since he refers to them as catechists, while the others are called *national* catechists, which is an identifier for Greenlander.[36] As noted above, the brothers were paid up to six times more than the national catechists, in addition to the rations supplied by the Trade. Furthermore, according to the 1787 report, both brothers had been trained in bloodletting,[37] a medical practice of the day in which they were apparently quite accomplished. The national catechists were as yet unable to perform this procedure, but Hveyssel would see to it that they were encouraged to learn it as soon as the appropriate instruments arrived. The ability to perform bloodletting, which sets Frederik and Joseph apart from their countrymen, would presumably have been much esteemed by their fellow Greenlanders because it would resonate with the practice of the *angakkut* and some of their healing practices.

Hence, to Hveyssel, Frederik and Joseph Berthelsen were in a different league than the others. This was attributable to the fact that their father, Berthel Laersen, was Danish *and* a very popular missionary in the district. This may help to account for why the Missionary Department might have wanted to look favourably on Joseph despite his fall from grace. I shall look more closely at this differentiation and preferential treatment in the following chapters, but I note for now that Hveyssel is clearly treating these two Greenlanders, sons of a Danish father, differently and seems to expect more of them. That is at least the impression one gets if we compare the punishment of Joseph with that of

35 Some catechists were paid in wage-rations. Via archival investigations, Gad established that in 1793, 12 of the 35 national catechists were given rations, and eight of these were given only half-portions (Gad 1972, 28; Lauridsen and Lytthans 1983, 254).

36 In a report from 1787, point 2, Hveyssel thanks the Missionary Department for the favour bestowed on Catechist Frederik Berthelsen. However, Hveyssel had clearly begun writing "National" but stopped and then wrote "Catechist" over the letters "N" and "a."

37 Bloodletting, a common medical practice until the late nineteenth century, consisted of drawing large amounts of blood from a patient after opening an artery, usually in the underarm near the elbow.

Isaak, one of the national catechists. Initially, Isaak received the following report (in 1789):

> Isaak, formerly one of the most accomplished and hardworking catechists, has stood at Kangisleet in the fiord Kangerdlugssuatsiaq last winter, where the seductress is staying and has let himself be deceived by her so that he politely defends her cause. He has (and I am ashamed to write this) been led by her to believe that he is Christ, and her husband Habakuk, who before his baptism was a murderer and two years ago a well-known whore-man and adulterer, she calls Jesus and says that he is equal to the big God. When I was told this, as well as numerous other absurdities and shameful things, I could not immediately get to them. In addition, when I was informed that they were heading off on the caribou hunt – since their Prophetess had postponed Judgement Day – I wrote them a letter and admonished them to open their eyes and not be deceived by her lies and blasphemy. But I can guess the extent of the effect of the letter on them by the fact that they immediately went off with her on the hunt.
>
> HVEYSSEL 1789, point 4, no. 5

Isaak seems to be in the thick of things, participating in the Habakuk community, embodying the teachings of Mary, and, above all, ignoring Hveyssel's admonishments. In the report from the following year (1790), Hveyssel tells of his decision regarding Isaak:

> Isaak at Akpamiut, who last year was on the side of the fanatic, but last autumn made good promises and assurances, has in the beginning of the winter not entirely given up on his propensity for this, since he had Elijah with him who was one of the false prophets. In consideration of his former work and accomplishments, his isolation from the fanatic of his own free will, and his strong assurances, he may in future show the usual hard work and loyalty for which I earlier have commended him, I let him stay in service, albeit first of all with a noticeable reduction in his salary.
>
> HVEYSSEL 1790, point 3

It appears that the punishment for Joseph is harsher, or that Hveyssel regards Joseph's dissent more seriously, since Hveyssel earlier requested of the Missionary Department that Joseph be favoured.[38] Following Joseph's dissent,

---

38 In the report dated 7 September 1786, Hveyssel thanks the Missionary Department for the decision to hire Joseph and give him 25 rigsdaler in salary and a half-ration (*Rigsarkivet*

Hveyssel expels him from the district[39] and wants nothing more to do with him. In contrast, Isaak, who seems to have been involved in the Habakuk movement at a similar level, is kept on as a catechist. It is worth noting another incident, mentioned in a letter dated 27 August 1787, in relation to Joseph. Here Hveyssel states that he wanted to keep Joseph at the colony to assess what use may be had of him in regard to language. Hveyssel writes: "But now that the Inspector has placed the infamously lustful Lund as merchant here, I have no choice but to let Joseph stay at one of the outposts so that his daughters will not be seduced."

By 1789, the tone has changed somewhat, for now Hveyssel says about Joseph that

> I have told him that if he wants salary and rations the following winter, he has to come and stay at the colony, but this he refuses. He gives this excuse: that he fears that his daughters would come in bad (illegible) because of the Danish crew, which he says has happened earlier at Fiskenæsset.

Joseph seems less than impressed with the sexual morals at the colony, and Hveyssel does not seem to think this is an adequate excuse – even though he fully shared these same concerns a few years earlier. There appears to be a complex struggle going on here: Hveyssel seems to be pushing Joseph to identify as a European by setting him apart from the others through favours and privilege. In response, Joseph seems to be resisting this push by joining the movement and refusing to stay at the colony, where his family would come under increased Danish influence.

With respect to the national catechists, Hveyssel retains most of them after the trouble has blown over. Only Titus and Sem, the two who, according to Hveyssel, assisted in killing their mothers, were dismissed. The rest (Isaak, Christian and Micka) are taken back into service due to their early repentance and hard work. Micka and Christian were initially taken in by Mary, but they had moved quickly to distance themselves from her. What is striking in these

---

[Danish National Archives]: *Missionskollegiet og Direktionen for Vajsenhuset: Indkomne sager den grønlandske mission vedk.* 1786–88, folder 1786, no. 14: Hveyssel's report to the Missionary Department, 7 September 1786, point 4).

39 Joseph is later employed by Missionary Heide in Holsteinsborg according to a letter from Hveyssel (*Rigsarkivet* [Danish National Archives]: *Missionskollegiet og Direktionen for Vajsenhuset: Indkomne sager den grønlandske mission vedk.* 1788–91, folder 1791, no. 13: Hveyssel's report to the Missionary Department, 23 July 1791, point 1). This is repeated in no. 24: Hveyssel's letter to the Missionary Department, 15 August 1791, point 3.

brief notices about the national catechists is Hveyssel's display of authority. He decides who goes and who stays, whether their salary is to be reduced or stay the same (salary raises are the privilege of the Missionary Department in Copenhagen) and has, in effect, established a situation of mastery and hierarchy in relation to the Greenlandic men. Hveyssel depicts their straying from his tutelage in sexual terms, as a seduction away from the 'correct' relationship, which at the same time is a 'correct' social order and patriarchal hierarchy. Therefore, he can say in his report (1789, point 3) that "Christian has consistently proved himself worthy of the high thoughts I have had of him," a statement which smacks of superiority and patriarchal benevolence.

In this section, I have drawn out how Hveyssel attempts to construct a position of mastery for himself. From this position, the Greenlanders employed by Hveyssel are placed in a hierarchical order that corresponds to their level of obedience and their Danish ancestry. Hveyssel has high expectations of Frederik and Joseph Berthelsen because of their Danish ancestry. However, only Frederik meets these expectations, while Joseph becomes a follower of Mary. Outside this realm of discipline, we have the Greenlanders, who appear to the reader as one big nameless mass with a handful of prominent names: Habakuk, Mary, Elijah, Alhed. Furthermore, Hveyssel also constructs himself as the embodiment of a rational detached masculinity very much in line with the general self-perception of the Danish/Norwegian missionaries in Greenland. This is particularly brought out in the dealings with Greenlandic "superstition" and "folly." The rest of the book argues the position that this rational masculinity is instilled in what was to become the Greenlandic elite. While this emergent masculinity was institutionalised in the mid-nineteenth century, I propose we can glimpse its inception and emergence in interactions between missionaries, such as Hveyssel, and catechists, such as Frederik Berthelsen.

In Hveyssel's report from 1789, order has been restored. In the next section, I analyse what Hveyssel considers the reason for the disruption of order, and in the subsequent chapters, I extrapolate the "order" to which he refers.

In the Manner of Women

I begin with Söderberg's point concerning Hveyssel's view of the conflict: Mary Magdalene is understood as a personification of the conflict between Lutheran orthodoxy and Moravian Christianity. In fact, this is the view taken by most church histories about the mission to Greenland; they tend to eclipse the contact with indigenous religious practices and overemphasise the struggles between the Moravian Brethren and the Lutheran mission (Koch and Kornerup 1951; Lidegaard 1993). A consequence of this emphasis is that the conflict becomes centred on theological ideas, while the every-day life and practice of Greenlanders is marginalised. Another significant point is that these noble theological ideas are conceptualised by men.[40] When Hveyssel reduces Mary Magdalene to a matter of doctrine, we are witnessing a masculine signifying universe,[41] where meaning is produced from an already-established masculine hegemony. This hegemony is in turn sustained by re-signifying Mary Magdalene, from being Greenlandic, different, dangerous, and unpredictable, to being the gendered expression of well-known and comforting theological heresies. This move erases her "Greenlandishness," subsuming it within an abstract theological framework whose gender-symbolism marks her as a superstitious "wench." In one move, she predictably comes to embody the symbolism of superstition as envisioned by Lutheran Christianity, while her distinctiveness as a *Greenlandic* woman is simultaneously emphasised and erased. It is emphasised because she is made the vehicle of these heretical ideas that place notions of doubled superstition (Greenlandic and woman) and deviant religious practices into a single person who from the outset must be prone to such tendencies (visions and heretical interpretations) because of her gender and race. It is, however, simultaneously erased because she, the flesh-and-blood-person Mary Magdalene, is unimportant. She is, after all, just a vehicle – it is the ideas she stands for which must be combated.

To elaborate some of the theoretical issues raised in the preceding discussions, I have chosen a theoretical approach to gender that emphasises historical developments. This is necessary in relation to the scope of the analysed material. The approach outlined by American labour historian Joan W. Scott (1986) in "Gender: A Useful Category of Historical Analysis" emphasises symbols, contesting interpretations, institutions, and social relations in gender analysis. Scott (1986, 1067) understands gender as "a constitutive element of social relationships based on perceived differences between the sexes" and as "a primary way of signifying relationships of power." In other words, in a worldview where men and women are seen as different and take on various socially-determined roles that correspond to these differences, gender is a significant and fundamental element in establishing and sustaining these roles. Consequently, this corresponds to the symbolic use of gender to signify power relations, a symbolism that also rests on the presumption of difference. Scott proposes the following four elements of gender: culturally-available symbols,

40 Merry E. Weisner frames this question in relation to her work on the Protestant Reformation and the Catholic Counter-Reformation (1998, 33).

41 This expression is taken from Lone Fatum's study on the history of theological discrimination (1982, 42).

normative interpretations of these symbols, institutional representation, and subjective identity (1986, 1067–68).

The task of the historian is to address these elements with questions such as: which symbols are evoked to represent gender, and in what contexts? At which times and under what circumstances do dominating interpretations emerge, and what are they trying to exclude? How are these understandings of gender related to wider social institutions and organisations, such as education, economy, and the labour market? And finally, how are gendered identities constructed and how may this be related to cultural representations (1986, 1068)? Interrelated but distinct is Scott's theorising of gender, which follows Bourdieu and Godelier, and which asserts that since gender is established as an objective frame of reference, it is deployed to structure and legitimise social relations: "[C]onceptual languages employ differentiation to establish meaning and...sexual difference is a primary way of signifying differentiation" (1986, 1070). Gender is part of the construction of meaning on the national and reproductive levels, while it also structures levels of knowledge. For gender to make sense at all as an objective frame of reference requires a preconceived notion of gender characteristics such as rational men and emotional intuitive women, as well as an assumption about gender hierarchies. I will show how these structures are manifested in the treatment of Mary Magdalene.

Within the colonial setting of Greenland, the mission constitutes an influential institution, and the missionaries, all educated in Denmark at the University in Copenhagen, bring their cultural assumptions of gender with them. Prevalent at this time is the connection drawn between women and superstition, which took on a life of its own in the Greenlandic context where what was seen as superstitious belief and behaviour abounded. The following quotation from the diary of Henrik Christopher Glahn, a missionary from 1763 to 1769 in Holsteinsborg (present-day Sisimiut) shows that while on the surface he seems culturally sensitive about different belief patterns and their cultural settings, he nevertheless does not challenge the predominant view that the Greenlandic epistemological structures are superstitious. I will explore this further in the next section, and here only draw attention to the prevalent gender pattern in Glahn's writing:

> Concerning this superstition which reigns among the Greenlanders, I had occasion to ponder the matter last evening. If one gleans from experiences in other countries, it is shown that nothing is so difficult to root out as an old superstition. It is imbibed as with mother's milk and the constant repetition by so many old wives makes an impression on the soul, which cannot be persuaded by the strongest of reasons. How does it

> stand in our own countries, where Christianity for so long has had its seat? I wonder: is all superstition rooted out from there? I recall being chased out by a minister's wife once in my childhood, because I was so unfortunate as to be suspected of having evil eyes. And is it not well known that in Jutland one will never have the luck to make good candles should a man enter at that very moment?
>
> 1921, 11–12

It is noteworthy that the women are portrayed as the active transmitters (many old wives, the minister's wife, and the candlemakers, which was a woman's occupation), *and* as providing the symbolism of the transmission ("mother's milk") of superstition, all of which is negatively defined and strongly opposed to reason. This characterisation is not limited to Glahn or, for that matter, to Greenland. It is part of a larger Danish Protestant Enlightenment discourse in which women are connected with superstition and 'papist' ritual, while men are inscribed as the champions of God's word, who with logic and enlightened Protestant rationality can see through and fight against these follies and figments of the human imagination. In 1736, on the 200th anniversary of the Reformation in Denmark, the Danish court theologian Erik Pontoppidan published a pamphlet on superstition – in Latin, so as to target only the "soul-doctors" and not the diseased souls of the unenlightened (Pontoppidan [1736] 1923, 4). In this publication, we also find the double connection between women and superstition, where women ("old hags") are repeatedly marked as the active performers of all kinds of heathen and papist "folly," as well as being the symbolic vehicle for superstition. Note the overt and explicit gendering of orthodoxy and superstition in the following quotation from Pontoppidan:

> It is much to be regretted that this Queen of Superstition, if we may call it that, still rules over poor fat-headed people, even though she is of great displeasure to the heavenly King, on whose will alone the dark or light forms of Fortune rely…
>
> 1923, 15

Pontoppidan's pamphlet is but one of a long line of theological dissertations and writings on superstition and magic that began in Denmark with a paper by the Reformation theologian Niels Hemmingsen called "Warning to Avoid Excess Belief [*overtro*, i. e. superstition] in Magic" from 1575 (Olrik 1923, iii). These writings address a larger issue on the symbolic role of women. In his study on witchcraft in Denmark between 1500 and 1588, historian Karsten Sejr Jensen notes the profound shift in the symbolic role of women that occurred with the Reformation, and the alterations within the "divine order." Before the Reformation, the figure of the Virgin Mary had played an important part in the order of the spiritual universe. After the Protestant reconfiguration and the exclusion of Mary from the divine economy, the godhead became solely masculine. Jensen notes that Luther did attempt to anchor the holiness of the woman exclusively in the domestic sphere, but without the religious symbolism in the divine sphere to underpin it, the attempt was unsuccessful (Jensen 1980, 65). Jensen argues that women and their power became something completely incomprehensible, and thus connected to strong and mystic forces (76). The attempt to control these forces took place by connecting women with any deviation from the norms of patriarchal society (77). Thus, Jensen does not see witchcraft as an expression of the free and conscious woman's reaction against patriarchal society, but as one of the ways in which patriarchal society could suppress and control women, as well as an expression of the deep anxiety towards the feminine that society instilled in men (77).

Bringing Scott to bear on Jensen's conclusions, we see how gender is used to configure the norm (masculine) and the deviation (feminine). Furthermore, this lends legitimacy to the control of women as a way for society to sustain its structure. This combination of women and superstition/witchcraft was vividly sustained through the centuries as a consolidation of Protestantism as a rational relationship to God. Hence, a new symbolic role was created for woman, namely as Queen of Superstition. It is difficult to avoid the suspicion that Pontoppidan is using this designation as a play on the Queen of Heaven, a title for the Virgin Mary. Note that in Pontoppidan's pamphlet the superstitious practices were of both heathen and "papist" nature, enabling him to conclude with the following: "[P]apism as an unholy cuckoo-mother has sat on these rotten eggs of heathenism…" (1923, 68). This gendered symbolism was the result of the collusion of "papism" and heathenism, and created a symbolic role that fed into many concrete ideas and suspicions about the power of women and the provenance of that power. But it was also the result of the removal of the female from the divine order, a removal which left the role of the witch as the chief locus for conceptualising women and power. In turn, this increased the accusations and convictions for witchcraft in the centuries following the Reformation. Hence, in the theological world of eighteenth-century Denmark, there was a prevailing tendency not only to identify sorcery and superstition with women, but also to conceive of "deviant" female behaviour as a fundamental threat to the patriarchal social structure (Fatum 1982, 51).

Paying attention to these conditions, and how they form the necessary backdrop to understanding missionary Hveyssel's presentation of events, helps avoid hasty conclusions such as the one in Inge Kleivan's analysis of another charismatic figure in the history of Greenland, *The Virgin Mary of Tasiussaq* (1986).[42] Kleivan emphasises this movement's "obvious feminist nature" – unlike the Habakuk movement. The reason for this feminist label is that Kleivan sees the Virgin movement as an expression of one woman's (Inequnarneq's) protest against, and attempt to influence her fate in, a male-dominated world (1986, 221). Kleivan's article is important and groundbreaking in its own right since, as she points out, the scholars who previously analysed the movement were all male and therefore failed to give Inequnarneq's social and economic background and motivations much notice, let alone take them seriously. In this sense, Kleivan's article certainly departs from earlier approaches. Yet it stays firmly within a gendered structure that she does not question. She never raises questions as to *why* previous scholars see Inequnarneq as cheeky, fanatical, or hysterical, and which notions and understandings of women, men, superstition and rationality are behind such labels. As indicated above, these presuppositions should be just as important as the economic and social issues, not least, as Joan Scott argues, because these presuppositions underpin the economic and social realities in which these movements, as well as the interpretations of them, take place. With this in mind, I want to contextualise Hveyssel's presentation of Mary.

How exactly does Hveyssel attempt to downplay Mary Magdalene's charisma, or popularity? Which understanding of gender does Hveyssel presuppose, and how is this expressed? First, it is interesting to note that Hveyssel, according to his first report, approaches Habakuk about his wife, and thus subordinates Mary to her husband. In the second report, Hveyssel casts her as spokesperson for the Moravian customs introduced by Berthel Laersen. She is denied any individuality or independence, but is in both cases represented solely in connection with a man. Hence, she is reduced to either a wife, who needs to be trained and subordinated, or a mouthpiece for a dissenting Christianity. This indicates that Hveyssel represents Mary from his own theological and cultural presuppositions. Consequently, he speaks from Danish understandings of gender roles and social patterns, which tie the woman to the life of the family and subordinate her to the authority of the husband. However, as I noted above from the brief discussion of Pontoppidan's pamphlet, *Fejekost*, women are also regarded as being simultaneously the symbolic bearers and the actual vehicles of superstition, whether of the heathen or "papist" variety. This in turn is closely connected to the above-mentioned

42 Inequnarneq of Tasiussaq, also known as the Virgin Mary of Tasiussaq, claimed in the winter of 1874–75 to have given birth to the baby Jesus, who then gave her a number of messages about the improvement of her social status.

reduction of Mary's visions and interpretations of the hereafter to a matter of doctrine, which places the situation within Hveyssel's jurisdiction, since with the questions regarding correct Christian doctrine and practice, he is one of the highest clerical authorities in the country. Hence, with scriptural authorities to back him, he can condemn Mary's teachings as being against the will of God. That the Greenlanders reject his exegetical manoeuvres and theological acumen as authoritative is seen in the reactions of Mary's followers: they either leave or sing hymns to block out his words.

There is another interesting designation for Mary, namely, seductress of catechists. This sexual symbolisation of her power over the catechists invokes a comprehensive legal sphere that understands non-marital sexual relations as a breach of public morality (Koefoed 2008, 187). As historian Isabel Hull notes in her study of sexuality and the state in eighteenth-century Germany, sexual imagery was used to discuss social issues. Its usefulness relied in part on the central role sexuality had played in the construction of the social order (1997, 230). The Reformation and its rejection of celibacy, its central positioning of marriage and upward valuation of marital sex, made the Protestant civil vision even more "resolutely heterosexual and family-centred." This shift in emphasis generated a different list of sexual sins than had been the case in the Roman Catholic tradition, where sodomy, bestiality, and masturbation were central. To the Reformers, non-relational, non-heterosexual activity was quite marginal to the marriage project and thus the important sexual sins became those that threatened marriage – fornication, adultery, and adulterous thoughts (1997, 21).[43] I do think that we need to go further than merely noting that sexual imagery is central in conceptualising social issues. For Luther, the references to licit and illicit intercourse, and appropriate interaction, were part of

43 In 1737, Pontoppidan also wrote the official exposition of Luther's small catechism, called *Sandhed til Gudfrygtighed* (Truth in Accordance with Godliness). This was adapted to Greenlandic circumstances by the earliest missionaries. Unfortunately, no copies of the Greenlandic versions remain. Within Pontoppidan's catechism, the proper code of conduct within a marriage is included under the discussion of the sixth commandment and its prohibition on fornication. This section consists of 22 questions and answers, and is thus the third-largest topic. Here we have the divine institution of marriage to reproduce, to prevent lust, to provide mutual help, comfort, and consultation (question 208); the code of conduct between husband and wife (questions 209–210); and the prohibition of fornication, adultery and adulterous thoughts (questions 213–218); as well as what may lead to weaknesses of the flesh, such as drinking (questions 221–224), and a host of circumstances, such as idleness, lascivious company, novels and loose love-books or images, frivolous games, dancing, acting, and all that which generates lust for the eye, lust for the flesh, and opulent living (question 225).

his larger political reformation programme and its attempts to intervene in the household structure of Roman Catholicism, thereby eroding the social structure supported by that household structure. Given the influence of marital morality in the Lutheran social structure, it is hardly surprising that sexual imagery is central in conceptualising social issues. It also gives us a sense of how grave Hveyssel considers Mary's offences to be. Not only does she refuse his authority, but she is threatening the entire social structure. The nature of this social structure is the object of the third chapter after a theoretical digression in the following.

CHAPTER 2

Complicating Governmentality

Colonialism, Protestantism, and Greenland

The relationship between the individual and the social structure is one of special importance in regards both to Hveyssel's tasks and Mary Magdalene's behaviour within the pastorate, and an important corrective to the traditional emphasis on the theological content of the whole affair. That the events surrounding Mary Magdalene have a theological import is evident. This is indicated by the references to God, Christ, and Jesus, which Hveyssel snatches from Mary's teachings, which are subsequently recast in terms of Roman Catholicism and Moravian Christianity as a way to take control of the situation. The theological import is further reflected in Hveyssel's attempts to refute the teachings through a stream of biblical exegesis. Presumably, Hveyssel never dreamed that Mary Magdalene would be taken seriously because he himself found her teachings so utterly ridiculous and unbelievable. But I propose that as the task of the missionary goes beyond that of making *Christian* subjects of the Greenlanders to making Christian *subjects* of them, so the resistance takes on a much broader sense. To theorise the relation between the individual and social structure in a way that takes the systemic role of religion seriously, Foucault's theory of governmentality and the central role of pastoral power works well, albeit with a few adjustments. This short chapter serves to introduce the theoretical apparatus of my analysis.

Pastoral Power and Governmentality

Simply named "Governmentality," Foucault's essay was originally one of the lectures from the *Security, Territory, Population* lecture series at the Collège de France between 1977 and 1978. This lecture was subsequently published as a discrete essay in *Aut Aut* in 1978, and later reprinted in the anthology on governmentality, *The Foucault Effect,* published by a number of Foucault's coworkers (Burchell, Gordon, and Miller 1991). The major points of Foucault's essay revolve around the notion of governmentality as signifying a certain type of power, an art of government, which "has the population as its target, political economy as its major form of knowledge, and apparatuses of security as its essential technical instrument" (2007, 108).

What Foucault sets out to do in this essay is map the difference between sovereignty and governmentality, as well as the development of the "art of government." The problem of government was particularly acute in the sixteenth century at the crossroads of two processes:

> [T]he one that, shattering the structures of feudalism, leads to the establishment of the great territorial, administrative, and colonial states; and a totally different movement that, with the Reformation and the Counter-Reformation, raises the issue of how one must be spiritually ruled and led on this earth in order to achieve eternal salvation.
>
> 2000d, 202

The issues of government are thus situated within the social and spiritual upheavals of the sixteenth century. In that context, Foucault traces questions of government and its focus on the various engagements with Machiavelli's *The Prince*. Foucault argues that the "reason of state" developed in the late sixteenth and seventeenth centuries, and its institutional structures, acted as an obstacle to the development of the art of government for historical reasons (2000d, 213). The historical impediments were the great upheavals of the seventeenth century—wars, rebellions, and financial crises. "The art of government could only spread and develop in subtlety in an age of expansion, free from the great military, political, and economic tensions that afflicted the seventeenth century from beginning to end" (2000d, 213).

Another obstacle was sovereignty and its institutions, which was the centre and purpose of all development. The outflanking of these obstacles was aided by a number of processes:

> [T]he demographic expansion of the eighteenth century, connected with an increasing abundance of money, which in turn was linked to the expansion of agricultural production through a series of circular processes with which the historians are familiar.
>
> 2000d, 215

Here we see the difference between modes of government. Sovereignty is an end unto itself, with laws as its instruments. Its workings are centripetal, drawing things towards the centre. Governmentality, on the other hand, is decentred, oriented towards the management of things, the welfare of the population, and perfecting the processes through multiple tactics (2000d, 211).

The separate publication of the essay makes it easy to overlook the place of pastoral power within the genealogy of governmentality and its central place in the power structure of governmentality as a whole.[1] The "Governmentality" essay focuses primarily on the differences between sovereignty and governmentality, and therefore does not draw out pastoral power for special emphasis. This setting aside of pastoral power—in one essay—has generated a common understanding of pastoral power as a purely religious form of power, distinct from governmentality, which is understood as secular (Blake 1999; Rud 2007; Thomas 1994; Scott 1995). Hence, governmentality too easily becomes a way of constructing a neat and ideal distinction between religion and the public sphere.[2]

Within a colonial context, a split is thus imposed between the missionaries as a distinct religious group focused only on religious matters, and to whom all matters of religion are relegated, and the colonial administration, depicted as a secular group. This idea of a split frames the mode of operation in many colonial societies as non-religious. However, not only were the missionaries extremely active in providing the ideological backdrop for colonial politics, as several studies show (Comaroff and Comaroff 1991, 1997; van der Veer 2001; Viswanathan 1989), but through its infusion in European culture, Protestantism (in this case) was pervasive in the attitudes of the colonial administration's understandings of gender, race, and civilisation. Compartmentalising religion thus becomes a way of ignoring its influence in ideals of social structure and the place of men, women, and non-white people within that structure.

This distinction between religion and the public sphere is also found in studies that apply Foucault's work to illuminate religious issues. These studies thus apply Foucault with an assumed and prior compartmentalisation of religion. Bernauer and Carrette's anthology (2004) on Foucault and theology is a rich collection of essays whose focus is on what use we can make of Foucault

1 The analysis of the pastorate stretches over five lectures (from 8 February to 8 March) of the 13-week course, linking government and *raison d'État* (see Foucault 2007, 115–237).

2 In his study of the disciplinary revolution, Philip S. Gorski (2003) argues that Weber theorised the relationship between religion and discipline, and Foucault that of discipline and the state, but that neither dealt with all three. It is important to note that Gorski regards Foucault's "History of Sexuality" project as a new one (2003, 25), while Matt Chrulew (see below) sees it as an integral part of Foucault's thinking on pastoral power. Indeed, the first volume of "History of Sexuality," *The Will to Knowledge*, was published in 1976, *before* the lecture series *Security, Territory and Population* of 1977–78. An explanation of Gorski's confusion could be that from a Roman Catholic point of view, there is no opposition between the individualising power of the pastor and the emergence of the discourse of sexuality, since for Foucault, the putting of sexuality into (Roman Catholic) discourse *was* an individualising technique.

within theology.[3] The one exception is James Bernauer's survey article, which links Foucault's thoughts on power, knowledge, and subjectivity to what Foucault calls "Christianisation in depth." A more detailed and painstaking study of the same themes is found in Matthew Chrulew's thesis, discussed below.

One significant exception to the compartmentalisation approach to Foucault is Danish theologian Mads Peter Karlsen, who problematises the distinction between the religious and the secular in his analysis of the Christian heritage of the Danish welfare system. Deploying Foucault's concept of pastoral power, Karlsen constructs a genealogy that traces the influence of Christianity beginning with the role of the clerical minister in the seventeenth century, through the beginnings of the health-care system, the destabilisation of the patriarchal structure in the nineteenth century and the emphasis on philanthropy, all the way to facing the truth about oneself in the treatment of obesity in the Danish welfare system (2008). Karlsen's study draws out the implications of Foucault for the study of the Danish welfare system, and how such insights may question the perceived secularism of the Danish state. As such, it points to where Foucault's probing could take us, namely, towards a critique of the narrative of secularism. Thus, while the theoretical benefits pertaining to the development of the Danish welfare system and secularism are important and innovative, the theoretical benefits in regards to Foucault and religion are secondary to Karlsen's project.

While these studies of Foucault and religion have yielded important results, I still find the basic approach somewhat problematic because Foucault's concepts are regarded as a fully-equipped toolbox, ready to use and apply to any given situation. A more genealogical approach to Foucault's own work on religion is needed to expose its weaknesses and blind spots before it is possible to deploy it usefully in other contexts. This genealogical line of questioning is at the forefront of Matthew Chrulew's careful study of Foucault and Christianity (2010).[4] Chrulew traces the general backdrop of Christianity in much of Foucault's work and provides valuable summaries and references for Foucault's increasing incorporation of Christianity within his work on the subject. I shall

3 There are also numerous scholars of the bible as well as of early Christianity who make extensive use of Foucault in their work, with interesting results and with significant theological importance, not least in the area of gender and sexuality. See especially the work of Virginia Burrus (2004), Elizabeth A. Castelli (1991, 2004), Elizabeth A. Clark (1999, 2004), Stephen Moore (1996, 2001), Kimberly Stratton (2007), Joseph Marchal (2008), and the Foucault-inspired anthology on 'natural' sex with an impressive list of contributors (Moxnes, Børtnes and Endsjø 2002).

4 I thank Matt Chrulew for generously making earlier drafts available to me.

focus on the section on pastoral power, which Chrulew situates between the confessional practices of the early to mid-1970s and the technologies of the self in the early 1980s. Chrulew classifies the central texts of pastoral power as the two lecture series from the *Collége de France* (*Security, Territory, Population* in 1977 and 1978, and *The Birth of Biopolitics* in 1978 and 1979), and the three lectures from various venues during that period, published as "Sexuality and Power" (1978), "What is Critique" (1978), and "*Omnes et Singulatum*" (1979) (Chrulew 2010, 31).

Chrulew notes that Foucault's research into Christianity is part of the genealogy of governmentality:

> He [Foucault] in fact seeks to distil, from Christian ecclesial history, a diagram or *dispositif* that he refers to under the general term of 'pastorate,' which is an essential precursor to where we are today.[5]
>
> 2010, 35

This is an important point, especially since the connection between the pastorate and governmentality is bypassed in at least two of the articles mentioned above ("Sexuality and Power" and "What is Critique"). The Christian political technology of the pastorate is modelled on the shepherd and flock, which enters Western rationality through Christianity (Chrulew 2010, 36). Deriving from the Hebrew theme of the shepherd in relation to a nomadic group, it takes on a different "ritualised diagram of power" when it enters the "concrete institutions of Christianity" (2010, 38).[6]

Foucault defines a number of significant elements of this technology of power, which vary according to the lectures. However, the recurring themes are those of obedience/submission, confession/knowledge/truth, and

---

5 My references are to the manuscript with which I have been working, and thus may vary from the final version.

6 Foucault goes to great pains to show that this is a unique mode of power relations, unprecedented in Greco-Roman thought. During my schooling as a biblical scholar, we were always taught (admittedly from a particular methodological perspective) to emphasise the *continuities* between Christianity and its Greco-Roman context—for example, how the masculinity exhibited by Jesus in the gospels and Paul in his letters actually *conforms* to particularly Stoic ideals of masculinity, another point that Foucault will not concede. Foucault cannot accept a notion of self-mastery because it goes against his notion of subjection within the pastoral mode of power. Hence, we again face the uniqueness of Christianity amidst Greco-Roman ideals. This seems to me a very theologically conservative position. See Jonathan Z. Smith for a comprehensive critique of Christianity as "Wholly Other" in *Drudgery Divine: On the Comparison of Early Christianities and the Religions of Late Antiquity* (Smith 1990, esp. ch. 2).

individualisation, which together comprise a "uniquely Christian mode of subjectification" (2010, 42). As Chrulew points out, this is an extension of Foucault's previous work on confession and examination, but brings in "an increased emphasis on the subjection (to the authority of the confessor) that accompanies such techniques" and, as Foucault puts it, "a mode of individualisation by subjection" (Foucault 2007, 184, in Chrulew 2010, 42).[7] Foucault identified this pastorate as "the apparatus from which emerged the arts of government characteristic of modernity" (Chrulew 2010, 46). The mutation and dispersion of pastoral power into modern government was a result of several "counter-conducts," which reached an apex in the Reformation. As a result,

> [g]overnmentality emerges as a political rationality through a process that can be defined as one of secularisation only ambiguously: insofar as it further instils and intensifies the configurations of the pastorate, it carries out what Foucault elsewhere calls a Christianisation-in-depth.
>
> CHRULEW 2010, 47

Chrulew continues: "Indeed, and of course, pastoral power itself emerged as a strategic response to other currents of practice" (2010, 47), namely the internal issues to pastoral power—in Foucault's words, "resistance to power as

7 In his development of pastoral power and its notion of subjectivity within the framework of a given ideological formation, the influence of Louis Althusser is quite apparent. The double subjection, by which the subject is created as a subject and is simultaneously subjected, is well-known from Althusser's analysis of the interpellation of the subject and the Ideological State Apparatuses. The strength in Althusser's model lies in its connections between the daily practices of the individual and the ideological desires of the state. Through its Ideological State Apparatuses, supported by the more overtly violent measures of the (Repressive) State Apparatus, the state inscribes its ideology in the subject, 'drumming it in,' so to speak, from childhood and throughout its life, so that the subject finally can enact the desired ideology on its own or by itself, while believing itself to be free. The difference between Althusser and Foucault is that the latter approached the state from, as it were, 'the bottom up':

> "Whether in the case of madness, of the constitution of that category, that quasi-natural object, mental illness, or of the organization of a clinical medicine, or of the integration of the disciplinary mechanisms and technologies within the penal system, what was involved in each case was always the identification of the gradual, piecemeal, but continuous takeover by the state of a number of practices, ways of doing things, and, if you like, governmentalities. The problem of bringing under state control, of 'statification' (*étatisation*) is at the heart of the questions I have tried to address (Foucault 2008, 77)."

conducting" (Foucault 2007, 195). Foucault identifies five forms of counter-conduct that "tend to redistribute, reverse, nullify, and partially or totally discredit pastoral power in the systems of salvation, obedience and truth ... which characterize ... the objective, the domain of intervention of pastoral power" (Foucault 2007, 204): asceticism, formation of communities, mysticism, interpretation of scripture and eschatology (Chrulew 2010, 50).

In his discussion of the "crisis of the pastorate" and how it "assumed the dimension of governmentality," Foucault (2007, 194) thus sets aside the "external blockages" to pastoral power, which are the unconverted populations, extra-Christian practices (witchcraft and heresies), and the relations with political power and economics. Instead, he looks to five themes of counter-conduct in the Middle Ages that mark opposition to the pastoral organisation of Christianity and "clarify precisely what it is that Foucault identifies as Christianity—the power relations set up in the pastorate" (Chrulew 2010, 51). The internal struggles led to the reshuffling of the pastorate and resulted in the new schismatic churches and the Roman Catholic church of the Counter-Reformation.[8]

Foucault discerns two types of pastorate as originating from the Reformation (which he sees as a pastoral battle rather than a doctrinal one), namely, the Protestant type, which was meticulous and hierarchically supple, and the Counter-Reformation type, which was hierarchised and centralised (Chrulew 2010, 52; Foucault 2007, 149). This generated an "intensification ... in its spiritual forms," which increased the level of control in the material or temporal dimension (Foucault 2007, 229–230).

But Foucault is not suggesting a transition from religious power to secular power. Rather, the sixteenth century is in general an "age of forms of conducting, directing, and government" (Foucault 2007, 231) of which the question of conduct within pastoral power was but one. This focus on conduct outside the religious sphere articulates "a domain of practice and reflection with its own objects, rationality and mode of intervention" (Chrulew 2010, 52), a situation, one might add, to which Protestantism managed to conform itself, inscribing itself into the genealogy of reason. Thus, "[t]he crisis of the pastorate made way for the emergence of governmentality" (Chrulew 2010, 53). This expansion into civil life of conducting conduct necessarily entails the counter-conduct of political resistance. The important point is that "what is at stake in such counter-conducts or – claims is precisely the same element that is targeted by

8 In "What is Critique?," Foucault draws the connection between biblical interpretation and critique as an example of resisting a certain form of government by seeking alternative interpretations of scripture (1996, 385).

governmental power: it is a battle over forms of conduct and the forces of life" (Chrulew 2010, 56).

Chrulew's emphasis on the connection between pastoral power and governmentality implicitly addresses Agamben's criticisms raised in my Introduction, namely, the connection between governmentality and technologies of self. By emphasising the role of pastoral subjection techniques in governmentality, Chrulew has shown how subjectification takes place within this power formation, and thus sets the coordinates for technologies of self.

All this means that Foucault has, as Chrulew notes, "identified a specific mode of contemporary secular power, one inherited from the church, [which] suggests a challenge to certain prominent ways of conceiving the question of religion and politics" (2010, 57), which in turn points to the necessity of "identifying the precise manner and effects of [the state's] nonetheless very 'clerical' apparatuses of governmental power" (2010, 58). This relationship between religion and politics is indeed the challenge, and one that will be taken up in the following chapter. In the following section, I shall engage with three studies of governmentality and colonialism, and their attentiveness—or lack thereof—to the clerical apparatuses of governmental power.

Colonialism and Governmentality: Outlining the Issues

Important to the understanding of the various interpretations of governmentality is whether governmentality is situated within a narrative of secularism, understood as the separation of religion from everything else.[9] Scholars such as sociologist Mitchell Dean, for instance, assume a compartmentalisation of Christianity in relation to secularism. Dean reduces Christianity, and thus pastoral rule, to a philosophy of the socially vulnerable: "[T]he exercise of pastoral rule rests on a specific conception of the potential inclusion of all humankind within the community, the solidarity of rich and poor, and the duty of almsgiving" (1999, 82). Even though Dean includes discussions of Christianity within his chapter on "Pastoral Power, Police and Reason of State" (1999, 73–97), his understanding of Christianity is already shaped by Enlightenment ideals of Christianity as "enchantment." He completely sidesteps the central role of

9 The importance and repercussions of the relation between Foucault and religion have been recognised and utilised in Education Studies. See, e.g., the work of Ian Hunter (1994, 1998, 2001). In Law, see Ben Golder's article, "Foucault and the Genealogy of Pastoral Power" (2007). The relationship between Pietism and governmentality has been noted by, e.g., Jørgen Ole Bærenholdt (2007).

Christianity in the shaping of the modern self because he operates with a preconceived understanding of Christianity as restricted to a religious domain and thereby separated from modernity and civil government. Foucault's own understanding of the social impact and extent of penetration of Christianity is far more sophisticated than what Dean's analysis would lead us to believe.

In his introduction to *The Foucault Effect* entitled "Governmental Rationality: An Introduction," Colin Gordon dismisses any unification of the role of "sacerdotal pastor" and the "secular ruler," and emphasises the autonomous rationalities of modern governmentality (1991, 8–9). He also hints at secular perpetuity as a concept "with complex Christian antecedents" (1991, 9), a secular hierocracy and the Catholic pastorate (1991, 12), the Reformation and religious problematization of the individual (1991, 12–13), and "detheologization" (1991, 13)—without unpacking any of these concepts. He does, however, note that the

> development of a secularised manner of reflection on personal ethics is a close corollary of this shift. The trend should not be mistaken for a move towards irreligion. It provided, as well, an instrument of active mobilization on each side of the confessional battle lines: Catholic, Calvinist, Lutheran—a kind of competition in moral armaments.
>
> 1991, 13

Gordon therefore does not conflate irreligion and secularism. However, what Gordon refers to as "a secularised manner of reflection on personal ethics" is not immediately apparent. According to the context, framed by references to Oestriech's work on Justus Lipsius and Neo-Stoicism, it would seem to refer to the particular Neo-Stoic inflection of the moral armament. However, Gordon (and Dean for that matter) misses the important point that Lipsius was Roman Catholic, and that one of his aims was to bring together Stoicism and Christianity (Dupré 1993, 129).

More forthcoming on the role of Christianity in the development of the modern self is Nikolas Rose, who distinguishes between Roman Catholicism and Protestantism. He sees the latter as central to the development of the disciplined character, both universalizing and individualizing (1999, 224). He notes that writing takes a central place as a replacement for the confessional. Sadly, his observation on writing remains within a religious sphere as strictly confessional writing, such as, for example, the Puritans' diary of sinfulness (1999, 224). Although his discussion of religion is a brief three pages, Rose nevertheless identifies religion as one of several self-disciplining forces in the formation of modern society, as well as one out of several mechanisms linking self-regulation with the organisation of social power (1999, 224).

In spite of the engagement of Rose, and to a certain extent Gordon, with religion in their work on governmentality, it constitutes a minor element of a larger argument. The impression is that pastoral power (Gordon 1991) and religion (Rose 1999) are not significant to the workings of governmentality. Although they acknowledge the presence of religion within governmentality, religion is nevertheless kept well in the background, providing a different emphasis from what Foucault emphasised in his own genealogy.

There are several problems with this sidelining of religion. Not only does it downplay the immense influence of Protestant and Roman Catholic Christianity on Western European forms of governmentality and the corresponding technologies of subjectification, it also sets aside the importance of Christianity in the subjection of colonised peoples. This sidelining is transported onto the mapping of colonial societies, where missionaries are cast as a distinct religious group focused only on religious matters and therefore the locus upon which all senses of religion may be deposited by interpreters. Over against the missionaries, we have the secular colonial administration. As noted earlier, this split sidesteps the ideological backdrop of Christianity in European culture and its influence on members of the colonial administration, especially in terms of Christianity's views on gender, race, and civilisation.

In their meticulous study of the role of Christianity in the colonisation of South Africa, Jean and John Comaroff show how influential the Nonconformist Christian missionaries were in terms of the political, social, and economic transformations that took place in South Africa:

> It follows, then, that the study of Christianity in Africa is more than just an exercise in the analysis of religious change. It is part and parcel of the historical anthropology of colonialism and consciousness, culture and power; of an anthropology concerned at once with the colonizer and the colonized, with structure and agency.
>
> 1991, 11

In volume one, the Comaroffs trace the influence of the evangelical encounter on self, consciousness, and culture, and in volume two labour, gender, value, clothing, domesticity, medicine, and rights, and they show how the Southern Tswana gradually became incorporated "under the European *imperium*, into a global order of capitalist relations" (1997, 407). While theirs is not a study of governmentality, it nevertheless shows the arbitrariness of the distinction between Christian mission and colonialism. The richness of their analysis shows how much is lost through this separation. In this present section, I engage with three very different studies of colonialism and governmentality.

I have chosen these three because each of them relate explicitly to religion, and thus pose problems that become an element of the argument in the following chapter: the separation of Christianity and colonialism (Rud 2007); the separation of religion and rationality (Scott 1995); and the separation of pastoral power and governmentality (Blake 1999).[10]

Danish historian Søren Rud brings governmentality to bear on the colonial history of Greenland in his doctoral work. In an article whose title translates as "Foucault's Concept of Governmentality and the Study of Colonialism," Rud (2007) attempts to show how the theoretical concept of governmentality may be deployed within a historical study. I will show how his approach completely ignores pastoral power and understands governmentality as arising from and affecting the realm of colonial politics. Such an approach simplifies some of the workings of power and the implementation of colonial ideology within the Greenlandic context.

In the first half of his essay, Rud takes Foucault's "Governmentality" essay as his point of departure and, after outlining the main points in that essay, proceeds to discuss the impact of governmentality on sociology and cultural studies, as well as some limitations with the concept. Rud notes that a significant point of criticism is the lack of sensitivity towards the "structuring social circumstances" and the fact that different social groups have varying conditions. So he suggests deploying some of Pierre Bourdieu's concepts as a way of differentiating groups within governmentality (2007, 185). In the second half of his essay, Rud moves on to discuss governmentality within a colonial context and introduces Nicholas Thomas's study *Colonialism's Culture: Anthropology, Travel and Government* (Thomas 1994) with specific attention to the chapter on colonialism and governmentality in late-nineteenth century Fiji.[11]

Rud argues that the expeditions to the remote and uncolonised East Greenland[12] during the nineteenth century prompted a new perspective on

10 As an example of a study that utilises governmentality in a colonial setting without attention to religion, see Hannah (2000).

11 Rud draws out a number of themes from Thomas's analysis in an elaborate misreading. Thomas argues for a restructuring of Fijian society that was in accordance with British notions of sanitation but is nevertheless *presented* as a re-institution of traditional Fijian society with the cooperation of the local chiefs. Rud, however, maintains that Thomas argues for "two contradictory intentions in the case of Fiji: the 'governmental' compulsion to clean, make visible and order, and the anthropologically grounded respect for Fijian 'originality'" (Rud 2007, 187; my translation). This is not only a misunderstanding of Thomas's point, but also misses the in-depth workings of governmentality.

12 The expeditions were initiated to search for the Eastern settlement of the Norse settlers, who were believed to have settled on the East Coast of Greenland because of the name

the West Greenlanders, who had been subjected to 150 years of Danish colonisation and European influences. This traditionalist view clashed with the one that advanced increased modernisation.[13] The traditionalist view privileged seal hunting in kayaks as the quintessential Greenlandic way of life, and promoted this lifestyle through education and colonial management, especially through the *forstanderskaber* (local councils). Ostensibly, local councils were an attempt to promote self-government and include Greenlanders in the government of the colonial districts. The establishment of the local councils was an attempt to regulate and order what previously had been dealt with through "uncontrollable" custom (Rud 2007, 189). This re-structuring of society also meant a subtle shift towards distribution, especially housing, which was ostensibly enacted for the protection of the Greenlanders, but was in fact a further step in a colonial politics of control. Finally, the issue of protection against epidemics and famine was central in the strategies of the colonial administration of the Greenlanders, resulting in, among other things, the re-ordering of their housing conditions to address dangers to their health and morals.

It is a significant problem that Rud completely ignores the role of the Danish state church in the colonisation of Greenland, and its central role in the various restructurings on both ideological and practical levels.[14] As I argued in the preceding chapter, the task of the missionaries reached well beyond just converting Greenlanders, to include a much broader civilising agenda informed by the values of Lutheran Protestantism. This set of values would also have been prevalent among some members of the colonial administration, primarily those from middle-class families. Rud mentions the restructuring of dwellings in response to threats to health and morals, which signals a certain ideological interest in the implementation of western-style housing. In this regard, he quotes a Doctor C.J. Kayser, who found the domestic arrangement of the Greenlanders problematic:

> The only separation which occasionally takes place between the different families occupying a Greenlandic house is a caribou hide, which by aid of

Østerbygden (Eastern Settlement). Eventually, explorers realised that both Vesterbygden (Western Settlement) and Østerbygden were situated on the West coast of Greenland.

13 A much more thorough assessment of colonial politics in Greenland regarding the contradiction between traditionalism and modernisation is found in Rud's 2006 article, translated as "The Conquest of Greenland: Expeditions, Ethnology and Local Board Arrangements in the Nineteenth Century." However, this article includes no discussion of governmentality. A close analysis of the 2006 article appears in chapter four.

14 Rud does mention this briefly in the 2006 article cited in the above note and discussed below.

> strings forms some sort of dividing wall, and reaches only circa one or one and a half foot above the plank bed. Here they all lie, young and old, married and unmarried, strangers and dwellers among each other in a fashion that is just as harmful in respects to hygiene as well as morality. It would not be correct to see this as the only cause for the gross immorality which is rampant among the Greenlanders, but it cannot be doubted that it is encouraged by this.
>
> C.J. KAYSER, in RINK 1856, 63

This control of health and morals through a specific regime of housing is an example of what Foucault describes as the constitution of the sexual confession in scientific terms, where (Christian) sexual morals are hidden behind concerns about health and sanitation issues (Foucault 1998, 65).

Hence, the sanitation issues are firmly connected to Western notions of family, which in turn are connected to Christian conceptualisations of family and sexuality. According to Pontoppidan's catechism, the official exposition of Luther's small catechism, a household consisted of those to be obeyed: father, mother, master, wives, guardians, benefactors, honest elders; and those who had to obey: children, grandchildren, stepchildren, servants, wards, and other youths (point 162). A household thus contains only one father and one mother, whereas it was not uncommon in Greenland for a household to consist of seven or eight "nuclear families" living together. This shift towards smaller dwellings took place in the second half of the nineteenth century and was completed by the end of that century (Petersen 1974, 171).[15]

Apart from the "hygienic and moral" benefits, the Trade also profited greatly from this movement, partly due to the lumber they could sell to build single-family houses, and partly because they could trade the surplus of smaller households that previously would have been distributed to other members of the larger households. Individual families would also have been granted economic benefits (Rud 2007, 190). As I will show below, the missionaries' understanding of the Lutheran family ideal, as propounded in the catechisms of the time, is one of the prime patterns for social restructuring of the Greenlandic population, and as such is a crucial aspect of colonial politics. However, this entire aspect is missing from Rud's analysis in the 2007 article, a lack related to his construal of governmentality as a secular mode of government.

---

15 See the description of longhouses and their demise in Petersen (1974). Thuesen (1988) discusses their decline and the general material poverty as part of the social background for the emergence of the revival movement, *Peqatigingniat*.

Another study on colonialism and governmentality is anthropologist David Scott's article "Colonial Governmentality," which is an attempt to reconceptualise colonial power, or rather to reconfigure how we talk about colonial power. Scott advocates moving from conceptualising a break between the colonial to the modern, to "how that break is configured" and "what it is understood to consist in" (Scott 1995, 194). The former line of inquiry tends to treat colonialism as a monolith, and "pre-empts an inquiry that would allow us to sort out those political rationalities that constituted colonialism in its *historically varied configurations*" (Scott 1995, 195; emphasis in original). Scott emphasises the need to historicise, or distinguish between earlier and later forms of colonial rule, because this will clarify "the distinctiveness of—and the transformation entailed in—the making of *modern* power in its colonial career" (Scott 1995, 196; emphasis in original). This line of questioning will have an impact on the issues raised because the shift in political rationalities will have a bearing on the material outcomes of certain social practices. This emphasis on the forms of political rationalities is a way of highlighting discontinuities within the colonial enterprise itself and the shifts within the configurations of power. Hence, according to Scott, the political rationality of the modern colonial state changes the political game, and thus also the terrain of the political struggle itself (Scott 1995, 198), shifting the points of application, the objects and instrumentalities, as well as the field of operation.

Scott argues that these two distinctive features of modern power (disabling one form of life by dismantling the conditions and through new conditions enabling governing effects on conduct) constitute a decisive break between what preceded modernity and what came after (1995, 200). The workings of modern political rationality, especially its double construction of the "space of free social exchange" and the rational and autonomous subjectivities within it, is what Scott sees as relevant to Foucault's analysis of governmentality and its focus on the two modalities of power, totalising and individualising (202). This has implications for the study of colonialism, since through an understanding of the political rationality of governmentality, we can "discern colonial power's point of application, its target and the discursive and non-discursive fields it sought to encompass" (204).

Scott's narrative of the break between what preceded modernity and what came after seems to eclipse precisely what he is calling for when he emphasises transformation, production and formation, namely, how one (premodern) rationality of power develops into another (modern) rationality of power—in other words, the continuity between the rationalities of power, without it necessarily being a unified march of progress and reason. Instead, Scott envisions a complete break, referring to the uprooting of conditions of superstition and its replacement with rational principles (1995, 199). This seems to conflate all kinds of religion (superstition, priests) in an oppositional stance to reason. However, tucked away in a footnote is the observation that "in this sense [i.e. the disabling of non-modern forms of life by dismantling their conditions with an aim to put in place new and different conditions] the Evangelicals were also but children of the Enlightenment" (1995, 217n21).

This note highlights an observation that I support: that Protestant Christianity from its inception envisioned itself in rational opposition to the perceived superstitions of Roman Catholicism.[16] This is evident from the conflation of heathen and Roman Catholic superstition found in the pamphlet by Pontoppidan that I discussed in chapter one, and from the connection between Protestantism and social structure and, as I will argue, natural law, all of which prompt this self-understanding. In its aggressive civil agenda, Protestant Christianity shaped the public sphere, as Peter van der Veer (2001, 34) argues. Furthermore, as the Comaroffs show (1991, 78), Christianity, in particular Protestant Christianity, also underwent an enlightenment process and became increasingly rationalised. Indeed, Kant is but one example of this rationalisation of Protestant doctrine, and Hegel another.

Finally, Foucault's concept of pastoral power hardly supports such a definite break in that it is envisioned as a technique of power developed from the medieval period and carried through into these political rationalities. As such, it is an old power technique, originating in Christian institutions, in a new political shape (Foucault 2000c, 332). Foucault distinguishes between two aspects of this pastoral power: its ecclesiastical institutionalization and its function. While its institutional aspect has diminished since the eighteenth century, its function has not, given that it has been dispersed outside this initial institutional framework (333). This continuity in the function of pastoral power unsettles the notion of a "break" between pre-modern and modern notions of power.[17] The continuity lies in the notion of pastoral power and, I propose, in

---

16 The most important proponent of this idea, apart from Ernst Troeltsch, is Max Weber (see especially *The Protestant Ethic and the Spirit of Capitalism*).

17 Scott similarly posits a difference in operation between disciplinary and governmental modes of regulation: "Whereas discipline is concerned to actively work upon subjects, government does not regulate in this kind of detail" (1995, 203). It appears to me that the disciplinary society is a prerequisite for the emergence of governmentality. According to Foucault, "we need to see things not in terms of the replacement of a society of sovereignty by a disciplinary society and the subsequent replacement of a disciplinary society by a society of government; in reality one has a triangle, sovereignty-discipline-government, which has as its primary target the population and as its essential mechanism the apparatuses of security" (2000d, 219). Michael Hardt and Antonio Negri (2000, 330) also

the configuration of "the rational," which is more complex than Scott would have us suppose.

My third interlocutor is Lynn A. Blake, who uses governmentality in her 1999 "Pastoral Power, Governmentality and Cultures of Order in Nineteenth-Century British Columbia." Blake analyses a particular event in British Columbia in 1876: an Oblate missionary, Father Charles Grandidier, developed a plan to police the insubordinate, secretive, and disorderly behaviour of Native people (1999, 79–80). The Superintendent of Indian Affairs, I.W. Powell, and the Chief Justice, M. Begbie, agreed on the need for a sober, orderly, and disciplined Native population, and hence on the necessity of Grandidier's plan, but the means to reach that goal, they imagined quite differently. Blake attributes these differences to their differing conceptions of order and the methods to enforce it, as well as the objects and products of the enforcements. Blake regards the fact that both groups agreed on the need to manage the population as a significant intersection of pastoral power and governmentality. However, she attributes differences in the conceptualisations of how to proceed to differences between pastoral power and governmentality.

In a sense, Blake pushes what is implicit in Foucault to its extreme, namely, the Roman Catholic nature of pastoral power. Blake's conceptualisation of pastoral power firmly connects discipline, surveillance, judicial violence, and self-examination to the institution of the Roman Catholic Church, and the enactment of pastoral power is carried out as a Christian regulation of the Christian population:

> Pastoral power, then, is a very old modality of power that can be characterized as: productive in its constitution of Roman-Catholic Christian subjects; disciplinary in its focus on individual bodies and minds; normalizing in its promotion of the self-regulation of its subjects; and sovereign in its juridicality and use of spectacular force.
>
> BLAKE 1999, 81–82

Blake's treatment of the relationship between pastoral power and governmentality is occasionally unclear; she appears to keep them separate at some times but brings them together at others. Following Karlsen and Chrulew's readings of Foucault, I question the separation itself—especially in the nineteenth

argue for the continuance: "The passage to the society of control does not in any way mean the end of discipline. In fact, the immanent exercise of discipline—that is, the self-disciplining of subjects, the incessant whisperings of disciplinary logics within subjectivities themselves—is extended even more generally in the society of control."

century. Blake chastises Foucault for not drawing pastoral power into the "anatomy of governmentality" (1999, 83) as a modality of power: "[H]e does not explore the governmentality of pastoral power itself ..." (1999, 90). Following Karlsen and Chrulew, this seems to be precisely what Foucault *does* argue: pastoral power as a technique of power derived from Christian practice is absorbed into strategies of governmentality, thus adapting the Christian subjection to a this-worldly situation (Foucault 2000c, 333–335). In this sense, Foucault's genealogy of governmentality is also a genealogy of a more complex and, indeed, sophisticated secularisation narrative.[18] I return to this matter in greater detail below.

The issue to which Blake directs us, namely, the very Roman Catholic nature of pastoral power, is nevertheless indicative of a larger problem: the eclipse of Protestant ideology within Foucault's work.[19] This problem emerges in Blake's article when she shows that the colonial administration in British Colombia was British Protestant, and thus held a different view of society and how to govern it. Therefore, the governmentality strand in Blake's argument presents itself as closer to a Protestant view of society, government, and civilisation. Blake does note that her argument could be taken in this direction: "I do not want to suggest that government and Anglican or Protestant missionaries saw eye to eye—there is ample archival evidence that they did not" (1999, 90). However, she does note that "[d]enominational strategies of conversion did vary significantly" and that "[t]hese types of strategy clearly aimed to produce a different kind of native subject than did the Oblate missions" (1999, 90–91). She concludes that "Catholic 'reasons of state' skewed the development of power, the nature of the spaces it was to invest, and its products, to a degree that made it *almost* incompatible with the projects of the provincial government" (1999, 91; emphasis in original).

While Blake does not want to suggest that the compatibility between the government and Protestant ideology is virtually seamless, her argument

18 The philosophical context in which Foucault is read is important for the genealogy of Christianity. Karlsen and Chrulew both situate Foucault alongside Nietzsche, and through this juxtaposition argue for a complication of the secularisation narrative—Karlsen by applying it to the Danish welfare state, and Chrulew by tracing Christianity within Foucault's own work. See also Michael Lackey's analysis of Foucault and secularism (2009).

19 Foucault notes in "What is Critique?" the importance of the Reformation (1996, 389) in the development of the *Aufklärung* in Germany (389) and refers to the importance of natural law as an important element of counter-conduct (385). Beyond this particular article, he does not return to an elaboration of the later importance of the intellectual development arising from the Reformation.

nevertheless does indicate a higher level of compatibility in purpose, strategies, and overall reason between the provincial government and Protestant missionaries. This comes as no surprise once we relinquish the insistence on a dichotomy between religious and secular governance and realise that the colonial foundations of law mean that the dominant beliefs of the settlers—in this case, British Protestantism—are built into the very structure of the legal arrangements (Randell-Moon 2008, 14).[20] Blake, however, relegates the conflation between government and Protestant ideology to internal British struggles and the prevalent anti-Roman Catholic bias, which in British Columbia means the Oblates took the predictable place of the 'Catholic other' inherent in nineteenth-century British nationalism (1999, 87).[21]

I suggest that the situation is slightly more complex. Blake indicates as much in her observation that the Roman Catholic pastoral power differs from Protestant pastoral power (1999, 83), thus hinting that it is not only an internal religious struggle, but that the different pastorates have different social agendas. In the following chapter, I will bring the Reformation into the genealogy of power that Foucault began to construct, in order to emphasise the role of theology within the genealogy of governmentality, thus complicating the religious /secular narrative of all of the above studies. The focus on the theological techniques of governmentality will also help us understand the aggressive social agenda of the Lutheran missionaries and the limits or coordinates imposed on the colonised society. Governmentality and pastoral power are thus useful tools with which to think in attempting to flesh out the relation between missionaries and colonial power without resorting to crude apologetics.

This chapter has highlighted some theoretical points that will be useful when we return in the following chapter to Hveyssel and his own ideological background. Hence, I now turn to elaborate this Protestant pastorate, which underpins my discussion of the role of the missionaries to Greenland in chapter one. This will provide a broader background with which to understand the operation of the missionaries in the Greenlandic context.

---

20 Randell-Moon's argument is carried out within an Australian context in her discussion of secularism and the Australian Constitution (2008).

21 We might also note van der Veer's argument that the separation of Church and State in Britain actually meant the enfranchisement of Catholics and Dissenters, and that this generated a shift from religious loyalty to national loyalty. Van der Veer thus argues (2001, 22) that nineteenth-century British nationalism *includes* Catholics, whereas Blake sees British nationalism as *excluding* Catholics.

CHAPTER 3

The Lutheran Pastorate in Theory and Practice

In the midst of explicating the relationship between the individual and the pastor in the first volume of *History of Sexuality*, Foucault mentions in a footnote that "[t]he reformed pastoral also laid down rules, albeit in a more discreet way, for putting sex into discourse"(1998, 21n4). Not only do Foucault's analyses and conceptualisations appear Roman Catholic due to his historical focus on the Middle Ages in the lectures on *Security, Territory, Population*, but his emphasis on confession and masturbation—not to mention the kind of relationship fleshed out between the individual and the pastor in *The Will to Knowledge* (1998)—are all within a Roman Catholic frame of reference.[1]

This distinction is important because it reveals the difference in subjectification between the practices of the Roman Catholic confessional and the Protestant catechism, which is where I would situate the Protestant subjectification process. If the Roman Catholic pastorate produced desiring subjects, then what kind of subjects did the Protestant pastorate produce? And what kind of shepherds? In the following sections, I trace the construction of the Lutheran social order and its relation to the order of the cosmos. I then trace the construction of the Lutheran subject, beginning with the individual in relation to the shepherd and then spreading out into the family as the locus for subjection. This will enable me to show the pervasiveness of colonisation and its fundamental restructuring of society into a new hierarchical system with new parameters and rules. This is firmly connected to—indeed enabled by—Lutheran pastoral power and its social ideal. As I argued in the first chapter, Hveyssel's display of mastery revealed that he followed an unwritten hierarchical order in which he was at the top and the brothers Berthelsen, whose father was Danish, immediately below him. The analysis showed that this hierarchical order was racialised, because the brothers' Danish heritage was the reason for Hveyssel's favouritism towards them. Next in the hierarchical order stood the national catechists, and, last, the other Greenlanders, men as well as women. Hveyssel's attitude towards the catechists under his tutelage was paternalistic and superior, an attitude which was endemic to the working relations between Danes and Greenlanders in the mission. The missionary was "in charge," and thus the one who could send recommendations back to the

1 The distinctive Roman Catholic dimension is also noted in the Introduction to the anthology on Foucault and theology (Bernauer and Carrette 2004, 5–9, esp. 6).

Missionary Department. As illustrated in the case of Joseph, however, the missionary could also withdraw his favour. This sense of hierarchy is built into the Lutheran social structure, a structure I will unpack in the present chapter.

In order to move beyond the religious overtones of shepherd/pastor, and to emphasise my Lutheran focus, I designate the shepherd as the master. This enables me to draw in the system of domination based on gender, class and race, and intermasculine issues raised in chapter one, and which I see at work in the social hierarchies of the catechism. Furthermore, the move from shepherd/pastor to master will stress the terrestrial realm of pastoral power and the extensions of its outreach.

The Protestant Pastorate in Practice

What divided the interpretations of Söderberg, Gad, and Lidegaard in the first chapter was the extent to which this movement was seen to have political significance; that is, to what extent did the movement constitute some sort of collective opposition to Hveyssel and the colonial apparatus he represented? Was the movement deliberately positioning itself against Hveyssel? While there is clearly room for such a political reading within Söderberg and Lidegaard's interpretations, Gad avoids such an approach and finds the reasons for the popularity of the movement in the hysterical nature of Mary Magdalene and the emotional nature of the Greenlanders. The effect of Gad's interpretation is a feminisation of the Greenlanders, understanding the feminine within a Western context as inherently hysterical and emotional. This coupling of the feminine and hysteria[2] is but one part of a larger epistemological structure, amply identified and testified to by a range of (feminist) scholars, namely, a masculine signifying universe which codes emotion, matter, and nature as feminine, and rationality and reason as masculine (MacCormack and Strathern 1980; Plumwood 1993; von Braun 2009 [1985]; Lloyd 1993; Rosaldo, Lamphere, and Bamberger 1974). Situating Gad within this frame, we see how he first identifies Hveyssel as a rationalist, which is positively coded, and then proceeds to place himself as an extension of this approach, albeit with a more mature insight into the larger historical picture, as the Hegelian spirit manifest.

2 The term hysteria derives from the Greek word for womb (*hustera*), thus connecting this affliction firmly with the female sex. Christina von Braun's *Nicht Ich. Logik, Lüge, Libido* deals at great length with hysteria as a female corporal contestation of the masculine signification process into which women are interpellated. I do not deal with this aspect of her study, but only with her outline of the masculine signification process in chapter four.

Gad interprets the movement as a psychosis that spreads because of a general "indeterminable dissatisfaction" (1976, 382). This places the source and cause of the movement inside a woman's head—literally—and considers the social factors as secondary contributors to the movement's growth. This seems to be an extension of Hveyssel's own interpretation that the entire movement arises out of Mary's jealousy coupled with Moravian influences. While Hveyssel never uses the words 'nature,' 'hysteria,' 'emotional'—or 'superstitious,' for that matter—he does place himself and the Greenlanders within certain roles and expectations that are inevitably governed by assumptions of gendered and racial superiority. As such, Gad's assertion of male rationality through which Greenlanders are feminised is an amplification of themes already hinted at in Hveyssel's reports to the Missionary Department in Copenhagen.

What interests me is the connection between the individual and the social—or rather the lack of a connection. In Gad's discussion, the movement grows because of popular dissatisfaction with the politics of trading, which he emphasises as working *against* the mission. In Hveyssel's account, the movement becomes popular because of a general sense of faithfulness to Moravian customs. They both seem to separate the dissatisfaction from the Lutheran mission—that is, the dissatisfaction is not seen as directed towards the mission as such. Such a conclusion sees the mission as something separate from the social and political world. I think, however, that Hveyssel's frustrations and outrage at this blatant disregard for his authority signals his awareness that something else is at stake.

The trouble in Evighedsfjorden, as recounted by Hveyssel, is from a time in Danish history when Evangelical-Lutheran Protestantism had been firmly anchored in Danish culture. Since the beginning of the absolute monarchy in 1660, Protestantism had become a crucial factor in Danish nation-building in two respects. First, it constructed a transcendent and divine role for the king. *Kongeloven* (The King's Law) of 1665 required the king's obedience to the Augsburg Confession, the preservation of this Confession throughout his kingdoms, and the protection of the kingdoms against heretics (Schwarz Lausten 1987, 146). *Danske Lov II* (The Second Book of Danish Law) of 1683 explicates the jurisdiction of the king's power. In theory, the king had power only over the church's external relations, and the clergy over the inner or spiritual sphere of the church. In practice, however, the king had full power over clerical appointments and the execution of their office (Schrøder 1959, 389; Schwarz Lausten 1987, 146). Nevertheless, the king was accountable to the God of the Lutheran faith and, as such, was a servant of the church (Schrøder 1959, 391).

The clergy, in turn, constructed the Danish monarch as God's anointed one, construed his ascension to the throne as a manifestation of the divine will, and assumed that he would reign under the fear of God—and that his subjects would fear him as such and obey him unconditionally. This is especially obvious in the anointment ceremonies of the absolute monarchs during the years 1671 to 1839 (see Hermansen 2005; Olden-Jørgensen 2001; Petterson 2012a; Stenbæk 1983). The king, in turn, forcefully imposed the new Christian regulations on the population. I return to the details later in this chapter, and note here only that in the course of the seventeenth century, theological doctrine was deployed to construct a fairly comprehensive system of sovereignty, borders, and believers within a tight patriarchal social structure. This system is possible only within a Protestant framework, which does not recognise the (external) authority of the pope; hence the monarch may appropriate the pastoral techniques within his rule.

This is what I meant in the Introduction by "a Protestant pastorate." As with Foucault's pastorate, this also had its internal issues, especially the struggle between Pietism and orthodoxy, which caused considerable unrest in Denmark. The struggle was resolved by the king in 1732 through a number of tactical manoeuvres that polarised radical Pietism and Lutheran orthodoxy, with the monarchy rejecting the more radical forms of Pietism such as the Moravian Brethren (who were sent to Greenland) and implementing moderate pietism as a state ideology (Bredsdorff 2003, 36).[3]

Pietism's more internalizing and individualising techniques, such as the revival, enlightenment, and conversion of the individual believer, were a sign of the times of the Enlightenment with its focus on the individual and the liberation from tutelage. Through comprehensive soul-searching, the individual would come to understand him-/herself as a sinner and, through repentance – or, more dramatically, conversion – be reborn. It is the possibility of the individual to recognise his/her own sin and take a decisive stand towards redemption that connects Pietism to early Enlightenment thought (Bredsdorff 2003, 90). As the argument unfolds, we will see how this imagery takes on a more menacing cultural significance in the colonial setting.

Pietism also had a social dimension, which expressed itself in the concern for schooling of peasants' children as well as care for the poor – a dimension which enabled the monarch to extend the care of the state to smaller groups in society that had previously been neglected. This care manifested itself through the establishment of the Vajsenhuset orphanage in 1727 (Pedersen 1951, 86) and the gradual establishment of schools all over the country.[4] Finally, the

3 See also Wallin (1999) for a description of this power structure in relation to the mission to Greenland.

4 I refer to the decree of 28 March 1721 on the establishment of schools on the equestrian estates, the 23 January 1739 decree on the establishment of general schools, and the decree of

influence of Pietism could be seen in the state missions, not only to Greenland (1721), but also to Tranquebar in India (1705) and the Sámi in Northern Finmark (1715)—endeavours whose administration was centralised in the *Missionskollegiet* (Missionary Department) established in 1714 by royal decree (Pedersen 1951, 52). After 1721 and the beginnings of general schooling, Christianity was spread among the population through the school system, confirmation, and catechism. In this connection, court theologian Pontoppidan was commissioned to compose an authorised catechism to be used in the confirmation lessons (Pedersen 1951, 162). *Sandhed til Gudfrygtighed* (Truth in Accordance with Godliness)[5] was thus completed in 1738. These pietistic influences all worked through the state church, which remained Lutheran.

But in the process of this religious disruption, a new role for the state was signalled, as Gauri Viswanathan (1998, 17) notes:

> As disruptive as it might seem, conversion also brings to focus an essential role of the state in modernity: the restoration of a fixed, unassailable point of reference from which cleavages within communities are addressed. If conversion precipitates breaches within the fold, it also sets in motion a dynamic social process that confers a new power and role on the state.

While Viswanathan refers to the function of an already-secular English state in the following century, the quotation nonetheless seems to address the situation at hand, or at least points to how the beginnings of a secular state administration arose from religious schism and how the king enthusiastically embraced the opportunity of "disempowering ecclesiastical authority" (Viswanathan 1998, 42).

In Greenland, the connection between Lutheranism and the social structure was compounded by the fact that the introduction of Lutheranism involved a fundamental restructuring of society. The missionaries regarded Greenlandic society as savage, although a few of them, including Paul Egede, did note that Greenlanders seemed to follow some law of nature that gave a sense of harmony to their lifestyle (see preface in Egede 1766). Generally, however, the missionaries considered Greenlandic society to be a contradiction in terms because of the absence of (Western understandings of) science, religion,

---

17 April 1739 on the abolition of more than half the Latin schools (Pedersen 1951, 82, 188–189).

5 The Danish title is taken from Paul's letter to Titus, 1:1. For the translation of the title into English, I consulted the New Revised Standard Version (NRSV).

ethics, and law.[6] Thus, the missionaries regarded their task as one of constructing a society where none was to be found. The theological justification for such a venture lies in the concept of Natural Law.

Constructing Lutheran Society in Accordance with Natural Law

In his article on the role of the Danish church in the development of the premodern Danish state, historian Mogens Christensen argues that while this arrangement subordinates the church to the power of the state, the state nevertheless made good use of the services of the church on three levels: First, on the level of sovereignty and territory, Luther's understanding of the civil authority as subordinate only to God functioned efficiently in constituting the monarch as God's representative on earth. Second, the particular 'brand' of religion was used as a political marker for the identity of the territorial state, which may be seen from the decrees forbidding Roman Catholics and Reformed adherents from settling in the kingdom.[7] Finally, at a more disciplinary level, the state deployed the church's local context and knowledge in its administration to control the parishes. Thus, the disciplinary measures of the church could be instituted as state discipline and as a way of regulating citizens (Christensen 2007, 146).

These contributions show how the state made use of the church as an administrative and regulating authority, thereby illustrating how Luther's two

6 Paul Egede states in his preface to the first Greenlandic translation of the New Testament (1766) how difficult the translation process had been because the Greenlanders know not of "Religion, Ethics, Law [and] Sciences," or even of the corresponding words. For an analysis of Egede's view on humanity and bible in this preface, see Petterson (2007).

7 I refer here to severe limitations on alien religious practice in the kingdoms in 1676, especially the restriction and control of Reformed (primarily Calvinist) immigrants, who were permitted only for the sake of profit, as well as the ban on Quakers in 1685. I should also mention such measures as the royal decree of 2 October 1706 that banned gatherings in conflict with the Augsburg confession; the decree of 13 January 1741 requiring all godly assemblies (which effectively included bible reading groups) to take place in a church; and the decree of 20 November 1744 that forbade certain unruly elements from visiting Herrnhut, the Moravian mission's headquarters in Germany. No one was allowed to send their children there and no one educated there could hold a clerical position in Denmark. This decree was sharpened on 29 January 1745 so that anyone leaving Denmark to go to Moravian Brethren headquarters would forfeit their property and their rights. There is also the decree of 5 March 1745 reinforcing the Danish law concerning permitted religious practice in Denmark, and the Great decree of 19 September 1766 codifying earlier measures against Catholics.

kingdoms dovetailed. This dovetailing is also evident in the doctrinal element, which fostered an understanding of Protestantism as the expression of the rationality of the universe—natural law—that is my focus in the present section.[8] This will allow me to highlight the various elements within a Protestant social order that sees itself as the expression of divine will and reason.[9] What I aim to show is that the issues at stake within natural law, such as the re-ordering of nature in conformity with the Lutheran understandings of family and social hierarchies, become central to the colonial administration of Greenland and subsequent social developments.

The phenomenon of natural law has a history before and beyond that of Luther's adaptation, but I will largely suspend this vast history here in order to keep my argument focused.[10] The specifically Christian notion of natural law is most often connected with Thomas Aquinas, who developed a very complex theory of natural law as part of a larger theological desire to push for a subordination of civil law to clerical law. This occurred at a time of general interest in the codification of Roman law, particularly as the power struggles between the pope and the emperor were increasing in intensity and scope. Aquinas developed his theory of natural law within a framework of natural theology, briefly defined as knowledge of God instilled in creation. Two-and-a-half centuries later, Luther worked natural law into his two-kingdoms framework by making it the basis of the positive laws to be elaborated and enforced by God's representative on earth, the magistrate (Witte Jr. 2002, 115). Hence, Luther explicitly emphasises the political context and potential of natural law instead of the heavy theological (but equally political) context that was pervasive in Aquinas.

One may, however, question the extent to which Luther's notion of natural law is any less theologically founded than that of Aquinas. For Luther, the Decalogue is "the Decalogue of the whole world, inscribed and engraved in the minds of all men from the foundation of the world" (*Weimarer Ausgabe* (WA) 39/1:478 quoted in Witte Jr. 2002, 114) and knowledge of this law comes from

8 As mentioned above, Foucault alludes to this in "What is Critique?" (see note 83), and also in the lecture series (Foucault 2007, 235, 237, 263, 349).

9 In conceptualising the relationship between Protestantism and reason through natural law, figures such as Kant or Hegel belong to the latter stages of a development connecting Christianity with rationality.

10 For descriptions of the development of natural law as a political theory, see Otto Gierke (1957, 1987). For discussions of the philosophical developments of natural law as well as an argument for a positive use of natural law, see Ernst Bloch's *Natural Law and Human Dignity* (1987). For a discussion of the function of natural law within Lutheran tradition from a legal perspective, see John Witte Jr.'s contributions to this field (2002, 2006).

two places: Scripture and reason. This understanding is founded on an interpretation of Romans 2:14–15, in which Paul states that even the Gentiles have a law written in their hearts and thus have a natural knowledge of good and evil.[11] Therefore, the natural law is written upon every heart, and rewritten in the bible. However, according to Luther, sin prevents humans from paying attention to the law, which is where the magistrate comes in as the one who contextualises the universal law of God.

Delving further into Protestant doctrine to determine the development of natural law as well as its social effects, one may note that the Lutheran Protestant doctrine of "justification by faith alone" completely veils the social context and material conditions for the enactment of this faith through a sustained suspicion of and bias against "works" that are seen as a condition for salvation in Judaism and Roman Catholicism. It is precisely the social context that is a key issue in Ernst Troeltsch's *Social Teaching of the Christian Churches* (1992, 524), which carefully analyses the Lutheran social order and its relations to Lutheran ethics, and provides a helpful starting point for relating theology to the "sphere of ordinary human life." In the chapters on Lutheranism, Troeltsch's main line of enquiry concerns Luther's ideas, and the centuries immediately following them, with indications as to where the ideas proceed in the Enlightenment and post-Enlightenment periods.

One of the fundamental changes from Roman Catholicism is the place of this world, or nature (usually meaning human nature), in the overall Protestant framework. In medieval Catholicism, matter and nature constitute a stage in the creation of the world, and as such are separated from the pure world of spirit. This means that nature is simply a step towards supernatural perfection, and Troeltsch speaks of an evolving or ascending from Nature into Grace. By contrast, Luther sees nature as the "sphere appointed by the Creator for the realisation of ideal values" (Troeltsch 1992, 475).

The separation of nature and grace are thus overcome in the "permeation of the existing forms of life with the spirit of faith and love" and becomes ideally what Troeltsch (1992, 512) calls an ecclesiastical civilisation.[12] For this to be

11 Romans 2:14–15 reads: "When Gentiles, who do not possess the law, do instinctively what the law requires, these, though not having the law, are a law to themselves. They show that what the law requires is written on their hearts, to which their own conscience bears witness ..." (NRSV).

12 This is effectively the same position Christina von Braun takes in her analysis of writing (2009), as I will argue in the following chapter. An important difference is that she relegates this (re)joining of spirit and matter to the New Testament texts, while Troeltsch sees it as a feature of the Reformation doctrine.

realised, one requires a general moral 'code,' which Luther found in the Decalogue. According to Luther, this objective revelation of the moral law had been confirmed and interpreted by Jesus and the apostles in the New Testament, and could therefore be taken as the expression of God's natural law. Troeltsch argues that Luther seized on the Decalogue because it enabled him to incorporate "'this-world' morality and 'this-world' institutions into his whole ethical scheme" (1992, 504).

Thus, Luther found within the Decalogue the entire Christian ideal, with the First Table (commandments one to four) concerning man's relationship to God as constituting the purely religious demand—faith, in other words. The Second Table (the remaining six commandments) includes

> the doctrine of the 'calling' and of the teaching on adjustment to existing conditions in the state and in society, and the idea that love is to be exercised not beyond, but within the natural order of human life.
>
> TROELTSCH 1992, 505

The Second Table, however, is only fully understood when it is carried out in light of the First: "Hence the Decalogue and the Natural law, when they are fully understood, constitute the pure Christian and spiritual ideal" (Troeltsch 1992, 505).

When one of the earliest missionaries to Greenland, Paul Egede, mused in his preface to the first Greenlandic bible translation over the fact that Greenlanders were unwittingly following the law of nature in their interaction with each other, Luther would probably have insisted on the incomplete or misunderstood nature of this observation, since "pagans ... were really only acquainted with the Second Table of the law; they had forgotten the First Table" (Troeltsch 1992, 505). Without the infusion of the Christian spirit, the Second Table was merely "cold self-righteousness and pagan self-love" (505), hence the need for missionary activity and conversion, which Paul Egede also considered necessary. The unconverted had forgotten, or were in some way unacquainted with, the First Table of the law and only fulfilled the Second Table. In Luther's view, therefore, the unconverted lacked the spirit that constitutes the Christian ideal. This is also expressed in the various attempts of the missionaries to civilise the Greenlandic population, that is, to make them live by the Second Table *through* the First, or to make the body into a vessel for the spirit. It is also indicative of the self-understanding of the missionaries as being beyond the body. This particular understanding shows up in the repeated references to the lust and desires of others, in particular the lusty sailors and workers at the various colonies, as well as in the severe penalties, such as expulsion, for sexual misdemeanours in the catechist colleges, where the men were taught to be embodied spirit.[13]

On this matter, Richard Dyer's observations on whiteness (1997) are highly pertinent. Dyer suggests that the embodiment of whiteness is constituted by three elements: Christianity, "race," and enterprise/imperialism. The crucial element is Christianity's founding idea of incarnation, along with the particular understandings of flesh and spirit that accompany this notion. Dyer sees the distinction between matter and spirit as producing a third notion of flesh, as the "good flesh" or the Christ-like flesh. Although he does not go into detail, Dyer (16) notes that the spirit-in-body is the body of Christ over against the body as such, which is inferior and sometimes evil. These two bodies become mapped out onto white and non-white bodies. Due to the historical connection between Christianity and Western Europe, the distribution of bodies as such—pure flesh and matter—characterised the non-white populations, while the European men became embodiments of the spirit. Dyer sees this perception of a link between body and spirit as one of two intellectual steps which together comprise a foundation for race.[14]

Following from this acorporeal nature of the spirit, Luther's idea of natural law is, as Troeltsch succinctly puts it, "that of the divine activity expressed in reason" (1992, 534). This reason is constituted by the ideas of Aristotle, Cicero, and the Stoics, as well as humanistic ideas of politics, economics, and social doctrine, which *as* natural law become appointments by God through reason. They just require the religious principle to become a Christian ethic (Troeltsch 1992, 508). One can thus see Luther's interpretation of natural law as governed by his doctrine of the two kingdoms; hence, the sphere of the state was governed by reason as the expression of divine activity and therefore the foundation of the entire Lutheran social order, which commands obedience to this sphere of the state.

As some have noted, this emphasis glorifies the power and authority of the ruler to the extent that all opposition to this power is, by extension, opposition to God (Troeltsch 1992, 529; Bloch 1987, 29; and Glebe 2010). In the civil or 'private' sphere, the natural law is expressed in Christian love, which entails

13 Thuesen (2007, 132–35) devotes a section to "moral failings" in his chapter on training, but notes also the importance of prudent sexual behaviour for the social order, as discussed in chapter one.

14 The other move is the fixing and domination of territories, along with the subsequent encounter with people of different physical constitutions, which was seen as a marker of intrinsic difference.

service to God at an individual level through the family and ordinary duties of citizenship, and at a societal level, since family, the state, and society in general and all labour are methods of exercising the Christian spirit of love and obedience (Troeltsch 1992, 541). The family, the state, the division of labour and economics all belong to the sphere of natural law—that is, within the sphere of the state.

However, as Troeltsch points out, Luther was so keen to emphasise God as the founder of these institutions, providing scriptural proof for family, state, economics, and division of labour, that this actually conflates the two kingdoms into one. According to Troeltsch, "this mixture of arguments, however, only proves that the assumption of an inward unity and conformity of Natural law with the Christian spirit is the underlying idea" (1992, 535). In effect, then, what Luther is trying to do—through the deployment of a sphere of natural law and reason (as indirect divine appointment) as well as a sphere of scripture and Christian love (as direct divine appointment)—is to construct a highly conservative and patriarchal social order and seek to prove its provenance with arguments from both spheres, which were in fact connected all along.

Lutheranism is thus firmly tied to the Protestant construction of social order, which is established by God and demands unconditional submission from the Christian. These demands to uphold the social order relied on each individual responding to his or her 'calling,' which in practice meant reinforcing and legitimising existing understandings of gender and class. The heavy emphasis on the monogamous patriarchal family as a crucial and fundamental aspect of society further intensified the inherent patriarchalism of Lutheranism, which also effected the economic organisation of society and locked it into its social hierarchies. Transgressing the limits of one's calling is a disruption to the social order and thus rebellion against God (Troeltsch 1992, 555). Thus, by incorporating a teaching on the state, as well as philosophical principles and ideas within a dualist framework that kept the Christian ideal as the "the truth of the natural order" (Troeltsch 1992, 509), room was created for a conflation of Lutheran Protestantism with the secularising forces of government in Western Europe. It is quite clear from dissertations, pamphlets, and diaries of the time that Protestant theologians understood themselves as directly in line with divine reason, in opposition to the 'scandalous superstition' practiced by heathens as well as Roman Catholics.[15]

15 As noted above in the section "In the Manner of Women." See also the detailed survey of publications from the Reformation to the beginning of the eighteenth century in Jørgen Olrik's preface to Erik Pontoppidan's pamphlet *Fejekost* (Olrik 1923).

However, we must consider another crucial dimension connected to Luther's social projects as well as the later contract theorists of the sixteenth and seventeenth centuries:, namely, the production of nature. Through the reconceptualising of nature in terms of a larger rational and social ideal, we see how these ostensible theoretical structures underpin colonial ventures and their reshaping of the colonised territories through an imperial master plan. This reshaping becomes the prerequisite for salvation, which thus entails a necessarily deprecating view of 'encountered nature' and immediately proceeds to change it, right down to the individual subjectivities. This will be the focus from now on, beginning with the individual and moving on to nature in the next two chapters.

Catechism and Family

One of the items within the Roman Catholic economy of salvation made redundant by the Reformation was the confession, that privileged social interaction between pastor and individual. Nevertheless, catechism, the instruction in faith, was retained.[16] In accordance with his notion of the priesthood of all believers,[17] Luther's move was to shift this instruction from the church to the home, where the father, as head of the household, was responsible for his own family. Thus, the unity of the family became a religious fellowship—the seed of the Church, in fact—and the exercise of prayers and catechism of the father/ head of the household establishes church life. This then begs the question: Which selves does the catechism foster? As I show below, the catechisms construct roles of gender and hierarchy into which individuals are subjected. A very important inflection is the individual and the hierarchy relations—both are vertically-oriented. The relationship between the believer and God is the primary relationship, and the foundation of the social relationships. The social relationships are in turn defined hierarchically, in terms of who is subservient to whom. In contrast, the self, which Foucault describes as generated by the confessional, is characterised by a vertical relationship to the priest or, in

16 A catechism is a manual of Christian doctrine, and was first used in reference to a written instruction in the early sixteenth century and Luther's Small Catechism. Before this, the term referred to oral instruction before Baptism (Cross and Livingstone 2005, 301).

17 As Peter Wallace outlines in his study on the long-term process of the European Reformation, Luther's programme consisted of three pillars: justification by faith; the authority of Scripture alone; and the priesthood of all believers. The priesthood of all believers meant that every baptised Christian was a priest before God and not dependent on anyone else for the reception of grace (2004, 79–80).

Foucault's terms, "the pastor," and a horizontal relationship to the rest of the flock, as well as the notion of desire, which is always directed at someone or something else.

The colonial context provides an important insight into the establishment of these selves. Whereas Roman Catholic missionaries were generally much more willing to incorporate indigenous religious practices within a Roman Catholic framework,[18] Protestant missionaries were uncompromising in this regard. Both approaches were undertaken for theological reasons, connected to their views on nature. Roman Catholicism regards nature as a signifier of the realm of the spirit, so indigenous practices are also regarded as signifiers of God. In stark contrast is the Protestant view that nature is the realm of ecclesiastical civilisation, as discussed in the previous section, in which indigenous practices have no place. This means that in order to enter into the Protestant framework, the former lifestyle should be firmly rejected in what thus becomes an attempt to shatter the social fabric from which the newly converted came.

The colonial context also adds a racial dimension to this patriarchal structure. Within the Greenlandic context, the missionaries came from Denmark and Norway, and employed Greenlanders as catechists. The tasks of these catechists included accompanying other Greenlanders on their summer hunting expeditions, and continuing the lessons they or the missionaries had been giving during the preceding winter. Another task was to help the European missionary with the difficult Greenlandic language. Their position was therefore clearly subservient to the missionary, and as such within a hierarchical structure, which was divided according to the perceived childishness of the Greenlanders—not to mention the perceived civilised status of the missionaries. The first Greenlandic missionary was appointed in 1874,[19] which indicates

18 See Vicente Rafael's masterful *Contracting Colonialism: Translation and Christian Conversion in Tagalog Society under Spanish Rule* (1993) for an analysis of the conversion of the Tagalog society in the Philippines that explains the Catholic epistemological structure underpinning this procedure.

19 A significant exception was Frederik Berthelsen, who was ordained as missionary in 1815. However, his appointment was due to extraordinary circumstances: the war between Denmark and England, a shortage of missionaries, and difficult communications. That this was an extraordinary appointment may be gleaned from the fact that 60 years would pass before a second Greenlander, Tobias Mørch, was ordained. Mørch was ordained as a minister in 1874 and remained the only minister in Greenland until 1905, when the Greenlandic Church was established. In the years that followed, three Greenlanders were ordained as missionaries: Jens Chemnitz and Lars Berthelsen in 1883, and Andreas Hansen in 1889 (Langgård 2004, 78).

that the Danes held on to their position of pastoral control for many years (Hans Egede, the first missionary, arrived in 1721).

I will return to issues of mastery and constructions of selves, but I again emphasise why it is important to distinguish between the Roman Catholic and the Lutheran Protestant pastorates, and their differing production of selves. While the primary locus for the construction of the self in Roman Catholicism was in the interrelation between the pastor and the individual, in Lutheran Protestantism it is the family that provides the primary setting for the inculcation of Lutheran subjects.

The monogamous, heterosexual, and patriarchal nuclear family is a central feature of Lutheran social philosophy. Not only is it the archetype of all social relations, but also the starting point of all social developments (established in 'Paradise') and economic conditions of management and service (economic theory is based on one-family households), as well as the cornerstone of the church itself.[20] I continue the exploration of power initiated in the discussion of Foucault and the pastoral, except that I focus more explicitly on gender roles and family as they were propagated in eighteenth-century Denmark.

In her 2008 study on gender, justice, and sexual morality in eighteenth-century Denmark, Nina Javette Koefoed analyses legislation on extra-marital sex and the various enforcements of its regulations. The point of departure for these analyses is the absolute monarchy and the king's duty as God's chosen to enforce a Christian society. Within this programme, and in line with the point noted above, Koefoed identifies marriage as receiving a very prominent social position after the Reformation (2008, 25). In Denmark, Luther's catechism was the code of conduct, disseminated through expositions by various Danish theologians. The exposition which interests Koefoed is Pontoppidan's catechism from 1737 (2008, 31). Pontoppidan chose not to allot a separate section to discuss Luther's *Haustafel*,[21] but instead discusses the ordering of society

20 Historian Marion Gray's study, *Productive Men, Reproductive Women* (2000) traces the restructuring of gender roles and the concomitant transformation of the household of the feudal period into that of the bourgeois family structure during the Enlightenment. Gray's work provides some of the historical background to Foucault's analysis in the *Security, Territory, Population* lectures.

21 Literally "house-table." Luther coined the phrase to refer to sections in the New Testament that describe an order of the household in which the various roles are defined and positioned within a structure of subordination. Examples include Ephesians 5:21–6:9; Colossians 3:18–4:1; Titus 2:1–10; and 1 Peter 2:18–3:7. While there is some discussion in New Testament scholarship as to what extent these household codes refer to internal community structures or the larger social fabric, there seems to be little doubt that Luther saw connections between household management and the larger social

under the fourth commandment, which in the Lutheran tradition is the commandment to honour the parents. The proper relationship to parents is then taken as a point of departure to include all authority figures, thus providing a good insight into the duties of the individual and the proper relations within a functional patriarchal society.

Catechism functions as a series of questions and answers. That the issues dealt with under the fourth commandment are of some importance may be seen by the amount of questions and their fairly detailed character. In Pontoppidan's catechism, there are 33 questions relating to the fourth commandment, a number exceeded only by those relating to the first commandment. The first two questions deal with the nature of the commandment (what is commanded, in question 159, and what is forbidden, in 160) and the third question addresses the meaning of "parents": "Our parents are first our natural parents, and then all those, whom in any way are obligated as authorities to command and rule us: guardians, masters, ministers, schoolmasters and the like, who all are parents according to their rank" (question 161).

The following question concerns the Lutheran tripartite authority structure: the rank of government, with the king and prince as parents and the subjects as children; the learned rank, with the ministers and schoolmasters as parents and the disciples and listeners as children; and the household, where the fathers and mothers, masters, mistresses, guardians, patrons, and honest elders should be regarded as parents by children, grandchildren, stepchildren, servants, wards and other youths (question 162). These issues are followed by a string of questions and answers, which confirm the divine appointment of these authority figures and the duty to obey. Towards the end of the text there are a number of items that address the duties of the Master and Mistress towards their servants, and the servants' duties towards their Master and Mistress, taking into account the possibility that the Master could be a difficult man (questions 184–186).

What we see is a programme for fostering subjectivities within a tripartite hierarchical order: king–subjects; minister–disciples; parents–children. Note that the parent–children function is the one used to describe the relation

fabric, and happily borrowed these structures to order society around the male leader. Foucault sees the expansion of Aristotle's "Concerning Household Management" to include the economy of the souls as a patristic innovation, attributed to Gregory Nazianzen (2007, 192). Foucault therefore does not take the New Testament household codes into account; nor, for that matter, Luther's appropriation of them. Gray's second chapter, "The Household as Economy" (49–88) samples a variety of household books from the seventeenth century directed at aristocratic proprietors and concerning the organisation of an agricultural estate. See also Richarz (1991).

between king and subjects, and minister and disciples. The father, then, is the central figure, encompassing the role of breadwinner, pastor, and priest of the household (Troeltsch 1992, 546). As such, the catechism construes him as possessing supreme authority. According to Troeltsch, we thus have an extensive masculine domination that is taken for granted, since Lutheranism and its systemic patriarchy considers the physical superiority of man as the expression of a relationship willed by God. The archetypical nature of family means that the terminology was stretched to signify other social relationships, such as the ruler as father of the country, the lord of the manor as father of the estate, and the employer as father-head of household. All these fathers look after their children (subjects, peasants, and servants), who in turn all serve God by obeying the master.

This theory was articulated in Luther's two catechisms, so "through a process of infinite repetition, this theory of Patriarchalism was hammered into the minds of faithful Lutherans" (Troeltsch 1992, 542). The catechisms thus construct and normalise a number of social and gendered roles which correspond to the hierarchies of social power, and which are naturalised through the practice of catechism and its questions and answers. This practice can be seen as a sanctification of the private sphere but also as a *de-clerification*, or in Foucault's words, a laicisation, of Christian instruction and a dissemination of the pastoral into the capillaries of every-day life (1996, 384). It is a displacement of sovereign power from the pope to all men in society who are heads of families, households, estates, and kingdoms. I suggest that this particular displacement of power is a crucial feature in the emergence of governmentality.

The fact that Pontoppidan did not maintain Luther's *Haustafel* as an independent point of catechism leads Koefoed to conclude that the *Haustafel* ideology was less significant in Denmark than was the case in, for example, Sweden. Furthermore, Koefoed (2008, 32) states that Pontoppidan only made use of the household codes of conduct and thus excluded the material that dealt with mastery over servants. This last point is simply incorrect since items 184 to 186 explicitly deal with relations between masters and servants. Furthermore, I disagree with the conclusion that the *Haustafel* ideology should matter less on account of its subsumption under the Ten Commandments. On the contrary, considering the centrality of the Ten Commandments in the legislative environment of the time as an expression of the natural law, and thus as the source of all justice, which Koefoed herself points out (2008, 20; see also Ingesman 2010), it appears that the inclusion of excerpts of the *Haustafel* within this law of God actually increased rather than diminished the importance of these excerpts. Within the Ten Commandments, the *Haustafel's* fundamental importance to social structure is emphasised—or rather the Fourth Commandment ("Honour your father and your mother") is expanded to accommodate the social structure of the *Haustafel*. Finally, as discussed above, Troeltsch argues that the explanation of the Fourth Commandment in the catechism made it the centre of all social ethics. The harsh and severe penalties for fornication show how central the model of the monogamous family is to the control of society in this period, and also how influential—indeed, fundamental—Protestantism was to the order of Danish society.

This is the order that was exported to Greenland, along with Pontoppidan's catechism, which was translated and modified to fit the colonial situation by Hans Egede's oldest son, Paul. The imposition of this understanding of family (that is, monogamous, patriarchal, a one-family household) as a model of society, reinforced by incessant repetitions of catechisms, had a significant social impact in Greenland. The place of the Lutheran family structure within a larger order, as well as its assigned roles of subordination and mastery, meant that the Danish and Norwegian men who came to Greenland assumed the position of master, whereby Greenlanders were subjected as children, or at the very least placed in a subservient relation to Danish men. Instruction via catechism would have implanted the notion of divine reason behind Danish mastery and Greenlandic subservience. In Pontoppidan's catechism, mastery unfolded according to three ranks: king, minister, and father, all of whom are anchored in God. This authority structure was likewise assumed in Greenland. However, both God and king were absent figures,[22] made known to Greenlanders only through the missionaries and merchants,[23] and sometimes used as threats if Greenlanders did not comply with the wishes of missionaries.[24] This was buttressed by Danish displays of power towards the Dutch[25] as

22 The first king to visit Greenland was Christian X in 1921.

23 See Hans Egede's summary of a talk he had with a group of Greenlanders on God, king, and his own role (1925, 174–5).

24 Hans Egede stands out as having a propensity for aggressive threats. See 1925, 110, 112, 151, 152, 155–56, 170, 205–6, 237, where he threatens to tie up a man and send him to Denmark for punishment, or 275, where he tells Greenlanders, who were dying of smallpox by the hundreds, that the epidemic was God's punishment for their lack of diligence towards the word of God.

25 In 1739, a sea battle between Dutch traders and the Danish colonizers allegedly terrified the Greenlandic population (Lauridsen and Lytthans 1983, 91). The ongoing struggles between Dutch whalers and traders are mentioned several times in Paul Egede's diary (1988, 81, 96, 110, 111, 112, 151, 181), as is the greed of the Danes and their display of power as a source of wonder for Greenlanders (1988, 122–123). Lauridsen and Lytthans also mention the many struggles with the Dutch (1983, 87–99).

well as the impressions related by Greenlanders who had been to Denmark and met the king.[26]

Backed by powerful forces, the missionaries and merchants gained their position of mastery, and Greenlanders, one by one, were compelled to enter into this relation. The missionaries were also 'parenting' Greenlanders in the sense that they chose, employed, and trained catechists; they also reported back to the Missionary Department on their progress, how hard they worked, and to what extent they were eligible for a pay raise, as demonstrated by Hveyssel's dealings with the catechists in chapter one. Another circumstance, which fortified Danish mastery was intermarriage and the physical paternity of the Danish and Norwegian men who married Greenlandic women and produced families. These relationships set in motion whole series of events that radically altered the Greenlandic social fabric. This new family unit was constructed through a significant curtailment of the social position of Greenlandic men. Polygamy was forbidden for baptised men—hence Habakuk's evil ways in the first chapter—and Greenlandic women began marrying European men.

'Mixed' families could thus be pioneers in showing a civilised way of life and cohabitation, a point that emerges in the following quotation from missionary Berthel Larsen, the father of Frederik and Joseph Berthelsen. He says that the task of the missionaries is to lead Greenlanders "to a realisation of their deep depravation and show them the way to the one who can save them from this and transform them into new people in heart, house and mind" (Lauridsen and Lytthans 1983, 124).

In his chapter on marriage, Gad notes that the attitudes towards mixed marriages differed among the Danes (1969). Some missionaries, such as Bloch and Peter Egede, noticed in 1752 that once Greenlandic women had their heart set

26 Between 1721 and 1740, four Greenlanders survived the round trip to Denmark: Pooq in 1724, Hans Pungiok (named after Hans Egede) in 1739, and Arnarsak and Tullimak, who accompanied Paul Egede when he left for Denmark in 1740. Arnarsak and Tullimak returned to Greenland the same year. According to Paul Egede, their impressions of the visit were marked by the unfathomable largeness of what they had seen. In particular, the houses are characterized as "man-made mountains" (1988, 35) or "mountainous" (1988, 113). Paul Egede describes the reaction of "his Greenlanders" as one of astonishment and speechlessness, being moved to point at "the land, the castle, and the many ships, which were under sail and anchored." Paul Egede estimates that there were between 200 and 300 ships (1988, 139). Their sheer number and size seems to be what most impresses the four, especially when compared to the scale of human construction to which they were accustomed in Western Greenland. According to Egede, Pooq states that "a master on a whaling boat is just a small master when compared to the big masters in our [that is, Egede's] country, and that they are also small masters in comparison to the king" (1988, 35).

on marrying a European, they scorned their former way of life and their old Greenlandic beaus (Gad 1969, 493). As noted in the Introduction, Missionary Glahn wrote in his diary in 1766 that Greenlandic girls would look down upon the most noble Greenlander but eagerly marry the lowliest and most worthless (Danish) sailor (1921, 63).

The complaints from Bloch and Egede were tied to a specific case, which in turn led to a list of conditions and demands in 1753 to be met by the prospective suitors. This list became a general marriage regulation, and conditions to be met by the suitors included an impeccable lifestyle; being healthy, hard-working and able; and the girl's consent and her family's permission (Gad 1969, 494). Once married, the man was tied to the country and the Trade for life, and was expected to lead a proper life and raise his children to work at the mission and in the Trade. When these conditions were met, the Trade would support the family; while the Trade reduced the husband's salary, it granted his family three rations of food.

There was still resistance towards these mixed marriages, which Gad notes was founded in the fear that Greenlanders would be drawn away from their traditional way of life, creating economic risks for the Trade if the supply of locally procured goods were to diminish. I return to these families in greater detail in chapter five.

In *Security, Territory, Population*, Foucault notes that the family unit went from a model of government under the management of the father to an instrument of government through which information, which contributes to statistics, may be obtained (2007, 104–105). The idea of family as model has a long pedigree, notably within the Christian worldview, and Foucault draws out Aquinas's analogies of government, where the father and, incidentally, the pastor are both his third analogy, after that of God and nature. The Lutheran understanding of family, which I discussed above, also corresponds to the model of government. Significantly, it was only after the shift in focus to population that the model of the family could be discarded as an insufficient way of conceptualising economy and government. The family could instead be subsumed *within* the population as an element, or indeed, as Foucault puts it, a "relay," which denotes its place as a privileged unit within this framework, as a connection which controls the currents of governmental strategies. Hence, the family could be deployed in governmental campaigns, which Foucault designates as campaigns of medicine, mortality, and hygiene (2007, 104–105; see also 1998, 100).

The shift in the understanding of economy in the eighteenth century consequently meant a shift in the understanding of family: where economy earlier indicated a form of government, it later denoted "a field of intervention for government" (Foucault 2007, 95). The role of the family underwent the same shift within this framework of governmentality to a renewed focus, privileging and consolidating this particular organisational unit. In colonial Greenland, however, the gradual implementation of the model-family, that is, the nuclear family took place as *an instrument* of government. The family was a part of the restructuring of society according to natural law or what was perceived as "civilisation." This is what Foucault calls "a permanent intervention in everyday conduct" (2007, 154); recall the heart, house, and mind in the Larsen quotation above, indicating the specific locations of this restructuring.

The missionary was not merely in charge of teaching Christianity, converting 'the pagans,' and conducting services – but he was also in charge of constructing and upholding a social morality framed within a patriarchal social order, thereby creating subjects from and according to this morality—in short, maintaining the ideological backbone of this society-in-the-making. This sense of responsibility is, as Lauridsen and Lytthans have argued, evident in the diaries of the missionaries, which emphasise the constant interaction with Greenlanders and unceasing attention to upbringing and education—in other words, to 'civilising.' The civilising aspect corresponds with the Lutheran understanding of nature, where the world is the site of salvation. In Lutheranism, therefore, it becomes imperative to change or reform nature in order to make it the home of the pure spirit, which contrasts with medieval Catholicism's construal of nature as in and of itself pointing towards the pure world of spirit. The following quote from Hans Egede, the first missionary to Greenland in 1721, sets forth this point of view:

> It is a matter which cannot be questioned, that if you will make a Christian out of a mere savage and wild man, you must first make him a reasonable man and the next step will be easier. This is authorised and confirmed by our Saviour's own method. He makes a beginning from the earthly things; he proposes the mysteries of the kingdom of God in parables and similitudes. The first care taken in the conversations of Heathens is to remove out of the way all obstacles which may hinder their conversion and render them unfit to receive the Christian doctrine, before anything can be successfully undertaken on their behalf.
>
> It would contribute a great deal to advance their conversion, if they could by degrees be brought into a settled way of life and abandon this sauntering and wandering about from place to place to seek their livelihood. But this cannot be hoped until a Christian nation comes to be settled among them (I mean in such places where the ground is fit for tillage

> and pasturage), to teach them, and little by little accustom them to a quiet and more useful way of life than that which they now follow.
>
> 1745, 216–17

Danish theologian Henrik Wilhjelm discusses the mission to Greenland (2005) in light of both these comments from Egede. Wilhjelm looks at the prerequisites for conversion demanded by the two competing missions working in Greenland in the early eighteenth century: the Danish mission (Egede's) and the Moravian Brethren mission. The Brethren demanded a complete conversion from sinful humanity. Human in Greenlandic is *inuk* (plural: *inuit*), which also means Greenlander. With this linguistic twist in mind, Wilhjelm points out that from an understanding of the human as completely corrupt, it was a short step to understanding the Greenlander as worthless precisely because he was a Greenlander. Thus, in order to be saved, the Greenlander had to discard human-ness, which in this case meant Greenlandic customs (2005, 4). The Danish mission, on the other hand, insisted on raising the Greenlanders up to a level of (rational European) humanity that could form the basis of a Christian identity—that is, civilising before Christianising. In both cases, the Greenlandic is to be discarded: in the case of the Brethren as sinful humanity, and in the eyes of the Danish mission as a form of pre-human existence (6). This is an extremely important point: from Wilhjelm's outline of the situation, it becomes clear that theology *produces* an understanding of nature, which in turn becomes the legitimate reason for the subsequent domination and domestication of that nature, be it sinful or savage.

What must be immediately contested is the ease with which Wilhjelm divides the production of the native into the Brethren's construct of a sinful nature and the Danish mission's construct of a savage nature. That the Danish mission was just as concerned with sin as with civilisation may be seen in translations of the New Testament into Greenlandic, where the conceptual universe of Greenlandic 'religious' practices was deployed to signify damnation (Petterson 2012b). It is also expressed in the various missionary diaries, where the category of superstition is frequently invoked in opposition to the faith of the Danish Lutheran mission. I do agree that the *formative* effect on Greenlandic society differed, in that the social effects of the Danish mission were much more influential and pervasive. However, this is due to the collaboration with trade and the mercantile framework within which the mission was cast.[27] This situation was different from that of the Moravian Brethren, whose

27 Anthropologists Susanne Dybbroe and Poul Møller compellingly argue that the settlement and conversion of the Greenlanders were of initial benefit to the Trade in that they

financial support came from Germany and who could therefore concentrate on the religious dimension without having to harness the labour power of their converts.

However, this did not mean that the Danish mission was less interested in the souls of the Greenlanders. The civilising process to which Egede alludes in the earlier quotes, and which Wilhjelm takes as a point of departure for his distinction between the two, is also informed by theology, namely, the cultural Protestant upbringing that follows codes of ethics and organisations of time, work, and family shaped by centuries of engagement with Protestant ideology and its implementation by the absolute monarchy, as noted above. Furthermore, I want to repeat that that the missionaries had a profound influence on the implementation of a Protestant work ethic through various paternalistic mechanisms and constant supervision (Lauridsen and Lytthans 1983).

The missionary was placed in charge of a profound cultural and social invasion that could be appropriately described either as subjection, in the case of converting the population, or as conduct, in the case of managing Christian subjects. Both these steps of 'civilization' work towards creating (or redefining) and orchestrating a social order. A reaction against this 'conduct of conducts' would therefore, not surprisingly, be aimed at the Protestant pastorate and its constant attention to subjection and subjectification. However, the effects of such a reaction would go beyond that of the mission. Consequently, the situation in Evighedsfjorden and the various refusals against Hveyssel—to listen to him, to take his exegetical refutations to heart, to stay with him at the colony—are all refusals of conduct, which he himself realises. Nevertheless, the reaction also affected the Trade and the hunt, which is why merchants were called in to assist. Likewise, the mode (writing) and chain of command that Hveyssel finds self-evident, namely, to admonish Habakuk to keep his wife in line, is futile, as are his attempts to get Habakuk to leave his second wife. All of these refusals and resistances discredit the Protestant pastoral power in its systems of social structure, obedience, salvation and truth, which, to paraphrase Foucault (2007, 204), characterise the objective, the domain of intervention of Protestant pastoral power. A retaliation, or reaction, should thus come as no surprise, since this is part of the consolidation of pastoral power. But perhaps the actual step seems somewhat counterintuitive.

---

facilitated direct contact with the Greenlanders, broke down Greenlandic traditional authority structures, and severely limited Dutch and English merchants, whose trade relied on the mobility of Greenlanders (1981, 143). Once these external hindrances to trade were broken, the Greenlanders were then regularly moved out to smaller settlements, accompanied by national catechists.

In 1791, annual state funding to the mission and Trade was cut as part of a larger budget adjustment. Following this reduction, the number of appointed missionaries and districts was reduced to five from ten, with the volatile district of Sukkertoppen left without a missionary after its incorporation into Holsteinsborg district.[28] This vacuum was filled by Frederik Berthelsen, who stayed at Sukkertoppen until 1814 (except for a two-year commission in Godthåb). The year 1796 also marked an end to the use of Danish-born catechists in Greenland; from then on, all the catechists were recruited from the indigenous population (Gad 1976, 435–6). As Gad notes in his historical exposition, this strengthened the mission because these catechists had closer contacts with the Greenlandic population, and the mission increasingly came to be regarded as a Greenlandic affair (Gad 1976, 412). However, it is also necessary to note that with the development of a catechist faction which favoured the legitimate sons of Danish fathers, the groundwork was also laid for a racialised stratification of Greenlandic society whose embryonic form may be discerned in the figure of Frederik Berthelsen. In this way, the Habakuk movement facilitated the extension of colonial power through its opposition.

28 See detailed discussion of the negotiations in Gad (1976, 401–412).

CHAPTER 4

Catechists in the Making

Labour, Writing, and Gender

> The importance of writing lies in its creating a new medium of communication between men.
>
> GOODY 1968, 1

Foucault characterises governmentality as the specific encounter between technologies of self and technologies of domination (2000a, 225). While the previous chapters were focused on a technology of subjection or domination, I now take a closer look at a technology of self. The present chapter offers an analysis of writing as a gendered governmental technique. Foucault's own observations on writing are restricted to a few essays analysing Stoic epistolary and notebook-writing as exercises in the formation of the subjects:

> In the case of the epistolary account of oneself, it is a matter of bringing into congruence the gaze of the other and that gaze which one aims at oneself when one measures one's everyday actions according to the rules of a technique of living.
>
> 2000e, 221

For Foucault, these kinds of writing (epistles and notebooks) are Stoic technologies of the self (see also 2000a, 238). My own aim here is to place writing in the colonial context established in the last three chapters and analyse how writing, as a technology of self, dovetails with the disciplining strategies of the colonial administration.

I am particularly interested in how alphabetic writing transforms oral tradition; how it functions as a medium of subjection and masculinity; and its production of 'reality.' Employing Christina von Braun's (2009) observations on what she calls linear writing and how it facilitated abstraction and generated a different perception of and relationship to reality (namely a linear logic), I argue that the recording of oral traditions in writing changes the medium of transmission and provides a way of objectifying Greenlanders.[1] Of course, as von Braun also points out, the understanding of alphabetised writing as a

1 I follow Rafael's line of argument that the Tagalog people of the Philippines were objectified as Tagalogs—in Spanish accounts—through the translation of their language,

medium with considerable social and political effects is not new, but has been advanced by many theorists of writing.[2] However, close analyses of the actual effects and their consequences in a colonial situation have not been advanced with quite the same fervour.[3] This is what I aim to do in the present chapter. The argument runs as follows: the recorded traditions, which are made available in writing function as a kind of mirror. In their schooling, the catechists—who were all men—participated in this process of objectification by copying the transmitted material as they practised their handwriting. In their very isolated employments along the coast, they were required to keep daily journals, a process that created distance between themselves, subjected as observers, and their surroundings, on which they reported. Finally, this production of nature is also performed in the literary production of the catechists, a production that initially emerged with the newspaper *Atuagagdliutit*, and continued in subsequent lyrics and novels.[4] I am particularly interested in the production of the hunter as the foil for a catechist identity, an analysis that is further developed in the subsequent chapters.

Writing, Gender, and Abstraction

> *... the anathema that the Western world has obstinately mulled over, the exclusion by which it has constituted and recognised itself, from the* Phaedrus *to* Course in General Linguistics.
>
> DERRIDA 1998, 103

This quotation from *Of Grammatology* brings out in characteristic condensed Derridean an important element within the argument of the present work, namely, the function of writing in Western self-consciousness as the means by which the West *constituted* and *recognised* its—this is an important inflection—*masculine* self. The following section introduces the discussion of orality and literacy, with its undercurrents of primitivism/savagery over against

the descriptions of their customs and politics, and the recording of their responses to colonial authority (1993, 16). Writing here is the practice of objectification.

2 Von Braun (2001, 59) mentions a range of scholars from fields as varied as political economy (Harold Innis), classics (Eric Havelock), literature (Walter Ong, Aleida Assmann, Marshall MacLuhan, Derick de Kerckhove), Ancient Near East studies (Ignace J. Gelb, Jan Assmann), and anthropology (Jack Goody).

3 Penny van Toorn (2006) is a notable exception.

4 See Langgård (2000) for a description of the views of nature in Greenlandic literature.

culture/civilisation, to argue for the centrality of writing for the constitution of the masculine self. Consequently, I begin with Derrida to discuss orality and literacy, and move on to discuss the connection between gender and writing, drawing out education and abstraction as key concepts.

In *Of Grammatology*, Derrida's deconstruction of the metaphysics of presence is exemplified in his engagement with Lévi-Strauss and Rousseau. The reading of Rousseau through Lévi-Strauss brings out the instability of the nature/culture distinction in the work of the former, and the latent ethnocentrism in the perceptions of nature of the latter. One of the principle points into which Derrida delves is the notion of writing as an external violation of the natural and innocent state, "bursting," as it were, upon the scene of nature, and enforcing civilisation upon native communities (Lévi-Strauss) or nature (Rousseau). In his discussion of Lévi-Strauss, Derrida refers to this notion as "epigenetist" (1998, 120), a term which evokes Aristotle's theory of reproduction, where the generative principle (male semen) imposes form on passive female matter.[5] The term "epigenetist," which is the name Derrida gives to Lévi-Strauss's theory of writing, has gender implications that link it to Rousseau's gendering of nature as feminine, although Derrida, Lévi-Strauss, and Rousseau never refer to the penetration of nature as masculine.

This gendering of writing becomes important in my ensuing discussion of phallogocentrism, but for now I focus on the charges of ethnocentrism that Derrida levels at Lévi-Strauss and Rousseau. Derrida's point is that although both claim that writing is something external to "native communities," it is always present in their description of these self-same communities. Therefore, Rousseau distinguishes between "writing of the heart" and "writing of reason" (Derrida 1998, 174), and Lévi-Strauss speaks of people "without writing." Hence, "[b]y one and the same gesture, (alphabetic) writing, servile instrument of a speech dreaming of its plenitude and its self presence, is scorned and the dignity of writing is refused to non-alphabetic signs" (Derrida 1998, 110). Derrida refers to this as "ethnocentrism *thinking itself* as anti-ethnocentrism" (1998, 120), that is, conceptualised within a progressivist narrative that is inherently ethnocentric.[6]

---

5 Aristotle expounds this theory in the text *Generation of Animals*. Epigenesis is seen as an important background text for (feminist) understandings of the generative principle in New Testament texts, especially in regard to Jesus in John's Gospel (Buch-Hansen 2007; Reinhartz 1999) but also to Paul (Singh 2007).

6 The full quotation, which encompasses these points, is: "I have earlier emphasized the ambiguity of the ideology which governs the Saussurian exclusion of writing: a profound ethnocentrism privileging the model of phonetic writing, a model that makes the exclusion of the *graphie* easier and more legitimate. It is, however, an ethnocentrism *thinking itself* as

Derrida's argument with Rousseau and Lévi-Strauss can also be seen as a comment on a larger discussion within the social sciences, namely, that of orality over against literacy. Anthropologist John (Jack) Goody, one of the pioneers of research on orality and literacy, is unimpressed with Derrida's construction of writing (as is Walter J. Ong, discussed below). Goody writes:

> To equate 'the writing on the wall' with writing on a blackboard is equally unacceptable for analytic purposes since it is to fail to distinguish between graphic absence and phonemic presence, to equate a premonition with an inscription.
>
> 2000, 114

For Goody, it is imperative that the entire dichotomy between orality and literacy be sustained, since a large part of his own academic production rests on this separation. Thus we see how he refutes Derrida's notion of writing, which does not distinguish between "writing on the wall" and "writing on the blackboard," as refusing to privilege the alphabet (phonemic presence). Goody insists on a distinction and thereby inadvertently reinforces one of Derrida's underlying points: that an insistence on a certain conception of writing (namely linear and phonetic notation) to construct literate *and* oral communities is already ethnocentric; Goody's example of premonition[7] and inscription, which barely conceals his moral judgement, is a case in point.

---

anti-ethnocentrism, an ethnocentrism in the consciousness of a liberating progressivism. By radically separating language from writing, by placing the latter below and outside, believing at least that it is possible to do so, by giving oneself the illusion of liberating linguistics from all involvement with written evidence, one thinks in fact to restore the status of authentic language, human and fully signifying language to all languages practiced by *peoples whom one nevertheless continues to describe as 'without writing'*"(Derrida 1998, 120; emphasis in original).

7 The reference is to the Book of Daniel in the Hebrew Bible, chapter five, in which a detached human hand writes on the wall during one of King Belshazzar's opulent banquets. None of the king's wise men can read the writing, but Daniel is summoned, reads the writing, and interprets it as the impending downfall of the Babylonian empire. One possible interpretation of the passage is that it is a self-referential narrative, in which the power and privilege of scribes, responsible for writing a text such as the Book of Daniel, is brought to the fore through Daniel's abilities in the narrative, reflecting the social context of the text and thus the status of the scribe(s) who produced it (see Boer 1996, 276–8 for such an interpretation of 2 Chronicles). Whether one accepts this interpretation or not, it seems quite clear that Daniel is in a privileged position as the only person in the empire who is able to read and interpret the writing, an ability he gets from God. This ability completely upstages all the king's wise

In a fascinating article on French orthography in seventeenth – and eighteenth-century France, historian Dena Goodman (2005) analyses the politics and gender of orthography and education. Some of her insights serve well as points of departure here. Goodman is interested in the gendering of orthographic practice, and its shifts from phonetic principles of the sixteenth century onwards to the norm of the written word in the later eighteenth century (197). The written norm was based on Latin, in which only elite men, the men of letters, were educated. The phonetic norm, *l'ortografe des dames*, underwent a shift from being the orthographic ideal, representing the natural and pure *parole*, to incorrect spelling (210).

What interests me here, apart from the gendering of phonetics and writing, is the aspect of education. In Greenland, too, it was the men who were subsumed within the educational system and instructed in the art of (alphabetic) writing, an institutional arrangement, which gave them significant social power. Goodman notes that while literacy was spreading in the wake of the Reformation and Renaissance (and with it, I might add, the printing press), the gender gap increased with the spread of 'Latinacy'—the classical education provided by the *collèges* for young men (2005, 199). This furthered the mastery of the written word by the men of letters. With the written word established by the academy as the incontestable authority above all others, the position of the elite men was further reinforced (206). In the *Port-Royale Grammar,* Charles Pinot Duclos declared: "The body of a nation alone has rights over the spoken language, and the writers have rights over the written language" (Goodman 2005, 208).

These struggles over language, the distribution of gender and the privileges of education, provide a sound backdrop for understanding the development of the notion of *écriture féminine* within French feminist philosophy.[8] I am less interested here in the concept of *écriture féminine* itself, and more interested in what it is reacting against: masculine, patriarchal writing, which excludes women from the sphere of writing and from the mode of expression that is writing.

The connection between patriarchy and writing has been explored by German cultural theorist von Braun in *NICHT ICH. Logik – Lüge – Libido*

---

men and seers. However, Goody equates the writing on the wall with premonition, which smacks of rational judgement of superstition, and this becomes, in effect, what he connects with oral communities.

8 *Écriture féminine*, a concept of writing conceptualised by Helene Cixous, is an exploration of the political and subversive possibilities of writing, which opposes itself to hierarchised cultural representations (Shiach 1991, 9). See also Toril Moi (2002, 106–108).

(NOT I: Logic, Lie, Libido).[9] Von Braun's work is a study of the history of Western thinking and its construction of gender and nature. I am particularly interested in the chapter "The Logos and the Lie," a sweeping history of writing and its implications for the way we construct the world.[10] As such, it is a genealogy of Western abstraction, tracing developments within Western traditions since 3000 BCE, especially the role of Christianity, as a religion of the book, in the process of abstraction.

Von Braun notes her agreement with Derrida in that they both perceive abstract thinking or philosophy as a product of writing. However, von Braun insists on the specific character of Western writing in order to account for the thirst for conquest and missionary zeal characteristic of the West.[11] For von Braun, missionary zeal and conquest are firmly tied to writing and the level of abstraction in Western thinking. Writing and its accompanying mode of abstraction have produced two distinct realities, one which must be subordinated to the other (2009, 86–87). Furthermore, von Braun argues that writing generated a sense of eternity (*Ewigkeit*) that points beyond human mortality. Only through writing was it possible to speak of eternity and the promise of individual immortality. Thus, from writing, two realities emerged: one was the world, which could be grasped with the senses, and the other was the promise, the otherworldly transcendent reality, which must be believed (2009, 78).[12]

Of central significance to my argument is the key role von Braun assigns to Christianity in this genealogy; her analysis foregrounds the ideological role Christianity has played in colonisation, as well as Christianity's influence in the process of abstraction—the idea of an abstract self and the creation of an externalised matter. The process which precedes Christianity is the process of abstraction, whereby the symbol assumes its primacy over the symbolised, thus permitting the spirit to dominate matter (von Braun 2009, 90).

9 *NICHT ICH* has not been translated into English; the translations are mine.

10 An English translation of the chapter title does not convey the manner in which these concepts are gendered in German: *der Logos* (masculine) as opposed to *die Lüge* (feminine).

11 It is important to note that von Braun works with a different signifying economy than Derrida. Von Braun's concept of writing is phonetic writing, thereby departing from Derrida; she operates with a distinction between writing as a practice and its representation of 'reality,' tracing abstraction at a different level of meaning than Derrida, who works with Saussure's distinction between signifier and signified.

12 In *Versuch über den Schwindel,* von Braun uses the film *The Matrix* to explain these two senses of reality and their relation (2001, 143–44).

Furthermore, the concept of *logos* has been separated from words such as *mythos* and *epos*, leaving *logos* as that which is verifiable or tested via an exercise of logic and reason, while the meanings of *epos* and *mythos* were relegated to those of poetry and 'tradition.' This distinction unearths the separation of pure abstraction and truth on one side, and 'traditions' on the other, transmitted orally from person to person and hence characterised as 'the lie' (von Braun 2009, 95).

From Plato on, *logos* is connected with that part of the human which is ungraspable by the senses—the soul. Thus the philosopher becomes the earthly representative of *logos* and its law. Stripped of all matter, *he* can contemplate the pure spirit. Von Braun argues (2009, 97) that in the figure of the philosopher, the transformation of humans into ideal *body-less-ness* is completed, and showcases how humans become symbols and step into the "linear eternity," the progressive logic of writing. With the incorporation of *logos* into the realm of the spirit, it is not only masculine spirituality and feminine corporeality that is created, but also the division between manual and spiritual labour, nature and culture, and from these the master-slave relationship is generated.

According to von Braun, the necessity of the reign of the spirit over matter is at the origin of all colonial conquests and settlements (2009, 98), hence the role of Christianity in colonisation. And here we come to a crucial point: the *logos* wants not only to subject all matter to its rule, but also to prove that its law is universal and has validity for all people and all societies—that all are expressions of the natural law.[13] *However, the spirit needs the matter to realise itself.* The more matter is configured as an opposition to the spirit, the more it is required for revelation. Spirit has no other mode of expression than matter, and is therefore simultaneously master and slave of matter (von Braun 2009, 98).[14] This leads to the materialisation of the *logos*, which follows the shedding of the body (*Entleibung*). The shedding takes place in philosophy, with Aristotle touting the ideal as a male being (since the female is an incomplete male) and devoid of body (von Braun 2009, 100). From this tradition arises the spiritual fatherhood of patriarchy. Christianity has played a crucial part in the materialisation of the *logos*, with the incarnation—"the word made flesh" (John 1:14). Von Braun emphasises that the incarnation

---

13 As noted in my discussion of natural law in chapter three.

14 In their introduction to German feminist thought, Beinssen-Hesse and Rigby (1996, 14) accuse von Braun of masking the fact that the reality produced by the *logos* could not exist without the material reality. However, I think von Braun recognises this, particularly in expressions such as spirit being "master" and "slave of matter."

is not the reconnection of spirit and matter, but is actually a further separation, since it requires that *logos* now controls and dominates matter (2009, 102).

In Christianity, then, the subjection of matter to spirit is completed. Within this subjection, Christianity *produces* two kinds of flesh or matter: 'good matter,' which is Christ and the body in the bodily resurrection, and 'bad matter,' signifying women and death.[15] The emergence of two planes of reality has meant a radical change of all concepts and values, not only in mythical thought but also in the social reality of Western culture (von Braun 2009, 104). The man who thus had become God took on a social significance in the Renaissance and Reformation in that the transcendent ideal began to be realised. Von Braun writes:

> In the nineteenth century, Marx proclaimed the teachings of the 'base,' which determined the 'superstructure.' At the end of the same century, Freud discovered the power of the unconscious over the conscious. The 'matter'—be it the proletariat, capital or the unconscious—becomes the determining factor in the sciences, the economy, sociology and psychology in the last 200 years. But this 'matter' on which one increasingly relies is nothing but a production of *logos*. Never mind whether it concerns 'capital,' this 'money from nothing' which determines economy, paper money, stock or people, it discloses itself as the creation of the *logos*: not until the *logos* has created its own matter can it explain history; and, likewise, the unconscious can only be discovered when it works according to the ideas of *logos*.
>
> 2009, 117

Although my study is different in scope from von Braun's, a number of her insights are immensely productive for the present analysis, particularly the linking of writing to patriarchy, and tracing the way it produces reality. Her point about how matter is a prerequisite for the revelation of the spirit is also convincing, especially since it complements Troeltsch's argument, discussed earlier, regarding Lutheran social structure. Von Braun's proposition that writing creates another world to which we ("should") relate through belief, while grasping this world with our senses, fits well within the colonial context that this book explores in that the indigenous visionary experiences were denigrated while Protestant belief in God was propagated. Von Braun's most relevant point, however, concerns that of writing as the vehicle for abstraction,

15 This production of two forms of matter was also a crucial factor in Richard Dyer's argument on whiteness and Christianity discussed in the previous chapter.

since this gives new meaning to the implementation of phonetic writing in societies that did not previously have writing as a prime medium.

I had hoped that von Braun would have tarried more with the social and institutional background for the development of abstraction. After all, literacy developments are implemented within institutions, as the discussion of Goodman's work shows, and learning how to read and write would have enforced the social discourses on gender and class. It is still worth emphasising, even if this is an obvious point, that writing constituted the prime *medium* for the dissemination of Western patriarchy and masculinity. Both Rousseau and Lévi-Strauss were quite aware of the social power of writing: Rousseau used a gendered imagery to convey the opposition between nature and culture, speech and writing, which, along with the connection between men and non-phonetic spelling as analysed by Goodman, completely accords with the literary movements of his time. Lévi-Strauss used writing and non-writing to distinguish 'civilised' societies from 'uncivilised' ones.

I concur with Derrida's point about an inherent ethnocentrism in Lévi-Strauss's distinctions, but I also find that Lévi-Strauss points to an important feature of writing, namely, that it is connected to colonialism and has the ability to *represent* indigenous populations:

> The only phenomenon with which writing has always been concomitant is the *creation of cities and empires*, that is the integration of large numbers of individuals into a political system, and their grading into castes or classes.
>
> LÉVI-STRAUSS 1989 [1955], 392; emphasis added

This is a crucial point in the development of an intellectual class in Greenland and the impact of this development on its social structure.

The Introduction of Writing in Greenland

This section continues my investigation into aspects of the orality/literacy debate, moving from the more theoretical deliberations to the concrete processes in Greenland. The point of departure is literary scholar Kirsten Thisted's analysis of oral traditions, which I will follow to examine the recording of these traditions by Henrik Rink and Knud Rasmussen, and to explore the significance of the recording for notions of an objectified Greenlandic culture. This will then provide the foundations for the analyses in the last section, *Cultivated Estrangement*.

Oral Cultures and Colonial Writing

In Thisted's important 1997 article on Greenlandic oral traditions as sources for the cultural encounter between Danes and Greenlanders, there is a minor contradiction with which I want to begin. Thisted notes that one of the problems with using the oral traditions as sources for eighteenth-century encounters is that they were not collected until the nineteenth century, and "[t]he delay of a century is a long time in oral tradition, where a special feature is precisely the ability to rapid adaptation, so that the past continually is kept up-to-date with the present" (1997a, 73–74). On the other hand, she notes in a reference to Knud Rasmussen's collections from the early twentieth century that

> [t]hese stories show great concordance with those that were collected earlier—a circumstance which may be used to confirm the stability of the tradition, but also to some extent has its explanation in the fact that many of the stories had been published in print in connection with H.J. Rink's collection, and therefore that the tradition at this time is transmitted in a combination of oral and written forms.
>
> 1997A, 84N8

While the first quotation notes the rapid and fluid nature of the oral traditions, the second suddenly refers to the oral traditions as stable. From the printing of Rink's tales (1863) to the literary expeditions of 1902–04, during which Rasmussen collected his tales, we have a period of 40 years—more or less a generation and certainly a considerable amount of time in an oral tradition already characterised by rapid adaptations. Nevertheless, there is great concordance with the earlier collections, a circumstance for which Thisted offers two possible explanations: the stability of the tradition, and the dual transmission through oral and written forms. I want to follow the latter explanation and pursue the question at which she hints, namely whether the written transmission could have contributed greatly to the stabilising of the tradition?

That some shift had taken place in the understanding of transmission is abundantly clear from Knud Rasmussen's preface to the publication of the West Greenlandic traditions, where he explains:

> I have preferred to reproduce the tale of Kunuk according to the old Greenlandic original from 1830, which is found in *kalâdlit oqalugtualiait*.[16] I also have records of this tale, none of which are so complete as this one,

16 This is Rink's publication, *kaladlit oκalluktualliait*, spelled in accordance with Kleinschmidt's orthography.

> which is why I have selected it as the best, since its narrative form corresponded to my own transcription in detail.
>
> 1921, 5

Rink's collection, or at least one narrative in Rink's collection, *Kunuk,* becomes the Greenlandic 'original' against which the other versions are compared and found wanting. This is an assessment of the oral traditions from the parameters of writing, but it also shows the 'logic' behind printing at the time: an attempt to obtain closure.[17] Knud Rasmussen is attempting to preserve or conserve the Greenlandic oral traditions before they disappear.

However, Rasmussen himself undertakes a great deal of editing and revision, thereby effectively creating another strand of tradition. Thisted (1994, 207) offers an example in the transmission of the narrative of Sinngajik's genealogy, a narrative which simultaneously combines hunting culture with Christianity while deploying features characteristic of the oral as well as the written tradition. The story was told by Esaias, one of the primary sources for Rasmussen's collection. Thisted notes that Esaias could write, but that this particular narrative was recorded by Hendrik Olsen, a student at the college hired by Rasmussen to record Esaias's stories. Thisted argues that Esaias's style is influenced by stylistic characteristics of writing due to his intimate knowledge of writing, prompting her to further argue that Esaias's stories exhibit both oral and literary styles. However, Rasmussen edited or removed some of the elements, which were characteristic of written narrative, such as detailed geographical descriptions of the area and chronological references (Thisted 1994, 208).[18] Thisted (1994, 214) argues that the oral tradition had been influenced by the stylistic conventions of European writing, and that Rasmussen, at the end of a complex process, had constructed a contrast between oral tradition and its indigenous context, and written literature and its modern context,

---

17 Closure is one of the features indicated as characteristic of print by Ong (1982, 132). While I find much of Ong's work questionable for reasons that will be explained in the following, I do agree that closure is a characteristic feature of print. However, following a Derridean line, I don't believe that closure is in fact possible, but that we rather should speak of a *desire* for closure. Nevertheless, for groups of people not trained in post-structuralist theory, and whose main encounters with writing are constituted by an overwhelming bureaucracy, there still is fidelity towards the written word, a fidelity which is supported by the binding nature of written agreements.

18 The scribe Hendrik Olsen handed over both his drafts as well as the "final" version. Hence, Thisted was able to identify how Rasmussen edited and revised the material (Thisted 1994, 208).

precisely by editing and revising the material to meet these presumed oral and literary criteria.[19]

Thisted is a literary scholar; as such, her focus has been on Greenlandic literature and its development in the context of the Danish-Greenlandic cultural encounter. In this particular respect—although not in others—she can be placed within the pioneering scholarly tradition of Ong and Goody. Ong's most famous work, *Orality and Literacy: The Technologizing of the Word* (1982), is a study of the shift in consciousness generated by the transition to writing from orality. Casting orality and literacy within a teleological narrative that begins from natural orality and progresses to literacy, Ong accepts a somewhat watered-down version of Derrida's argument in *Of Grammatology* while simultaneously incarnating the ethnocentricity Derrida identifies in Rousseau and Lévi-Strauss (Ong 1982, 165–170). Ong argues that consciousness changes through writing, and becomes disembodied without a cultural, social, and political context.

This de-contextualisation is the main point of Penny van Toorn's critique of Ong (and Goody and McLuhan) and the argument that "writing in itself has played a determining role in the biological and cultural advancement of humankind" (van Toorn 2006, 8).[20] Van Toorn calls this the "autonomous model" in that it does not take account of contextual matters such as ideology, institutions, and socio-political relations. For van Toorn, whose study deals with the entry of writing and literacy into indigenous lifeworlds in Australia, the colonial context is crucial. Van Toorn's study focuses on the subversive use of writing by Aboriginal agents in the course of colonial history, such as the communication of their ill-treatment to the authorities. While there certainly are examples of Greenlanders who use writing in a similar way to give voice to the ill-treatment they suffered at the hands of Danes,[21] subversive uses

19 This argument was developed through an analysis of the stories recorded by Aron of Kangeq in her 1993 thesis, *Som perler på en snor. Fortællestrukturer i grønlandsk fortælletradition – med særligt henblik på forholdet mellem de originale og udgivne versioner* (As Beads on a String: Narrative Structures in Greenlandic Oral Traditions, with Particular Emphasis on the Relationship between the Original and Published Versions).

20 A similar critique of Ong is found in Anthony K. Webster's article (2006, 312) on literacy and orality in Navajo communities. Webster notes that "'artifacting' the word on the page has implications. I do not know if they so much change 'consciousness as they involve social, political, religious, and linguistic consequences (both intended and unintended)."

21 In 1791, seven whalers wrote a letter of complaint to the king about how little they were paid for their catch, having practically been left to starve (See Gad 1976, 248–255 for description of the letter and the context). However, letters to the king had to pass through several hands, so this one never reached its destination. A similar episode occurs 130 years

of writing is not the object of my analysis.[22] Instead, I aim to trace the impact of writing on those who were granted access to writing and used it as tools of power to construct Greenlandic society. I agree with van Toorn that this cannot be done without close attention to the ideological, political, and social context. In fact, the notion of a disembodied word, which propels the world towards fulfilment, is the most obvious indication of the theological and logocentric bias in Ong's study. This bias becomes glaringly apparent when Ong is read through the eyes of von Braun.

Concerning systems of signification, I do not regard alphabetised writing as a superior or more civilised form of signification than the Greenlanders' system of signification before colonisation, but I do regard it as a *different* system of signification. I also presuppose that its implementation in communities which were not accustomed to this system of signification placed the Greenlanders at a disadvantage because it was an unknown system with a different set of rules. The differences lay not just in the rules of grammar and orthography, but also the very means of communication, abstraction, and representation, as well as interaction with the page. These are not qualities inherent in the act of decoding alphabetised script; they are acquired through training and education. As discussed above, Foucault argues that writing is a technology of the self, which was one of the first uses of writing (2000b, 277). From the analyses of self-writing in his other essays ("Technologies of the Self" and "Self-Writing") and its focus on the classical philosophical tradition (Pythagorean, Epicurean, and Stoic), Foucault makes it clear that this is a particularly Western technology of the self, one that has been developed for at least 2000 years (2000b, 277).

later, when Peter Gundel writes the king to complain about the lack of a just legal system in Greenland—for Greenlanders. Gundel sends the letter to his patron, Jørgen Hvam, who decides not to forward it to the king. The procedure in both cases is the same: Greenlanders write to the highest authority to complain about unfair treatment; they forward the letter to an intermediary authority, and it goes no further.

22 Apart from van Toorn's study, see also Hackel and Wyss (2010) and Rafael (1988) for analyses that discuss subversive uses of writing. An example of writing used subversively in the Greenlandic context may be gleaned from the Habakuk affair, in which Frederik Berthelsen's brother Joseph functioned as Mary's scribe, writing down all her words. Furthermore, Andreas Ginge, the missionary in Godthåb (Nuuk), notes in his report back to Copenhagen that the heresy attracted converts from other districts through letters and envoys. *Rigsarkivet* (Danish National Archives): *Missionskollegiet og Direktionen for Vajsenhuset: Indkomne sager den grønlandske mission vedk.* 1789–91, folder 1789, no. 29: Report from Andreas Ginge to the Missionary Department, 27 August 1789, point 4).

In other words, while Foucault acknowledges that technologies of self exist in all cultures, the forms differ. Furthermore, technologies of self play a fundamental role in governmentality, in that Foucault (2000a, 225) characterises governmentality precisely as the encounter between techniques of self and technologies of domination. I will argue that this is what occurs in the training of the catechist. Foucault (2000b, 277) briefly notes this encounter in the education system: "[I]f we take educational institutions, we realize that one is managing others and teaching them to manage themselves."

Therefore, the technology of the self is always already a social act. One of the principle differences in cultural (and political) thought is determined by the position of the self in relation to the social. In writing—that is, the Western mode of self-writing—the self is placed as though it stands *outside* the social, and proceeds in accordance with the logic of the *logos* to produce the social in relation to the self. The introduction of writing thus enabled the coordination of complex social action (Collins and Blot 2003), a skill that required much labour to acquire and deploy. Access to education, and the ability to decode and understand the workings of the colonial apparatus and the logic of its system of literacy, was not granted to everyone. This was reserved for those who entered the catechist colleges, which were established in the mid-nineteenth century. Thus, the effects of writing (subjectification and objectification) were reliant on an already-established system of distinction and privilege that moved along racial lines.

Recording the Oral Traditions

This section begins with a discussion of the written recording of oral traditions, and how the process of subjectification/objectification occurred within this practice. I also introduce the agents of this effect, the trained catechists, who constitute the subject elaborated in the last section of the current chapter.

In 1823–28, the missionary in Egedesminde district in Northern Greenland (present-day Aasiaat), Peter Kragh, began a local collection of Greenlandic oral traditions. Several decades later, starting in 1858, inspector Rink initiated a nationwide (West Greenland) collection of oral traditions. Then in 1902–04, Knud Rasmussen undertook the Danish Literary Expedition. Since Kragh's collection was handed over to Rink, I will not discuss this venture any further; instead, I focus on Rink's collection, and its contexts and significance. My discussion of Rink's collection will provide the social and institutional background for further developments. This in turn will frame the particular aspect of the oral/literacy debate which is relevant in the present context: whether the oral tradition changes through its recording in writing, and what the social significance of such a shift may be.

On 22 April 1858, Rink published the call for tales, sermons, drawings, and so on. The plan was that Greenlanders themselves should gather material from these various genres, put them in writing, and send them to Rink. He would then publish them at the newly established printing press so that Greenlanders could use them for education and entertainment.

This call took place between 1845 and 1861, within a period of profound institutionalisation. In 1845, the catechist colleges were established;[23] in 1851, the excommunicated Moravian Brother Samuel Kleinschmidt published his grammar of the Greenlandic language, *Grammatik der groenländischen Sprache*;[24] in 1856–57, the local councils were established;[25] around 1857, Rink's printing press was founded; in 1858, the call for gathering traditions went out; and in 1861 the Greenlandic newspaper *Atuagagdliutit* was established. Ostensibly these various initiatives were undertaken to promote Greenlandic self-respect and pride, and intended to grant Greenlanders greater influence over their own affairs. However, in reality it meant a further implementation of colonial control, a consolidation of the coordinates within which Greenlanders could and would operate. A brief example may be borrowed from Danish historian Jens Christian Manniche's study, *The Mastery of Language and the Language of Mastery*,[26] in which he argues that written Greenlandic is a colonial construction and that Kleinschmidt, in making a certain kind of Greenlandic the norm (that is, from the Godthåb [Nuuk] district) privileges one area and makes this the standard for proper Greenlandic (2002, 25).[27]

Furthermore, as Manniche notes, the Greenlandic written language also functioned as a means of communication between Greenlanders. This certainly

23 This is the usual dating of the establishment of the colleges even though the buildings were not finished and the curriculum and teaching only took definite shape a few years later. The college in Godthåb (Nuuk) was opened in 1847 and the college in Jakobshavn (Ilulissat) in 1848 (Thuesen 2007, 73).

24 This was not the first Greenlandic grammar, but it was the first to be acknowledged as the norm for modern Greenlandic that, along with the dictionary from 1871, established Greenlandic orthography.

25 I have mentioned these briefly in connection with Rud's work in chapter two, and will return to them in the next chapter.

26 Manniche is inspired by Bernard Cohn's essay, "The Command of Language and the Language of Command" from Cohn's *Colonialism and its Forms of Knowledge: The British in India* (1996, 16–56). Manniche's paper is a similar analysis of language, dictionaries, phrasebooks, and colonialism in Greenland. The title of Manniche's work in the text is my translation of *Sprogbeherskelse og herskersprog*.

27 This is an example of what Benedict Anderson (2006, 44–45) defines as a unification of fields of "exchange and communication," which is one of the ways in which print language laid the basis for national consciousness.

opened up new ways of communication over longer distances, enabling an "imagined community" (Anderson 2006 [1983]), but other ways, means, and limits of communicating would have ceased to exist. This is the point I want to argue in relation to Rink's initiative for gathering the traditions. The text of the invitation runs as follows:

> At the Expense of the Royal Trading Company, a small printing press has been established, belonging to the Inspector's residence at Godthaab (Godthåb) in southern Greenland, in which – for the future – printing of Greenlandic writings or announcements will be carried out by the college's assistant teacher in cooperation with one or two natives, trained for that purpose, under the supervision of the Inspector and the principal of the college.
>
> The aim is thus partly to serve as means of notification for the Trade and the Mission, and partly to provide the Greenlanders *something for entertainment or general instruction.*
>
> Therefore, anyone who would want to contribute to this is requested to send in, to the address 'South Greenland Inspectorate,' such announcements as could be used for that purpose, including in particular:
>
> *Greenlandic legends or compositions, which are now maintained among the inhabitants of certain districts through oral transmission or singing, sermons delivered by missionaries on special occasions, sermons or essays written by the native catechists,* and especially, moreover, *anything that could serve as amusement or entertainment for Greenlanders* [and] *maps and drawings* done by natives which serve to describe the land, especially the lesser-known fjords, as well as their travels, caribou hunts and so forth.
>
> The natives who provide such a useful contribution for printing, will for this obtain payment in relation to the size and quality of the work.
>
> From reproduction in THISTED 1997b, 9; emphases in original

I have two initial observations: First, it seems strange that this is addressed to Greenlanders, but they are spoken *of* in the third person rather than spoken *to* directly. Second, the message appears to assume that Greenlanders lacked the means to entertain themselves, since it is necessary to begin the process of collecting materials to provide them something for their amusement.

To begin with the second observation, the contradiction is apparent. The fact that there was something—*a lot,* in fact—to collect means that these stories were already in circulation and functioning as entertainment. Thus, if Greenlanders really lacked entertainment, there would be nothing to collect.

Did Rink not know about the entertainment practices of Greenlanders? That is highly unlikely; the call explicitly mentions legends and compositions maintained through oral transmission or singing. Or did Rink want Greenlanders to amuse themselves in a different way? That these collections go beyond the desire to provide entertainment for Greenlanders may be noted in the encouragement to send maps and drawings of lesser-known fjords, as well as the routes taken by hunting expeditions. The Greenlandic text brings out an important underlying assumption, in that it states "fjords unknown to the *kavdlunak*" that is, the strangers, usually Danes.[28] This suggests that an underlying interest is a deeper penetration of the country, a wish to know all the crevasses and fjords where Greenlanders hunt. Through drawings and maps provided by local informants, Rink wants to explore Greenland's lesser-known areas.

Furthermore, as Hanne Thomsen (1998) has argued, the collections were also an attempt, via the evocation of the hunting identity of the forefathers, to boost the seal hunt, which had suffered a significant decline, a decline that had serious effects on the local economy and, in turn, on the colonial one. Thus, if the objective was to boost self-confidence and instil pride in hunting, one way to accomplish this objective would be to present Greenlanders with an image of themselves as a hunting people. This could be carried out by writing down accounts of their forefathers that Greenlanders could then read. While this might seem a rather banal observation, I find it crucial to note the process of objectification in all this, and how it fits the first observation above: Rink speaks *of* Greenlanders *to* Greenlanders. It is not just a matter of writing down and publishing oral traditions; it is a matter of presenting Greenlanders with an image of themselves through a medium that objectifies them as Greenlanders, while subjectifying them as hunters.

The prerequisite for enabling this subjectification through objectification is the maximum truth-value assigned to the written word. At a more abstract level, this subjugation of individuals by mechanisms of power that appeal to a truth is central to Foucault's (1996, 386) notion of governmentality. Writing as a medium of truth is connected to the materials printed in Greenland. Until 1850, approximately fifty books had been printed in Greenlandic, and only a few of these were not of a religious nature (Frandsen 1999, 205).[29] Hence, most of the materials accessible for reading in Greenland before the mid-nineteenth

28 I thank Henrik Wilhjelm who confirmed this translation for me.

29 In Greenland, the first grammar reader was printed in 1739 (Frandsen 1999, 202), followed by a number of catechisms, bible translations, and sermons. Frandsen notes that the first non-religious publication was a book of drinking and patriotic songs (1999, 202).

century would have been religious. This is a crucial aspect of the production of a notion of truth. The entire conversion process was reliant on the notion of a truth to which the Greenlanders were subjected. Over against this 'Truth,' the Greenlanders' own traditions were cast as false, deceptive, and superstitious, as described in chapter one.

In light of this discussion of truth, I want to return to the question of objectification, particularly in terms of Rink's publications involving a dual process of the objectification of Greenlanders *as* Greenlanders while simultaneously subjectifying them as hunters. Apart from requiring a connection between writing and truth, this process also requires that Greenlanders had access to published versions of their stories. Rink published four volumes of the manuscripts in Greenlandic as *kaladlit oĸalluktualliait* between 1859 and 1863 (Thisted 1996, 253). These volumes would not have been financially available for primary producers or casual labourers, but they would nonetheless have been widely circulated. Archivist Niels Frandsen's case study of book ownership in North Greenland in the years 1791 to 1850 shows that a relatively large number of books were sent to North Greenland during this period—so many, in fact, that it "seems plausible to assume that most persons had received an ABD[30] and a catechism, and that most families possessed an exposition [of Christianity] and a hymnbook" (1999, 208). Frandsen cites documents dealing with the administration of estates of deceased persons to show that of forty-six people, only six owned more than seven books each—and all six were from 'mixed' families (1999, 210). Books, then, were apparently not a high priority for any average Greenlander not employed in the colonial apparatus. However, this should not lead to the assumption that books were inaccessible. Reading material, such as the newspaper *Atuagagdliutit,* circulated widely. Moreover, it is through the transmission of the image of themselves as hunters that Greenlanders were subjected as hunters as well as objectified as Greenlanders.

Another significant issue is the question of *who* carried out this dual process of identification—who sent in the manuscripts, and who handled them. Thisted notes that most of the texts were submitted by Greenlandic catechists (1997a, 75). However, the two principal contributors were the colonial manager Jens Kreutzmann and the hunter Aron of Kangeq.[31] Nonetheless, students at the catechist colleges were assigned to copy and transcribe the manuscripts in

30 The letter C was not included in the construction of the Greenlandic alphabet. Hence, the reader is called ABD instead of ABC.

31 Thisted has edited and published translations of both their works, which consist of a large number of stories as well as watercolour paintings (Aron 1999; Kreutzmann 1997).

their writing classes so that the texts would be easier for Rink to work with (Thisted 1997b, 35; Wilhjelm 1997, 89). Thus, as part of their training, students at the colleges copied manuscripts about "the Greenlanders," who in the process became a group distinct from themselves.

Furthermore, the students learned how to relate to others through the medium of writing; how to transmit through writing and how to understand other written texts—in short, how to understand oneself as sender and receiver (Thuesen 1988, 199). Thuesen quite rightly considers that these comparatively advanced writing skills placed the catechists in a superior position of power. Whereas Thuesen goes on to analyse the ways in which the catechists influenced the population through the newspaper *Atuagagdliutit*,[32] I look to how the catechists *constructed* the population in writing. This shifts the line of argument; instead of focusing on how Greenlanders were objectified and subjectified through reading the written versions of their oral traditions, I examine the role of the catechists in this process as the ones who, through writing, objectified their fellow Greenlanders. The following section is therefore an analysis of the training of catechists in the colleges, and of the specifics of learning how to express oneself in writing. Of particular interest is how writing fosters a certain sense of self—as well as a certain sense of masculinity.

Cultivated Estrangement

After his training at the catechist college, Jens Chemnitz spent two years in Denmark and then arrived in 1885 (after a brief intermezzo in his hometown) at Holsteinsborg (present-day Sisimiut) to serve as head catechist (Thuesen 2007, 316). In his journals, Chemnitz draws attention to the feelings of estrangement that he experienced upon arriving in a different part of the country, but it is also an estrangement, which he himself seems to exacerbate by writing in Danish and referring to the surrounding population as "the Greenlanders" (Thuesen 2007, 321, 328). When an English whaling ship arrived just before Easter 1886, Chemnitz was displeased because he "sensed that a flurry of activity arose amongst the Greenlanders to produce small things to sell to the strangers, which thus gave them other things to think about than the

32 Thuesen's analysis looks at how the newspaper contributed to the spread and popularity of the nationalist revival movement, *Peqatiginiat* (Thuesen 1988). This study emphasises the objectification strategies of Greenlandic nationalism, while I focus on the agents of subjectification.

impending feast" (quoted in Thuesen 2007, 335).[33] This "estrangement" is the central theme of Thuesen's study, *Fremmed blandt landsmænd* (*Strangers Among Countrymen*), which regards the catechists as "middle-men,"[34] as "homeless" and positioned between the experience of the new and the old. Thuesen's aim is to assess "how catechists in concrete West Greenlandic local societies master 'homelessness', the experience of estrangement: briefly put, how they negotiate the position of the middleman" (2007, 26).

Thuesen's study thus foregrounds those Greenlanders, who actively appropriated the Danish worldview, as well as those who were born into it.[35]

---

33 See also Pedersen's analysis of interviews with young Greenlandic actors from the late 1970s who had staged a production entitled "Authentic Greenlandic" but thereafter displayed a similar distance to their cultural heritage as something out there in the settlements they wanted to capture (Pedersen 1997, 166). The theatre industry of the 1970s thus continued the objectification process.

34 Thuesen's concept of "middle-men" is borrowed from anthropology, in particular Robert Paine (1971), where middlemen stood between the population, whom they had to advise and inform, and the Danish civil servants to whom they were expected to pass on information about the local population (Rønsager 2006, 23–24).

35 Theologian Henrik Wilhjem's three volumes (1997, 2001, 2008) on Greenland's catechist colleges is an impressive piece of historical work that deserves to be cited here. The first volume, *De store opdragere* (*The Great Educators*) presents the three catechist colleges in Greenland and their principals (the Danish word *opdrager* also connotes a person who brings up or raises children). The title of the second volume, *af Tilbøjelighed er jeg grønlandsk*, is a quotation by Samuel Kleinschmidt that translates as: "of inclination I am Greenlandic." This volume is a historical biography of Samuel Kleinschmidt (1814–1886), the father of Greenlandic orthography, teacher at the catechist college in Godthåb (Nuuk), and mastermind of the first and only Greenlandic translation of the Old Testament from the Hebrew text. The third volume, *De nye grønlændere* (*The New Greenlanders*) describes what happened to students after they graduated from the various colleges: the issues and problems they encountered in their new homes, how they approached their work, and how they understood their own position within Greenlandic society and in relation to the colonial administration. The works can best be characterised as empiricist historiographies, based as they are on extensive archival studies coupled with little or no conscious reflection on knowledge production and ideological commitment. As such, Wilhjelm provides plenty of useful data. Despite the objectified nature of the works and their illusion of presenting things simply as they were, there are nevertheless, and inevitably, underlying assumptions. For Wilhjelm, the catechist institution is a uniquely Greenlandic institution. It developed due to "particular Greenlandic circumstances," (a small population spread over a vast area), but became an important way of negotiating colonial culture and adapting it to the transformed Greenlandic society. In his understanding of the catechists as cultural agents, Wilhjelm is in complete agreement with Thuesen.

A primary medium for this appropriation was writing. Indeed, *Fremmed blandt landsmænd* is the result of an analysis of eighty official journals from the districts of Holsteinsborg (Sisimiut) and Sukkertoppen (Manitsoq) from the years 1853 to 1932, during which a series of reforms led to an increase in Greenlandic participation in various parliamentary councils[36] and in mass communications (Thuesen 2007, 10). Thuesen assigns special significance to the catechists' journals as a way of producing self and other. He compares his own findings with ethnological analyses of Danish peasant diaries from the nineteenth century. Thuesen's research shows that in the early part of the century, the peasant diaries chiefly registered in a few words the events of weather and labour. In the middle of the century, more reflective journals began to appear, presumably generated by religious revivals and folk high schools[37] (Thuesen 2007, 262). Thuesen understands the activity of writing as a selection process in which 'happenings' become 'events;' something that happens undergoes a transformation from merely occurring to becoming something of social significance. Thuesen is particularly interested in the struggle to generalise one's own experiences and self-representations. Hence, by keeping the journal, the catechist selects important events and is consequently constructed through the writing as an individual subject, standing outside the local community (Thuesen 2007, 265). He notes that the initial entries of the catechists are less reflective and take shape as recording, but they also stand out as trivial and repetitive.

One example is the 1853 journal of Filipus. At the time, there was no tradition for keeping journals, or writing as such, and this is reflected in the very brief entries in Filipus's journal. Thuesen gives the example of an entry: "4th. Thursday. In the morning we worshipped. The children read. In the evening we worshipped" (Filipus in Thuesen 2007, 274).[38] Every Sunday, Filipus records: "I read the Gospel. In the evening I read the epistle." (Filipus in Thuesen 2007, 275). In contrast to this, Thuesen refers to the journal of Morthen Egede, who wrote forty years later (1893), and with greater fluency and confidence:

---

36 For example, the local councils mentioned in connection with the analysis of Rud's article in chapter two. I return to this in chapter five.

37 "Folk high schools" is the English translation of the Danish *Folkehøjskole*, an adult-education institution founded in the mid-nineteenth century to help enlighten the general population. Danish pastor and politician Nikolaj Frederik Severin Grundtvig is commonly regarded as the founder of this institution, which has had—and continues to have—a significant impact on Danish nationalist ideology.

38 Thuesen's examples are translated from Greenlandic by himself and Daniel Thorleifsen. My translations are from these Danish translations.

"Since shoals of *ammassat*[39] have arrived, making us busy storing for winter, I will cease to record every day in this journal" (Egede in Thuesen 2007, 279). This entry, Thuesen argues, displays a consciousness of the text through its reference to the act of recording. Thuesen also offers an example from an 1870 journal entry by Samuel Olsen, who was trained at the college and was head catechist at the time of writing:

> Now that the missionary is leaving, and I am in charge of the place on my own, I feel powerless in body and soul. But I also have faith in God, that he is with me and strengthens me in the name of Jesus Christ. After doubting and feeling downhearted in my thoughts, I now am in good spirits, since God usually cares for his children when they approach him and sing hymns to him.
>
> OLESEN IN THUESEN 2007, 283

While Thuesen regards Olsen's journal as a depiction of the catechist as a person of action, I also think that his journal demonstrates an interaction with the page—an interaction not present in the other examples. Olsen is not just recording events; he is writing about his own feelings and beliefs, demonstrating a level of *intimacy* with the page. This level of intimate engagement differs from those catechists who had not received training and who tended to dutifully record events in the community. However, regardless of whether the catechists were college-educated, this dutiful recording contributed to the construction of the catechist as an individual subject standing outside the community. Whereas the Danish missionary would have had no trouble seeing himself as the rational detached self, this would have been a comparably new situation for the catechists, one that demanded more effort to construct and maintain.

In her study of Victorian autobiography, Regenia Gagnier opposes the "modern literary subject" with "working-class subjectivities" and shows how Cartesian subjectivity was not a given for working-class autobiographers (Gagnier 1991, 141). The modern literary self is "a mixture of introspective self-reflexivity, middle-class familialism and genderization, and liberal autonomy" (31) and

> assumed individual creativity, autonomy, and freedom to create value by satiating its subjective desires as a right; it considered self reflection as

39 *Ammassat* or capelin, a small salmon that spawns off West Greenland in May and June, and an important resource (Dahl 2000, 111).

> problem-solving, and thus valued reading and writing; and it developed in a progressive narrative of self in gendered familial relations and increasing material well-being. This was the self of Victorian literature as it was studied in the academy (28).

Gagnier's point is that such a level of introspection and reflection is fostered in the academy. Consequently, for people outside the academy—working-class autobiographers—such discourses were not readily available. Although Gagnier's analyses concerns autobiography in Victorian Britain as well as presumably white, working-class subjectivities, I find a number of her observations useful for the task at hand, which is to trace the emergence of a new sense of self in the work of the catechists. Her analysis presupposes a certain genre and how it rests uneasily with a certain group due to a lack of instruction in this perception of self required to produce the desired genre. Thus, in Greenland, the Danish missionaries who report back to the Missionary Department in Copenhagen are obviously quite comfortable within this genre of journal-keeping and reporting. Hveyssel, we recall, reflects, analyses, and observes—but he is schooled within an academic tradition, and has therefore learned how to negotiate himself in relation to his surroundings. In contrast, we have Greenlanders who are not accustomed to this form of writing and expected to relate to their surroundings in an observing and objectifying manner that required training and practice that they had not yet received.

Where Thuesen reads the catechists' journals as "the catechists' constructions of local society" (Thuesen 2007, 268), I *also* read them as narrative constructions of the self—a very different self from the one which existed within an "oral" community where the social dimension is the basis of the narrative. The writing self is an individual. Writing is an individual occupation and thus, through the entries, the catechists are learning to become individual abstracted selves. That education plays a significant role in this abstraction process, as discussed above, may be discerned in Thuesen's grouping of the journals into three types: (i) uneducated catechists' journals, which are very insecure, brief and relatively silent; (ii) college-educated catechists' journals, done in an extensive and confident writing style, but still reveals a discomfort about genre and a tendency to say too much; and (iii) the ordained, head catechists' journals,[40] which were reflective as well as interpretive, and thus akin to the

40 The ordained head catechists were Greenlanders who in the course of the 1870s and 1880s received further theological education in Denmark. They replaced missionaries, were paid higher wages, and were not under the immediate jurisdiction of a Danish missionary.

journals of Danish missionaries (2007, 273). Thuesen argues that the catechists increasingly placed themselves in the centre of their written world. He sees it as a shift in perspective, from the outside to the inside, which takes place from the 1850s to the twentieth century (2007, 310). Furthermore, in the course of living in a mixed economy of hunting and wage labour, the catechists become increasingly dependent on money. This dependency generated a separation between the catechist and the world 'out there' that increasingly takes on a presence of 'nature' (Thuesen 2007, 310).

My line of enquiry parallels Thuesen's, but with greater emphasis on writing itself. The catechists' writing about the weather, people's movements, and events, plays an enormous role in producing the world 'out there' as nature *and the catechist himself as an abstracted subject.* The journal, which the catechists are instructed to keep, effectively distances them from others and increases the sense of estrangement. However, the journals that the catechists kept were also part of a larger system of observation and control. Hence, the catechists were to report on their work, how many services they performed, their classes with children, their house calls, and any unusual events. This journal was to be sent to the missionary, or shown to him (Thuesen 2007, 264).[41] The merchants had a similar system of control and reporting duties (Thuesen 2007, 264). In their recording of community, the catechists also wrote themselves into a hierarchical structure. The formal structure of reporting to the missionaries, who in turn reported to the Department of Culture in Copenhagen,[42] was undergirded by the ideological structure of the Protestant pastorate and its social inflection.

This hierarchical structure would have been more prevalent in trained catechists, in whom the self is disciplined and shaped to enter into the larger institutional structure (as noted earlier in the section "Colonial Writing"). A more euphemistic term for this could be "vocation," where the individual is called to enter into this office, a prime example of Althusserian interpellation. Thuesen lists Samuel Olsen as the earliest example of a catechist who displays a sense of vocation, and argues that this vocational understanding of the catechist-office becomes more prevalent among the college-trained catechists. Thuesen then continues: "It is precisely in the journals of this group of catechists

---

However, because they were Greenlandic, they were not 'ready' to become ministers according to missionary politics (Thuesen 2007, 315).

41 The instruction, which contains the directive to keep the journal, is dated ca. 1864. One of the journals analysed by Thuesen is older (1853); indeed, Thuesen cites Missionary Kragh as noting that some catechists began keeping journals as early as 1820 (2007, 269).

42 The Missionary Department was subsumed under the Department of Culture in 1859.

that a rupture in consciousness may be traced—this is where the hunting universe is refracted and encounters Christian and modern interpretations of life" (2007, 306). It is this refraction and encounter to which I will turn in the final two chapters, for the present study is driven by an interest in how the hunter identity is "put into discourse"—that is, how the encounter between catechists and hunters is transmitted, and what purpose the hunter identity serves within the catechist discourse. By regarding writing as a technology of the self, it is possible to focus on how the institutionalisation of written works functions to construct colonial subjects and its others. In the colleges, the catechists were not only taught a mode of representation (objectification through writing) but also the discursive constraints of colonial representation. which, as anthropologist Jeffrey Sissons notes, are associated with primitivism (2005, 147).

CHAPTER 5

The Ontological Status of the Hunter *or* The Production of Nature

The "ontological status of the hunter" is how I designate the hunter identity constructed by the catechists, and the objective of this chapter is to trace the emergence of this identity. The first step in this process is to examine how colonial politics worked to create various groups within the Greenlandic population.[1] I approach this task by analysing the *Instruction* of 1782, which established the racial parameters for social stratification. Following a more theoretical engagement with race and class, I then continue the analysis I began in the preceding chapter of how writing buttressed this process of distinction by producing the hunter and nature as a part of the self-construction of the catechist. As I argued in the previous chapter, one of the preconditions of the estrangement between the catechist subject and its others was the perfunctory recording of the surroundings, which as Thuesen convincingly argues became increasingly objectified as nature. My argument is that even as they move beyond the particular lifestyle associated with hunting, the catechists are reliant on the hunter for a sense of ethnic identity. In a sense, this chapter also broaches the question of class formation in that this book shows how the catechists came to define themselves as a distinct group. For such an undertaking, I deploy anthropologist Hans Erik Rasmussen's analysis of Greenlandic clothing, and use its basic structure and argument as a point of departure for a discussion of nature and hunting in the world of the catechist.

The *Instruction of 1782* as Racialised Discourse

From early on, the colonial administration targeted Greenlandic individuals to make them function within that administration, disciplining them in accordance with Western notions of subjectivity. However, not every Greenlander was subjected in this manner; the primary targets were men with a Danish

1 I am thus interested in how the hunter emerged out of various masculine identity options and not over against women as prey, gatherers, or other inter-gendered binaries. For such an approach in a more general setting, see Darlene M. Juschka's interesting analysis of the development of what she calls the Eurowestern mytheme of "Man the Hunter" (2009, esp. ch. 3).

father. This tendency became more pronounced in the second half of the eighteenth century, and was manifested to a certain extent in the *Instruction of 1782*, the regulation for employees of the Trade. Hence, the technologies of self, which could be deployed in conjunction with the domination techniques of the colonial apparatus, were inculcated and encouraged within a certain segment of the population. By directing these efforts towards men with Danish fathers, this particular governmental strategy had a gendered as well as a racial dimension. This issue is the focus of the present section.

The *Instruction of 1782* is a crucial document in the colonial history of Denmark and Greenland. Gad describes it as a *husorden* (1976, 19), that is, an "order of the house," the Danish equivalent of the German word *Haustafel* (as discussed in chapter three). It is thus not a law for Greenland, but a set of rules and regulations for the employees of *Det Kongelige Grønlandske Handelskompagni* (KGH, the Royal Greenlandic Trade Company) and, to a certain degree, for the missionaries, although this is not completely clear (Gad 1976, 19). The document consists of fifteen 'posts' with an Introduction, and signed by KGH's management. Of particular interest here is the second post, "Concerning Marriage." While the *Instruction* as a whole addresses the interaction between Europeans and Greenlanders, this particular post concerns the Danish administration's population-management policies, which had a decidedly racial element. Prior to 1782, there had been some informal regulations regarding who could marry whom.[2] However, this was one of the issues that the *Instruction* set out to regulate in some detail.

Roughly paraphrased, the regulations ran as follows: Trade officers were not allowed to marry "real Greenlandic women" (*virkelige Grønlænderinder*), but could, upon receiving permission from the Inspector, marry either European women or women of "mixed" heritage. Before the wedding, the groom would have to give a sum of money to a "widow-chest" so that the bride would have some means of livelihood should the husband die before her (a likely event). The sum required for European women was higher than for women of "mixed" heritage. The next group of employees in the Trade, coopers (barrel-makers), carpenters, and labourers, were neither permitted to marry European women nor "real Greenlandic women." However, if the Inspector found that the applicant had good qualities *and* the means to support a family, he could grant permission for the applicant to marry a woman of "mixed" heritage, again on the condition that he paid a sum to provide his wife with a yearly pension in the event he predeceased her. This pension was tiered, so that the

2 See the section on "Catechism and Family" in chapter three.

widows left behind by coopers and carpenters received 25 rigsdaler a year while the widows of labourers were given 20 rigsdaler (post 2, item 4).

Finally, men of "mixed" heritage were free to marry either "real Greenlandic women," in which case they committed themselves to staying in Greenland, or "mixed" women. If these men were employed by the Trade as storekeepers, assistants, or in other functions for which they were paid 50 rigsdaler, they needed to apply for permission to marry, and they had to provide for the same widow's pension as coopers and carpenters (post 2, item 5). Apart from the racial aspect of such a measure, there is also the matter of class: while European women were to receive the highest pensions, the pension of the "mixed" women was tiered according to the profession and race of their husbands, with the widow of a cooper or carpenter receiving the same as the widow of a "mixed" Greenlander, whatever his position.

I will return to these questions of race and class, but for now I focus on what the *Instruction* has to say about the children of these marriages. Item 7 (under post 2) states that the children should be trained in Greenlandic life and culture, and fed Greenlandic food, so as not to be a burden to themselves or the country. Boys were to be channelled through one of four streams: (i) raised to be good Greenlanders and learn from an early age how to use the kayak; (ii) trained as coopers or carpenters; (iii) employed by the Trade; or (iv) employed in whaling and other kinds of fishing. The important thing was that they did not waste time or grow accustomed to European food and operating on the basis of personal favours because these behaviours were regarded as promoting laziness, and would render them unable to earn a living in the manner of Europeans or Greenlanders.

Furthermore, the Trade would support the parents' endeavours and assist the children in the most effective ways possible, so long as fathers raised their children properly. This set of regulations only applied to "legitimate" children. Illegitimate children are mentioned in the first post, with its focus on a Christian lifestyle. The father of an illegitimate child was to pay six rigsdaler a year for the upkeep of the child until its twelfth year. The missionaries would place the child in care. Boys in particular were to be trained to become good providers, preferably in hunting and other necessary Greenlandic skills. The *Instruction* notes that if the money from the father was handled wisely, there should be enough to buy a kayak, rifle, tent and *umiaq*[3] for the young men, or an *umiaq* and a tent as dowry for the young women.

3 An *umiaq*, or "wives' boat," is a large vessel traditionally rowed by women. It can hold up to 20 people and their belongings, and was used to move families between settlements.

An important issue is the jurisdiction of the *Instruction* and its implications for understanding the Greenlanders as civil subjects. As mentioned above, the *Instruction* was not a 'Law for Greenland' in any formal sense. It dealt with rules and regulations for those employed by the Trade for regular wages, not those who sold their products to the Trade (Gad 1976, 18). First, this placed the Greenlanders outside any notion of rights, and thus left them in a 'state of nature' in which they were presumed to function well (Gad 1974, 140).[4] Furthermore, even though 'ordinary Greenlanders' were not part of the *Instruction's* jurisdiction, it nevertheless had a profound effect on their lives and trading patterns. The item of particular interest here is the *Instruction's* fourth post, "Concerning the Greenlanders." It outlines the various ways of dealing with Greenlanders, how to encourage them to hunt, and how to encourage them to store food for winter.[5] This shows the subsumption of Greenlandic practices within the Danish colonial apparatus: Greenlanders had been hunting for centuries, and they had developed various means of storage. However, the directive propagates the notion that hunting and storage—that is, "proper" Danish modes of hunting and storage—are practices that Greenlanders need to be encouraged to follow.

Finally, the *Instruction* distinguishes between Greenlanders according to racial 'mixing,' focusing on Greenlanders with a Danish father, as mentioned earlier, and those who worked for the Trade and were thus included in the directive's jurisdiction. This distinction has profound effects in that it created and enforced a view of the 'non-mixed' population as belonging to nature, subservient to the laws of nature, and that they should—ideally—be left alone to carry on as before.[6] In practice, they were left alone, once their lives had been

4 Gad quotes whaling assistant Peder Hanning Motzfeldt's *promemoria* (the official name for reports to Copenhagen) from 1799: "I daresay that the Greenlanders' simple nutrition and way of life make civil laws necessary only in very few cases, especially since they, in their mutual relationships, accord with old customs and regulations. These (as far as I can see) are in close congruence with the laws of nature and fairness when one excludes what their superstitious ideas of witchcraft may lead them to, as well as the matter of inebriation, which, according to the present order of the Trade, rarely takes place"(Gad 1974, 143).

5 These are examples of how the directive repeats and thus institutionalises some of the attempts by the missionaries to control the labour power of the Greenlanders. See Lauridsen and Lytthans (1983, 168–73) for descriptions of how the missionaries encouraged hunting and proper food storage.

6 This dynamic may be seen in the handling of the Habakuk affair, where the only way Hveyssel could intervene was doctrinally. Frederik Berthelsen, however, was better placed to arbitrate due to his 'mixed' provenance, and he is the person credited for the dissolution of the "heretical movement."

honed to match the desires of the mission and Trade. In contrast, 'mixed' Greenlanders were regarded differently; their placement within the directive's jurisdiction meant they were included within a sphere of 'civilisation.'

The main aim of the *Instruction* therefore seems to be to sustain this distinction, thereby keeping the sphere of 'nature' apart from the sphere of 'civilisation.' This was primarily maintained via the regulation of marriage and, hence, reproduction. When something occurred to trouble this distinction—a Greenlander stealing from a Dane, for example—it was to be punished. While the *Instruction* was a set of rules only for colonial employees, an actual law for the Greenlanders was not implemented until 1908. Employees of the Trade and mission remained accountable to Danish law after 1908, while other Greenlanders came under the jurisdiction of the new Greenlandic law.

In his historical survey of the developments in twentieth-century Greenland, Axel Kjær Sørensen comments that while this legal distinction *seems* to discriminate against Greenlanders, one would get the opposite impression if one looked at what actually was punishable and which punishments were handed out (1983, 35). Such an assertion is decidedly unconvincing; this is systemic discrimination that places one segment of the population under Danish law and the rest under another set of rules and practices. Furthermore, the distinction is based on a view of Greenlanders as uncivilised and childish. While these rules and practices were ostensibly milder, the division itself nevertheless placed Greenlanders outside Danish law and its entitlements. Hence, the entitlements of Danish law only befell the ruling powers. Sørensen is not taking the different living conditions and power dynamics into consideration; his judgement is based on the laws and not their practice, which he acknowledges could make a difference (1983, 37).

Let us consider a case that illustrates the arbitrary nature of the practice of Greenlandic law.[7] Peter Gundel was a hunter and fisherman from the settlement of Illumiut near Jakobshavn (present-day Ilulissat). Suffering from tuberculosis and gout, he was unable to hunt, and he used his spare time to write novels, letters, and, sometimes, reports for the doctor. He was paid only sporadically for his work as a scribe; he otherwise lived in relative poverty on welfare while his wife made some money sewing. He struck up a friendship with a Danish doctor, Jørgen Hvam, who had spent three years in Jakobshavn

7 It is a case which that Sørensen could not have known about because it dates from 1928 and the archival restrictions on legal cases meant that the legal documents have not been available before 2008. The letters, which give us one side of the story, were in private possession until their "discovery" in 2002. The following vignette is based on the letters, which have since been published (Gundel and& Tølbøll [ed.] 2004).

(Ilulissat), and it is Gundel's letters to Hvam from 1923 to 1930 which have been published. Peter Gundel died on 8 March 1931 at the age of 36.

Gundel was apparently regarded as a troublemaker, and he seemed to attract misfortune. The case in question begins with a fight between Gundel and another fisherman, Jonathan, after their nets become entangled. According to Gundel, it was Jonathan's fault, which meant that Gundel was within his right to cut Jonathan's nets to free his own (Thisted 2004b, 91). This enraged Jonathan, and he attacked Gundel. Gundel threatened to report Jonathan to the authorities for assault. Jonathan's stepson then stepped forward and claimed he has seen Gundel steal some fish from the Trade and sell them. Gundel admitted to the deed—without adding that this was common practice because the Trade generally underpaid fishermen.

Gundel now had to face the district council[8] and plead for a mild sentence. While trying to explain to the chair of the council, Knudsen, how easy it was to err, he chose the unfortunate example of Knudsen shutting himself in the stockroom with a local woman, Mariane—an incident Gundel had witnessed. Knudsen reacted by imposing a more severe sentence: loss of civil rights for five years, a 25-kroner fine, a 10-kroner liability fee, public announcement of his guilt, and a warning of deportation if he was ever charged again (Gundel and Tølbøll 2004, 213–14).[9] This was just the beginning of a long line of charges and accusations of rape and theft, grudges and finger-pointing, within a very small community. Gundel was so desperate that the only way out of this network of enemies waiting to pounce was to appeal to the king of Denmark.[10]

Kirsten Thisted concludes that "everyone already has lots of stories about everyone else; no one is impartial and the case may serve as a cautionary example of what happens when small communities have to manage legal issues by themselves" (2004b, 94). However, it is also important to keep in mind the deplorable material conditions: the nets that were slashed, the fish that were stolen, the sewing work for which no pay was received—are all indications of the poverty of the community, and the extent to which people struggled for the same work, the same fish, and the same money to survive. These conditions have shaped Greenlandic social fabric, or rather the racial Danish state in

---

8 Sysselråd, located between the municipal council and the national council, were implemented as a result of an administrative restructuring in 1925. The chairman was Danish and the rest of the council (two to four people) were Danish and Greenlandic men in equal numbers.

9 This was Gundel's second sentence after a 1925 conviction for illegal trade and hosting a small party for a ship's crew and local girls (Thisted 2004b, 92).

10 The appeal never reached the king. See chapter four, note 21.

Greenland. This is what led Greenlanders like Peter Gundel to state in 1923 that Greenlanders are treated like slaves by the Danes (Gundel & Tølbøll 2004, 10). Gundel records that Greenlanders mean nothing to the Danes, and that the Greenlanders are kicked out whenever the Danes see fit to do so (Gundel and Tølbøll 2004, 24).[11]

I have included this vignette on Gundel to show how Danish law and its segregationist practice functions as a marker of race and class. Gundel lived 150 years after the *Instruction*, which was replaced several times with subsequent directives, as well as the implementation of a Greenlandic law in the early twentieth century mentioned above. Nevertheless, I want to argue that the *Instruction* of 1782 articulated and formalised practices, which laid the foundations for inequality between Danes and Greenlanders, as well as creating a new group of Greenlanders.

Race, Class, and Nature

These preliminary points concerning racialised discourse and use of the *Instruction of 1782* and its distinctions will be developed as a point of departure for a specific discussion of race and how it laid the foundations for a stratification of Greenlandic society. In Denmark, there is a profound reluctance to address race as a structural factor in the social politics of the Danish state.[12] Race is usually reserved to denote either extremes, such as National-Socialist eugenics and South Africa's apartheid politics, or individual attitudes. Both these tendencies are not uncommon in studies dealing with state and race (Goldberg 2002, 3, 149). Issues pertaining to skin colour and difference are

11 Gundel was in the process of translating *Uncle Tom's Cabin*, so his comparisons are founded in contemporary literature. Greenlandic environmentalist and cultural critic Finn Lynge (2002, 72) also mentions how the grandparents' and great-grandparents' generations had to grovel before some merchants, how Danish homes had a door for Danes at the front and another for Greenlanders at the back, and how ordinary people did not have access to the same goods as colonial managers and civil servants.

12 This reluctance is also identified by Rikke Andreassen from Malmø Högskola and Anne Folke Henningsen from Copenhagen University. As of this writing, Andreassen and Henningsen were working on a research project on the exhibition of indigenous people from all over the world in the Copenhagen Zoo at the turn of the twentieth century. In a newspaper article describing their project, Andreassen points out: "In contrast to France and Germany, Denmark has not settled accounts with its racist past, which might be a sound move to make, because many of the old ideas are still going strong in our culture today"(Richter 2009).

usually euphemistically termed "ethnic." Danish research on Greenland is no exception to this rule. Anthropologist Ole Høiris published an account in 1986 of how Danish anthropologists embodied a general anthropological racist attitude to non-Europeans, and more particularly in relation to Greenlanders right up to the Second World War (Høiris 1983). Several studies, such as Høiris's indicate that Denmark was an active participant in racial studies from the late nineteenth century until the Second World War. The same studies indicate that Greenland played a significant role in this research, in that Greenland provided the data for analysis.

Nevertheless, the studies usually present this racial research on a synchronic level with the racial research of other nations (Duedahl 2003; Høiris 1983, 1986). This synchronic approach effectively separates Danish race research from its own colonial history, and conveniently exempts the Danish state from any involvement in matters of race. However, I argue that the practices enforced by the 1782 *Instruction* effectively structure Greenland on racially-based social taxonomies and on developed policies by the Danish state to deal with social interaction between Europeans and Greenlanders. The Danish policy of using primarily 'mixed' Greenlanders in lower positions within the colonial apparatus not only expressed a view of difference, but also generated a range of social consequences that demand further scrutiny.

In his study on racism and culture, David Theo Goldberg distinguishes between racialised discourse and racist expression in order to show how law, moral discourse, and the social sciences quietly deploy racialised language without overtly expressing racist viewpoints—or even when claiming to be anti-racist (1993, 42). In other words, racialised discourse enables Goldberg to expose the workings of systemic racialisation from which racism emerges as *one* object among others from such a racialised field of discourse. Furthermore, there is no singular form of racism; it "transforms in relation to significant changes in the field of discourse" (Goldberg 1993, 42). Racialised discourse is informed by: (i) hypotheses about human beings and their differences; (ii) ethical choices, such as domination and subjugation, entitlement and restriction, disrespect and abuse; and (iii) institutional regulations, directions, and pedagogic models. Goldberg refers to *apartheid*, separate development, educational institutions, and choice of educational and bureaucratic language (1993, 47).

In the Greenlandic context, the *Instruction* marks an institutionalisation of racialised practices, which were already in process before the formal edict. The *Instruction* is ideologically supported by a view that Greenlanders belong to nature, as well as an understanding of Danish entitlement to the products of the land, which the Greenlanders were obliged to produce. Thus, every-day interaction in Greenland was underpinned by a belief in difference, subjugation, and separated development.

The term *blanding*, literally "crossbreed," is usually modified in the secondary literature, either by preceding it with the words "so-called," or with quotation marks. Both Gad (1976, 29) and Wilhjelm (2009, 25) emphasise that the distinction between *blandinger* and "real Greenlanders" is social, not biological. Gad notes that in the *Instruction*, the understanding of *blanding* was fixed: a child born to a Danish man married to a Greenlandic woman, and it did not matter whether she was a 'real Greenlandress' or from a 'mixed' marriage. Therefore, children born out of wedlock, or those with a father from a 'mixed' marriage, were not regarded as *blandinger*. For this reason, Gad concludes that the *blandinger* constitute a socially-determined group rather than a biologically-determined one (Gad 1976, 29).

Henrik Wilhjelm follows this argument and notes that the distinction between real Greenlanders and *blandinger* was not, biologically speaking, completely clear, because a European forefather was not sufficient to be categorised as a *blanding* (2009, 25). Given the tendency to connect racism exclusively with twentieth-century eugenics and its biological pedigree, the emphasis here on inconsistent biological criteria could be seen as an attempt to refute any claims that the distinctions were racially motivated.[13] Such a restricted understanding of racism does not make sense according to Goldberg's theorisation of racist discourse. Within Goldberg's analysis, biological racism or eugenics become one manifestation from several possibilities, conditioned by material as well as ideological circumstances. This means that the social distinction may also be considered as a manifestation of racialised discourse determined by its own material and ideological circumstances (as discussed above).

In an examination of race and ethnicity in Greenland, linguist Karen Langgård notes that culture and way of life were decisive factors in determining who was to be raised as Danish (2008a, 93). She observes that the sons of colonial agents and missionaries would be raised as Danes, and the rest as Greenlanders.[14] However, as explained above, the restrictions in the *Instruction*

13 Gad, for example, denies racism in the categorisation and regulation of Greenlanders. He notes that "these 'blandinger,' as they crudely were called, were regarded as Greenlanders by the authorities, solely because they were born in the country, not from any racial point of view" (1969, 434; see also 1974, 192; 1972, 30). Gad construes racism solely in terms of its twentieth-century manifestations.

14 See, e.g., Peter Gundel, who had Danish ancestry but was a "Greenlander" by virtue of his lifestyle.

meant that only a child born to married parents could be regarded as a *blanding*, and thus have the privileged opportunity to continue within the system. I would modify Langgård's statement slightly and argue that along with race, class was a decisive factor in this process of distinguishing.

That social stratification was an increasingly important issue in the construction of Greenlandic society after colonialism is argued by anthropologist Hans Erik Rasmussen in his work on the reproduction of the upper class (or the "upper social stratum") through social endogamy in West Greenlandic society.[15] Rasmussen's research implicitly deals with the colonial politics of race, although it is never mentioned by that name, in part because he is dealing with the internal workings of the Greenlandic upper social stratum. Rasmussen's analysis does not concern the boundaries and rules set by colonial politics and administration, but rather how the Greenlandic upper social stratum negotiates the boundaries that have been set by colonial politics and rule. Thus, when Rasmussen separates ethnic issues from social ones, and understands the relations of the emerging stratum to the Danish upper class as "social," as well as the relations to the Greenlandic lower social stratum as "ethnic," he is expressing the views of his sources.

However, part of the negotiation process of these colonial boundaries involves dealing with categories that spring from racialised politics—for example, the primitivism/civilisation dichotomy.[16] Rasmussen argues that social endogamy may be seen as an expression of sustaining the dichotomy between primitivism and civilisation: *the upper social stratum adopted the viewpoint of the colonial administration, namely, that the 'mixed' group was situated between primitive natives and civilised Danes.* After the 1850s, when this group had established itself as Greenlandic, the colonially defined ethnic tripartite structure (Europeans–'mixed'–Natives) became a division between Danes and Greenlanders. It would seem that 'ethnic' here is a euphemism for race, since the tripartite structure is the racialised structure common in Europe in the mid-eighteenth century, modified through class.

Within Greenland, then, colonialism had different economic outcomes for different groups. In particular, the group of Greenlandic men (and, eventually, Greenlandic women) with Danish fathers had easier access to education and

15 This work is chiefly presented in his unpublished dissertation from 1983, as well as in a number of articles and papers (1982, 1986a, 1986b, 1986c, 1987).

16 Rasmussen also analyses the contradictions in the views on the nature/culture dichotomy by the primary producers (the hunters, fishermen, and sheep breeders) and the upper social stratum. From his analysis he concludes that the primary dichotomy is seen as the one between primitivism and civilisation, into which other dichotomies feed.

employment within the colonial apparatus, which meant easier access to desirable commodities and greater ease in identifying and thus operating within the colonial coordinates. In order to analyse these differences and their social implications, I consider the terminology of class distinction necessary. Yet class is another issue that several studies into the workings of colonialism and/or Greenlandic society have been hesitant to deploy: Thuesen and anthropologist Jens Dahl carefully refer to the "elite," while Hans Erik Rasmussen, inspired by Nicos Poulantzas, speaks of the "upper social stratum." Only the analysis of Jørgen Viemose (1977) speaks of class as such. It is apparent that some division took place in the population during the colonial period, a division that needs to be conceptualised, be it in terms of class, elite, or social stratum.

Social stratification as a result of colonial politics is not restricted to the situation in Greenland. Neither is the reluctance to analyse this stratification process restricted to it. One of my main quarrels with postcolonial theory (in particular Edward Said and Homi K. Bhabha) is the general failure to address questions of class. While this is not an innovative point—it has been made several times, most forcefully perhaps by Aijaz Ahmad (1992)[17]—it is a point well worth repeating: the intelligentsia cannot represent the material realities of "Third World" society.[18] I have modified Ahmad's argument slightly, since he vents his rage against migrant English-writing intelligentsia as representatives of India's national literature (1992, 76) and because I want to use his critique in a different situation. In Greenland, the intelligentsia is neither migrant nor Danish-writing, but nevertheless holds a privileged place within the overall social structure. In terms of education, income, and living conditions, the indigenous intelligentsia cannot compare to, let alone speak on behalf of, the indigenous lower classes. Furthermore, Arif Dirlik's point about what constitutes a postcolonial subject (1994, 332) should be considered. Dirlik argues that the subject position of postcolonial discourse is not only contingent on global capitalism as conditioning the emergence of postcolonial criticism, but also, as O'Hanlon and Washbrook note (1992, 165–66, cited in

17 Others include Dirlik (1994) and Brydon (1989). While Anne McClintock does not engage in criticism of those who leave class out of postcolonial analyses, she does herself include the concept as part of her articulated categories (1995, 4–9).

18 I put 'Third World' in quotation marks to signal Ahmad's critique of the term, to which I return in chapter six. See the succinct summary of the arguments and its various participants in Bart Moore-Gilbert's study (1997, esp.14–22). See also a very illuminating discussion introducing Graham Huggan's analysis of postcolonialism and its relation to Western consumption (2001, 1–33).

Dirlik 1994, 344), the material conditions and class relations of the postcolonial intellectuals. A postcolonial subjectivity is, in other words, firmly connected to class, particularly the upper middle class. In most cases, this class is a result of colonialism, either as a stratification of society, as in Greenland, or a consolidation of already existing social structures, as in South Africa (Mamdani 1996; Comaroff and Comaroff 1991, 1997) or India. One of Dirlik's issues —and there are several—with postcolonialism is the *reluctance* of postcolonial intellectuals to address the economic system (global capitalism), which established the conditions for postcolonial criticism—namely, the postcolonial critics themselves—in the first place (1994, 330–31). To repeat the above point, this also applies to the act of postcolonial criticism and the tendencies of its proponents to bypass the economic issues that enable the hybrid subjectivities under investigation.[19] In Greenland, as I have thus far argued, racial politics of the Danish colonial administration meant that the men who received a formal education were in most instances the legitimate sons of Danish fathers. This group in turn became the Greenlandic intelligentsia, who went on to form the Greenlandic literary tradition. As shown in the previous chapters, they were economically advantaged, since they earned wages, which by far exceeded what their countrymen could earn through hunting. This group of educated and employed men thus came to occupy an elite position in Greenland, and they expressed in their writings their sense of being caught between their own background and a colonial power towards which they were ambivalent. Thus, hybridity, which denotes this in-between-ness or ambivalence, is *not* a feature of *every* postcolonial condition, but more precisely constitutes a subject position characteristic of the elite or bourgeois postcolonial condition, of which Homi Bhabha also is a product. This cannot be emphasised enough: hybridity is conceptualised within relations determined by particular material conditions.[20] For this reason, class analysis is crucial in any colonial context.

19 See for example Thisted (2011) and Seiding and Toft (2011) and the focus on the 'new' Greenlanders, who are beyond colonial representations: "This musical self-representation [reference to the television programme in which these new Greenlanders appeared] was an effective contrast to the usual Danish-Greenland stereotypes of proud hunters or socially abject urbanised victims, stereotypes with deep roots in the colonial heritage, born and nurtured by the categorisation-apparatus of the Danish colonial administration and viable far into the postcolonial twenty-first century" (Seiding and Toft 2011, 273).

20 Rey Chow also draws attention to this feature of Bhabha's conceptual apparatus when she notes that "What Bhabha's word 'hybridity' revives, in the masquerade of deconstruction, anti-imperialism, and 'difficult' theory, is an old functionalist notion of what a dominant culture permits in the interest of maintaining its own equilibrium" (1993, 35). See also Anne McClintock's engagement with Bhabha in *Imperial Leather* (1995, 61–65).

Marx's notion of class as the difference between the exploiters/owners of the means of production/bourgeoisie and the exploited/direct producers/proletariat with only their labour to sell has more to say about the structural relationship *between* Denmark and colonial Greenland than about the social situation within Greenland itself. In Marx's sense, there is no bourgeoisie in Greenland: everyone in Greenland, including the Danes, belongs to the proletariat, with the bourgeoisie residing in Denmark. This is Jørgen Viemose's position:

> The purpose of Danish activities in Greenland has always been to achieve financial gain, not to the advantage of the entire Danish people, but for parts of the Danish bourgeoisie; always at the expense of the Greenlandic people and the Danish lower class, who mostly, through taxes among other things, have contributed to ensuring the bourgeoisie's yield from the colonies.
>
> 1977, 7

In 1905, during the reading of the budget bill in the Danish Parliament, Social Liberal politician C.T. Zahle offered a stinging critique of The Royal Greenland Trade (KGH)'s administration of Greenland: the net cash yield of trade and commerce, as well as the total cost of administration in Greenland, had been paid by the labour of 2000 hunters (Thorleifsen 1999, 68). The administrative costs would have included salaries for the Trade, with the missionaries being paid by the Department of Culture. Both, however, were part of the state administration. This means that the surplus generated by the 2000 hunters over the years not only paid the salaries of the employees of the Trade, which included Danes as well as 'mixed' Greenlanders—but produced a profit. The technical term for this is of course *exploitation*, which occurs when one segment of the population controls the surplus produced by another (Himmelweit 1985, 157).[21] The segment in control, however, was Danish, which brings us back to Viemose's position.

Turning to the situation within Greenland, the picture becomes slightly more complex than what Marx's categories allow.[22] While the owners of the

21 That this appears to have been the source of some tension between the catechists and the hunters is indicated in catechist Henrik Lund's 1915 article in *Atuagagdliutit*, where he states that "wages of the civil servants do not come from the hunters but from the Danish state" (quoted in Wilhjelm 2009, 513).

22 Nicos Poulantzas is one of the theorists who developed a much more complex class theory, one encompassing differences between manual and intellectual labour and making

means of production were situated in Denmark, there was still social stratification in Greenland, and not just between Danes and Greenlanders; there are also clear class lines within the Danish group,[23] and within the Greenlandic group it is possible to trace, through the politics of the Danish administration, the emergence of a new class of Greenlanders. Thus, the class status of the emerging Greenlandic upper social stratum is, in its inception, determined by colonial politics. Hans-Erik Rasmussen's argument is that the *blandinger* emerged as a distinct upper social stratum and, through clothing in particular, attempted to distinguish themselves from the primary producers, i.e. the hunters and the fishermen.

Here it is important to bring in one of the main features of class as defined by Marx in *The Eighteenth Brumaire of Louis Bonaparte*:

> Insofar as millions of families live under economic conditions of existence that separate their mode of life, their interests and their culture from those of the other classes, and put them in hostile opposition to the latter, they form a class. Insofar as there is merely a local interconnection among these small-holding peasants [of nineteenth-century France], and the identity of their interests begets no community, no national bond and no political organisation among them, they do not form a class.
>
> 1979, 187

In this quote we note a distinction between an objective situation and the subjective awareness, as well as the prerequisites for the determination of a class (Fetscher 1985, 79). In the first instance, both are fulfilled. The families do live under distinct economic conditions and regard themselves as different and, hence, form a class. The peasants do not have this collective understanding of their own economic and cultural conditions, and therefore do not form a class. Using this to illuminate the Greenlandic circumstances, we see that the *blandinger*, or Rasmussen's upper social stratum, would fulfil both the objective requirements (economic conditions) and the subjective ones (distinct mode of life, interests and culture, which are used to distinguish themselves

possible a host of distinctions or strata within a single class. Hans-Erik Rasmussen's class analysis (1986b) derives from Poulantzas' 1975 book, *Political Power and Social Classes*.

23 As indicated in the *Instruction*'s hierarchy of husbands, as well as in the frequent comments from the missionaries about the lusty sailors, and missionary Glahn's comment cited in the Introduction about Greenlandic women who scorning the most dignified Greenlander, but "will not hesitate in entering into matrimony with the worst and lowliest sailor" (1921, 63).

from other classes) for class status. The primary producers, however, while fulfilling the objective class criteria, do not possess the 'class consciousness' necessary for comprising a class in and of itself.

These questions are important insofar as there were distinctive groupings within Greenlandic society from the mid – to late-eighteenth century. These groupings were distinguished along lines of labour, a distinction that coincided with criteria of race. The questions are also important in the face of the political tensions between the groups and the political aspirations of the 'upper social stratum.' An examination of Rasmussen's analysis can shed light on these issues. Rasmussen argues that in Greenland at the beginning of the eighteenth century, there are two occupational categories: the direct or primary producers, and the colonial administrators/transmitters of ideology. These categories are also divided according to 'ethnic' categories: Danish and Greenlandic. The combination of occupational categories and ethnic characteristics effectively produces three socio-economic categories, in that the colonial administrators/transmitters of ideology are divided along ethnic lines. So there was a Danish category of colonial administrators/transmitters of ideology as well as a Greenlandic category of colonial administrators/transmitters. This is the category in which Frederik Berthelsen was located. In addition, there was a Greenlandic category of primary producers.[24]

Furthermore, Rasmussen argues that through complex "rules" of intermarriage, the Greenlandic administrators/transmitters—the 'upper social stratum'[25]—enforced themselves as a distinct social group over against the primary producers. The upper class asserted its position by incorporating the cultural practices of the Danish socio-economic category, while retaining their ethnic identity through incorporation of cultural elements of the primary producers. By designating this group as 'upper social stratum,' Rasmussen avoids categorising them as a distinct class. But, we may ask, upper social stratum *of what*? And the answer is: the primary producers—in other words, the Greenlanders.

My analyses proceed to argue that in the process of establishing themselves as a socio-economic category, the 'mixed' group *produce* the category of the

24 See Rasmussen's triangular structure (1986b, 140).

25 Rasmussen canvasses the material foundations for the emergence of the indigenous upper social stratum as a social category. These foundations include the colonial marital regulations from 1753 and 1782, as well as the conditions of employment and education, which targeted children of Danish fathers (1983, 14). Rasmussen then traces the various marriages and alliances between families and the various employments within the colonial apparatus, and determines the control of marriage and sexuality as social endogamy constructed on the social layer's perception of primitivism and civilisation (1982, 50).

hunter as an *ontological* status, as part of the process of becoming conscious of their distinctiveness as a group. While Rasmussen's 'primary producers' in principle includes hunters as well as fishermen and sheep-breeders, the latter two occupations have no significance when it comes to symbolising ethnic identity. *The hunters are thus singled out as a particular group with certain significance for the identity construction of an emerging Greenlandic ruling class.*

This brings me to the line of reasoning in the European epistemological tradition where nature has a certain place in the conceptualisation of the world.[26] Plumwood explains:

> To be defined as 'nature' in this context [of reason] is to be defined as passive, as non-agent and non-subject, as the 'environment' or invisible background conditions against which the 'foreground' achievements of reason or culture (provided typically by the white, Western, male expert or entrepreneur) take place. It is to be defined as a *terra nullius*, a resource empty of its own purposes or meanings, and hence available to be annexed for the purposes of those supposedly identified with reason or intellect, and to be conceived and moulded in relation to these purposes. It means being seen as part of a sharply separate, even alien lower realm, whose domination is simply 'natural,' flowing from nature itself and the nature(s) of things.
>
> 1993, 4

I discussed above how the Instruction *of 1782* functioned to place Greenlanders not employed by the Trade outside both the jurisdiction of the *Instruction* and outside Danish law. These Greenlanders were instead understood as being governed by the rules of nature. It is this connection between Greenlanders and nature, which requires further exploration. The Plumwood quotation emphasises a number of significant articulations of Western conceptions of nature, and how it is seen to function within the realm of reason. First, Plumwood points to the construction of a static nature as a backdrop for white Western entrepreneurial activity. Second, it is also a resource, simply available to be harnessed for entrepreneurial purposes. Finally, this construction defines nature as being in a realm of its own, on a lower scale, waiting to be dominated as is its inherent nature.

The term "entrepreneurial" is an important one because it connotes activity, energy, will, ambition, and the ability to build nations and divide labour.

26 I argued in chapter 4 that this is the objectification practice in which the catechists were trained.

It signifies the divine activity of creation, as alluded to by Dyer in his connection between enterprise, spirit and its effects (1997, 31). The biblical creation myth shows the same kind of entrepreneurial arrogance towards matter. In Genesis chapters 1–2, the earth appears to be already in existence when God begins the process of creation: "In the beginning, God created the heavens and earth. And the earth was chaos and shambles, and darkness was over the void and God's spirit/wind/storm whipped over the waters."[27] There seems to be something already there for God to work with. But is it a "formless void" (Revised Standard Version), which gives the impression of shapeless, lifeless matter—or was it instead chaos and shambles, which gives a sense of movement and rebellious matter?

By juxtaposing these questions with the Plumwood quotation, it becomes clear to what extent certain qualities, or rather lack of qualities, have been imposed on "nature" and its inhabitants to legitimate its conquest and domination. We thus have a passive, non-agent, non-subject, 'environment,' a *terra nullius*, a resource with no purpose or meaning of its own, yet capable of expressing the need for domination. The empty void, the *terra nullius*, the passive matter, is thus a production by someone who desires to be the beginning, erase the slate, clear the land, and start creating, or in von Braun's terms, the *logos* creating its own matter, in which it can realise itself. This means that people *within* nature cannot be seen to express this entrepreneurial drive, but are instead caught within a circuit that generates nothing *new*, but is only capable of reproducing itself.[28]

The construction of Greenlanders as part of nature is evident in the jurisdiction of the *Instruction*: they were required to remain within their own circuit, albeit with a number of alterations, in order to generate the means for the colonisers to undertake the process of creation. This process meant that the Greenlanders were cast as belonging to a nature as distinct from and *generated* by culture. In this chapter, I will focus on the role of the catechist in this

27 I have translated from the Hebrew text because the sense of an already-existing matter is more prevalent in the Hebrew than in the Revised Standard Version (RSV) translation: "In the beginning when God created the heavens and the earth, the earth was a formless void and darkness covered the face of the deep, while a wind from God swept over the face of the waters." This sense of existing matter is enhanced when we consider that the initial Hebrew words, usually translated as "In the beginning ..." may also be translated as "When God began ... "

28 This derogatory coupling of indigenous people and nature has been contested by various indigenous scholars. Linda Tuhiwai Smith's *Decolonizing Knowledge* (1999, ch. 2) engages this issue. See also Roberta James' work with 'Rousseau's knot' (1997) and Erik Gant's discussion of the Eskimo in anthropological research (1996).

production. I begin by examining historian Rud and anthropologist Hanne Thomsen's arguments for the colonial invention of Greenlandic society as a product of nature, which I call "the discourse on the hunter." I then extend this argument by identifying Greenlandic writing which supports this discourse. Finally, Hans Erik Rasmussen's work on ethnicity and clothing is recalled to support my argument.

The Discourse on the Hunter

In the early twentieth century, an intense discussion took place in the newspaper *Atuagagdliutit* about what it meant to be a "real Greenlander." Was the real Greenlander a seal-hunter, or was Greenlandic identity reliant on language, love of Greenland, and history? While these questions were—and are—important to Greenlandic identity, they are also questions firmly connected to labour, relations of production, and economy within a colonial context. And they are obviously also related to questions of masculinity, since the types of labour advocated in these positions—the hunter over against the catechist—are, generally speaking, men's labour. The question, then, is underpinned by another: what is a real Greenlandic *man*? That this is a salient question for Greenlandic identity today may be seen from its central role in the movie *Heart of Light*, which is analysed in chapter six. These questions were also part of the debate on orality and literacy (see chapter four). While oral traditions were configured as part of hunting culture (from the point of view of writing), I advanced the position that the literary tradition was related to a different kind of masculinity.

The question "what constitutes a real Greenlander" is the point of departure in Thomsen's article, "Real Greenlanders and New Greenlanders: On Different Perceptions of 'Greenlandic-ness'" (1998). Thomsen begins her article by pointing out the contradiction between the discourse of authentic "Greenlandic nature" as marketed in films, the tourist industry, and fiction/non-fiction, and every-day life in one of the bigger cities in Greenland. This contradiction between modern lifestyle in the urban sprawl and the *expectations* of Greenlandic culture is resolved by designating city life as Danish, while authentic Greenland is to be found in the settlements, personified in the hunter.[29] This image of an authentic Greenland is, according to Thomsen, the result of Danish

29 Note that anthropological investigations very often take the settlements and/or remote communities as their place of research (Breinholt Larsen 1997; Petersen 2003; Dahl 2000; Nuttall 1992; Williamson 2006; Robert-Lamblin 1986; Gessain 1970). Important exceptions

colonial politics and the attempts by the Trade to retain the population within a hunting mode of production (1998, 23). This meant that while seal-hunting was promoted as national labour, waged labour was deemed un-Greenlandic in the sense that Greenlanders were not 'mature' enough for this kind of work.

However, while the colonial administration sought to preserve hunting as the primary occupation through references to protectionism, it simultaneously attempted to erode the internal distribution practices between Greenlanders (Thomsen 1998, 24).[30] The establishment of local councils (*forstanderskaberne*), discussed in chapter two, is seen as a move in this direction. Local councils were established in each colony with representatives from the colonial administration (the colonial manager, the missionary, and the doctor) as well as from the local population (the head catechist and prominent hunters), and their most significant task was the administration of council funds. The funds, obtained by taxes on goods, were to be distributed to the needy, the unsuccessful hunters, and the lazy, and what was left over was to be distributed among those hunters who had not received aid. The hidden motive was that the less paid in aid to the poor meant that more would be left over. This would give the hunters an incentive not to distribute excessively (Thomsen 1998, 25). Heinrich Rink ostensibly designed these councils around hunting and the hunters in order for the indigenous population to regain its self-respect, which had been corroded under colonialism (Thomsen 1998, 26).[31]

Thomsen also points to the establishment of cultural institutions that corresponded to the councils and were also intended to instil national pride in Greenlanders. She cites the catechist colleges, the newspaper *Atuagagdliutit*, and the collection of myths and legends by Rink as examples of the colonial administration's attempts to forge an "imagined community" (Anderson 2006; Thomsen 1998, 27–28).

---

include the work of Gitte Tróndheim (2004, 2010) and Bo Wagner Sørensen (1991, 1994, 1994, 1997, 2001, 2003), which focus explicitly on urban settings.

30 Niels Egede had already suggested that this tradition of distributing meat, blubber, and skin according to who had participated in the hunt and transport, cut into the profits of the Trade. He suggested that flensing (stripping the blubber from the whale) should take place on Danish ships at sea to avoid these distribution rules, which only took effect when the whale was landed (cited in Lauridsen and Lytthans 1983, 174).

31 Rink discusses this as well as possible remedies in "*Om Aarsagen til Grønlændernes og lignende, af Jagt levende, Nationers materialle Tilbagegang ved berøring med Europæerne*" (On the Cause for the Material Decline upon Contact with the Europeans of Greenlanders and other Nations Dependant on Hunting) from 1862, discussed below. I would like to thank Søren Thuesen for this reference.

The image of Greenlanders as ideally in unison with nature but corrupted through civilisation was an increasingly popular trope and was propagated by, among others, the famous explorer Knud Rasmussen.[32] Thomsen notes how this image became the prevailing one at the beginning of the twentieth century, and posits the conclusion that is inevitably drawn from this, is:

> ... a division of labour that states that the Eskimo and the Greenlanders are the masters of nature, but the modern world is the white man's world. The result is also a dual image of the Greenlanders: the noble savage, that is the hunter, and then the semi-civilised and lazy colonial Greenlander or half-Greenlander, who must be provided for by others.
>
> 1998, 30

Thomsen's article continues to trace these trajectories into present-day Greenland, but my present task is to consider how Rud develops this particular line of thought. As discussed in chapter two, Rud brings together governmentality and Greenland in his work on governmentality and colonialism. While his theoretical article (2007) was the object of my analysis there, I will consider the more ethnographical contribution here (2006). Rud's 2006 article tracks the conflict between protection and modernisation of Greenlandic culture in Danish colonial politics. He finds Thomsen's analysis too one-sided in its emphasis on economic motives, so he seeks to buttress her analysis with a cultural dimension. He argues that the ethnological expeditions to remote and uncolonised East Greenland in the course of the nineteenth century prompted a new consideration of West Greenlanders, who had been subjected to 150 years of Danish colonisation and European influences. The ethnographic analyses undertaken on these expeditions presented an understanding of East Greenlanders as 'real' Greenlanders—that is, self-sufficient hunters. This construal was to have an immense influence on colonial politics (Rud 2006, 498).

This configuration, which Rud terms "the traditionalist view," clashed with the position that pressed for increased modernisation. The traditionalist view privileged seal hunting in kayaks as the quintessential Greenlandic way of life, and thus promoted this lifestyle through education and colonial management, especially through the local councils. As explained above, the council members included Danes and Greenlanders—but only those Greenlanders who were accomplished hunters. As Rud (2006, 504) dryly remarks, "the Greenlanders who wanted control over their own conditions could only be

32 Knud Rasmussen's mother was of 'mixed' descent, and as such he had Greenlandic lineage, although his ethnic and social affiliation was Danish (Thisted 2009, 247).

granted this influence if they met the criteria for the ethnological-national ideal established by the colonial powers." Rud thus attempts to develop an analysis that deals with the interaction between the personal and economic motives of various colonial actors.

I am sceptical concerning Rud's distinction between traditionalists and modernists, an issue that is not analytically addressed in his article. It arises from an exaggeration of the difference between advocates of traditionalism and modernity. I will take Rud's discussion of the catechist colleges as an example. Following Wilhjelm's history (1997) of the catechist colleges, Rud discerns different attitudes towards Greenlandic and Danish culture. While the catechist college in Godthåb (present-day Nuuk) placed great emphasis on lessons in hunting and kayak skills, the college in Jakobshavn (present-day Ilulissat) did not (Rud 2006, 499; see also Wilhjelm 1997, 115–116). Likewise with languages: the college in Jakobshavn emphasised Danish as a highly prioritised subject, a subject that was less prioritised in Godthåb (Wilhjelm 1997, 308–309). Rud determines the line taken at Godthåb as preserving tradition, while the college in Jakobshavn represented a more modernising approach. He understands the disagreements over the civilisation project in Greenland as crystallised in these educational approaches:

> On the one hand, there was the traditionalist wing, which cultivated hunter culture and wanted to protect Greenlanders against European culture; on the other hand, there was the modernist wing, which was keen to introduce Greenlanders to European culture at a quicker pace. These wings were found within the employees of the Trade/administration and mission—the discussions regarded subjects such as whether or not Danish should be taught at the colleges, whether or not Greenlanders should be sent to Denmark on (civilising) educational trips and the central free-trade or monopoly issue.[33]
>
> 2006, 500

Rud connects the traditionalist view with the understanding of kayaks and seal hunts as quintessential Greenlandic traits, and sees the situation as a matter of two opposing attitudes towards civilisation (that is traditionalism/modernism) between which a choice must be made.

33 In most accounts (Rud 2006, Thomsen 1998, Marquardt 1999, 11) the proponents of the monopoly system were the traditionalists, who used the argument of a "fragile" Greenlandic culture as an excuse to postpone the development of free trade. The Royal Greenlandic Trading Company monopoly lasted until 1953.

While the discussion in question occurs in the mid-nineteenth century, it resurfaces again in the mid-twentieth century with this difference: the earlier debate was over how to govern Greenlanders, and the opposing positions were all Danish, while the later debate witnessed the entry of Greenlandic opinions. In both situations, a critique is required of the question of *choice*, or the nature of the choice itself. We have here what Talal Asad calls a "Western choice," and *not* a question of whether or not to choose the West (1992, 345). As philosopher Slavoj Žižek would put it, following Lenin, the choice is presented as a formal freedom—that is, it is a "freedom" that operates within the terms of existing power relations.[34]

The traditionalist wing, with its emphasis on kayaks, hunts, and so on, represented the popular perception of the 'real Greenlander,' a position Rud argues arose following the expeditions to the east coast of Greenland. However, the dispersion of this perception into society was carried out in terms already determined by modernity, especially through the colonial administration. It came from the catechist colleges and in *Atuagagdliutit*. And so, as Rud points out:

> Both the national catechists and the newspaper *Atuagagdliutit* were thus part of the formation of a common Greenlandic feeling of identity, where the principal values were traditional cultural elements such as the hunt and kayak sailing. The initiatives for these steps towards identity formation came from the colonial power in the shape of certain circles within trade and administration and certain circles within the mission. In that way, the Danish colonial power was deeply implicated in the formation or determination of the Greenlandic national character. At a time (in the

---

34 Žižek writes: "And here one should risk reintroducing the Leninist opposition of 'formal' and 'actual' freedom: in an act of actual freedom, one dares precisely to BREAK the seductive power of symbolic efficiency. Therein resides the moment of truth of Lenin's acerbic retort to his Menshevik critics: the truly free choice is a choice in which I do not merely choose between two or more options WITHIN a pre-given set of coordinates, but I choose to change this set of coordinates itself." (2001, 121; emphasis in original). Here it might be worth following Ernesto Laclau's practice of deconstructing Marxist categories (see Laclau 1990; Laclau and Mouffe 2001), and question whether actual freedom is possible, or whether this changing of the coordinates themselves entails a shift in power relations that could be as oppressive as the ones it replaces. Žižek himself oscillates between a pessimistic view, which denies the possibility for social change, and a more optimistic, revolutionary view, which is open to the idea of actual freedom. The first position occurs when he remains within his Lacanian framework, while the second appears when he incorporates Judaeo-Christian concepts into his thinking (Boer 2007, 335–390).

> mid-nineteenth century) where the colonial administration of Greenland was faced with a choice between free trade/monopoly, modernisation/protectionism and Europeanisation/(re-)traditionalisation, the scientific romanticising of traditional hunter society was very influential.
>
> 2006, 503

Thus, in nineteenth-century Greenland, it was not a question of choosing more (modernist) or less (traditionalist) Danish influence; it was a question of what *kind* of Danish influence they wanted to adopt and *how* to apply the power relations most efficiently so as to optimise the outcome—for the colonial administration. It was *not* a choice between modernity and non-modernity; it was a modern Western choice. While Rud's argument sometimes seems to move in this direction, at other times it is locked into the framework of traditionalism/modernisation, an opposition with which he begins.

I do not deny that there were differences in opinion between traditionalists and modernists who wanted to industrialise and develop the labour market; the entire debate over fishing is a case in point.[35] However, I critically question the idea of traditionalists as culture-*preserving*, especially since Rud provides ample evidence that they are not; the institutionalisation of hunters into the local boards was an attempt to regulate and order what previously had been dealt with through 'uncontrollable' custom, breaking down old forms of distribution and creating new ones (Rud 2007, 189). These moves were, as previously discussed, a further step in a colonial politics of control. Simultaneously, the cultural institutions were promoting this ideal of the seal hunter, thus supporting the institutionalisation of the hunter as marker of Greenlandic identity. This is Thomsen's point—as well as mine.

In order to understand how this discourse is framed, it is necessary to draw out the alternative masculinity ideal fostered by the catechist office. However, I argue that it is not possible to separate, as was the case in all of the above-mentioned analyses, the institutionalisation of hunters from the institutionalisation of catechists, because what is taking place is a *construction* and subsequent *consolidation* of two different masculinities in two different

35 In the beginning of the twentieth century, fishing began to be considered a commercial endeavour, and was experimented with as such. Before then, although fishing had always been part of the household economy of Greenlanders, the Trade (see Introduction, note 24) focused solely on that part of the fishery dealing with seal products, thus generating a discourse of fishing as unmanly and little more than an emergency solution when starvation loomed (Langgård 1999a, 46). As a material foundation for this discourse, the Trade purchased fish at low prices, thus making it difficult for fishing to become a livelihood (Thorleifsen 1999, 70).

settings, but *within* the same colonial coordinates. When they are separated and institutionally compartmentalised, it becomes easy to overlook the fact that the hunter is crucial for the identity formation of the catechist. Going back to elements from Rasmussen's analysis, the maintenance of an ethnic (Greenlandic) identity meant integrating selected cultural elements from the primary producers: attitudes, behaviour, language, and dress. Simultaneously, the maintenance of a social (class) identity meant weeding out some cultural elements characteristic of primary producers while adopting certain cultural elements from the Danish 'upper class,' such as attitudes, dress, and interior decoration (Rasmussen 1983, 87).

The example of Frederik Berthelsen reinforces this point; Frederik's consumption habits indicate that he regarded himself as European to some extent.[36] One of the merchant lists also notes that Frederik Berthelsen purchased eight sealskins.[37] Assuming that Frederik was fully permitted (and expected) to hunt for his own consumption, his choice to buy the skins rather than

36 As discussed in chapter one, Berthelsen's salary and his purchases at the store far exceeded those of his fellows. His purchases are also of interest in this context; they included silk scarves, blue and white linen, several types of socks and stockings, and a pyjama top (1785–86). The same items figure on the list from 1786–87, along with the eight sealskins. In his analysis of the Trade's activities from 1747–1774, economic historian P.P. Sveistrup notes that Berthel Laersen (Frederik Berthelsen's father) was a major consumer of such goods as brandy, flour, tea, coffee, and raisins (1943, 50). His son, Frederik, who became head catechist after his father's death, apparently inherited the same expensive tastes, while the other son, Joseph, did not. Joseph's consumption was limited to tobacco, ammunition, and some bedding cloth. Frederik Berthelsen bought mostly luxury items; they could in no way replace clothes and food in every-day life, but instead supplemented them. These items, as well as the fabric used for clothing, indicate that Greenland was at that time part of the larger mercantilist economy and patterns of commodity exchange. Calico, kersey, silk, and linen were part of the larger network of trade between Denmark and its colonies in the East Indies. To this may be added the luxury goods cited above and in previous chapters, which were all part of the three-way trade between the African continent, the West Indies, and Denmark, an economy which relied mostly on the slave trade.

37 The *Instruction,* which was an attempt to regulate business in Greenland and to set certain standards for the future, included a directive (post 3, item 4) that seal skins were one of several monopolised commodities (blubber, whale-oil, whalebones, skins of bear, caribou, seal or fox, narwhal-tusk, walrus-tusk, eiderdown ... "or any kind of commodity which belongs to the Trade") that had to be purchased through the Trade. However, these regulations applied only to Europeans in Greenland. Greenlanders were free to catch what they needed for their own consumption, and were more or less compelled to sell the surplus to the Trade. This distinction between Europeans and Greenlanders posed a problem when it came to the *blandinger*. Were they to be reckoned as Europeans and thus subjected to the regulations of the *Instruction*, or as Greenlanders free to follow the

hunting them (not to mention having his wife subsequently flensing and parting the carcasses and preparing the skins) signals not just financial excess but a self-distancing from the hunter identity, a distance which also extends to his wife's chores. This behaviour is an act, which effectively 'makes' him more European than any silk ribbons or linen clothing ever could.

We thus see the tendency, which Rasmussen indicates in his analysis, that the emerging elite pulls away from the primary producers and increasingly adapts the lifestyle of the European upper class. Rasmussen draws attention to the growing importance of pecuniary economy in households which meant: (i) the size of income would constitute and further consolidate the upper social level as a distinct socio-economic category; (ii) the size of income would allow different patterns of consumption than those of the primary producers, which would also enhance the significance of consumption for sustaining social status; and (iii) the diminished role of women in preparation of the harvest and hence a shift in the role of women, labour, and their social consciousness (Rasmussen 1983, 92).

As argued in chapter one, the missionary avidly encouraged this distancing in the case of Frederik and, initially, his brother Joseph. The ontological status of the hunter, I argue, plays a similar role in the construction of the ethnic identity of the catechists. Hunting, as part of the every-day practices of pre-colonial Greenlanders, becomes ontologised as the 'true' identity of Greenlanders. It is construed as the 'true' identity of Greenlanders because it has always been like that, namely the forefathers were hunters. While this way of life is transmitted through storytelling and training from father to son, it also becomes fixed on paper, in the recording and subsequent publishing of the oral traditions, lending it, as von Braun argues, a sense of "eternity." In the course of the latter part of the nineteenth century, hunting was idealised as *the* Greenlandic way of life in the newspaper *Atuagagdliutit* (Langgård forthcoming: 6). Alongside translations of contemporary literature, such as *Robinson Crusoe,* and descriptions of other peoples from Australia, the Pacific Islands,

customs outlined and approved by the Trade? According to Gad's studies (1974, 1976) they were subjected to the *Instruction* if they were employed by the Trade; however, the *Instruction* does not discuss the mission or its employees. As far as the mission goes, it was presumed that the national catechists supported themselves through hunting, in addition to the token payment that they received. However, as I argued in chapter one, Hveyssel did not regard Frederik as a Greenlander. Hveyssel explicitly avoids calling him a *national* catechist and insisted on Frederik being granted full board and proper wages, which would enable Frederik to maintain a higher standard of living than other Greenlanders.

Patagonia, and Tierra del Fuego, Greenlanders could read local news and stories by and about themselves (Langgård 1999b, 180).

But these stories appeared next to descriptions of Australian aborigines as stupid, lazy, aggressive, and pagan, as well as beggars and alcoholics; stories about the natives of Patagonia and Tierra del Fuego as thieving seal hunters who killed all the missionaries; accounts of Pacific islanders as pagan warlike cannibals; and even accounts of Canadian Inuit as cannibals. By comparison, Greenlanders could see themselves as peaceful Christian seal-hunters, a self-image which, in light of the negative publicity surrounding other "natives," was highly suggestive. Hunting narratives were published, the most famous being stories of the hunter Ungaaralak that appeared in *Atuagagdliutit* between 1877 and 1884 (Kleivan 1995, 97) and the 13 narratives reprinted (in English translation) in Rink's *Danish Greenland* (Rink 1974 [1877], 230–267). All assume a hunting lifestyle as their frame of reference. In writing about the hunter past and present, the figure of the hunter slowly becomes abstracted from the daily practice of hunting.

Langgård notes that the articles in *Atuagagdliutit* were written by the Greenlandic elite in its broader sense, encompassing catechists, trade employees and hunters (1998, 91). Even though hunters also used the newspaper as a medium for promoting their way of life (1998, 91), I argue that this use of the newspaper already takes place within the coordinates established for the intellectuals, who have a printing press, a newspaper and a literate population at their disposal—and thereby the power to represent. When catechist Niels Lynge stated in 1911 that "the one who lives as a hunter, thinks like a hunter, and the one who lives as a catechist, thinks like a catechist" (in Wilhjelm 2009, 510), the separation indicates that the hunter has become an abstraction.

From here, the hunter and hunting culture may now be used as symbols. In Augo Lynge's novel, *Ukiut 300-nngornerat* (*300 Years After*), hunting culture is used to symbolise a superstitious and impoverished lifestyle that belongs to the past.[38] In contrast, we have catechist Ferdinand Clasen and his contribution to the debate on Greenlandish-ness: "Certainly this development [demise in the condition of hunting] is very much to be deplored, since we Greenlanders—constituting a nation of our own, living in Greenland and

38 In her analysis of the first two Greenlandic novels (Augo Lynge's is one), Kirsten Thisted uses Benedict Anderson to link the Greenlandic written language and nationalism, arguing that the emergence of a written tradition enabled national consciousness. Within this argument, abstraction (the use of a story as an image of something else) is recognised as something not possible within an oral tradition. Abstraction thus becomes that which facilitates national identity over against local patriotism (see Thisted 1990, esp. 115–116).

named Greenlanders—should be involved in occupations which reflect our Greenlandic way of life" (in Langgård 1998, 84). In other words, hunting should be that which defines Greenlandic-ness.[39]

To sum up, then, the Greenlandic elite's relationship to 'the hunter' is highly ambiguous. On the one hand, Greenlanders seek to distance themselves socially from the 'primary producers' (to cite Rasmussen's language); on the other, they nonetheless use 'the hunter' in their construction of a Greenlandic identity. The precise workings of this utilisation may be best described by returning to von Braun's argument on the production of nature (discussed in chapter four above). To recapitulate, von Braun asserts that with the advent of (phonetic) writing, a process of abstraction began that was consolidated with Christianity. In this process, the *logos* would replace reality with its own "reality" or "rewritten materiality," thereby shaping this rewritten materiality to suit its own purposes (von Braun 2009, 116–119).

As explained in the previous chapter, the writing of the catechists in their daily reports had the effect of distancing the catechist from the world 'out there' as 'nature,' thus producing the catechist as an abstracted subject. The elite is itself a product of the *logos*, which then goes on to produce its own nature, to put it crudely, from which it may distance itself through technologies of the self, and becomes an "I." Von Braun's argument highlights the constructed nature of both *logos* and nature, which constitutes a considerable strength of her argument.

In order to argue for this production of nature, she relies on a grand narrative of origins that may be open to question. However, in a colonial context, it is possible to see how profoundly a restructuring according to Western notions of truth, nature, and civilisation affected the colonised structures of societies, even in ostensibly 'untouched' places. And so, even though the reservation politics[40] meant that hunters were left to carry on life in the same fashion—'business as usual'—the valorisation of this form of life and its living standard was drawn into a different system of representation, power,

39 In her analysis of the glorification of the past that takes place in Greenlandic literature from the 1970s onwards, Birgit Kleist Pedersen notes how young Greenlandic authors were influenced by the radical left political movements of the time, especially the ecological consciousness, which suddenly placed indigenous people at centre stage, embodying a lifestyle that must be emulated to regain authenticity in the face of capitalism (1997, 164). See also Ter Ellingson's more general analysis of the "ecological noble savage" as a distinct feature of contemporary anthropology (2001, 342–58).

40 Reservation politics means preserving the population in its 'original' state. See Kjærgård (1982, 132), Felbøl (1983, 8), and Marquardt (2000).

and hierarchisation as a crucial means for the elite's own identity formations and expressions, while the lifestyle itself was considered undesirable.

In this way, the catechist colleges constitute part of the *conditions* established by the colonial powers to frame the possibility of social action.[41] That this is a deliberate colonial tactic may be seen in Rink's article "*Om Aarsagen til Grønlændernes og lignende, af Jagt levende, Nationers materialle Tilbagegang ved berøring med Europæerne*" (On the Cause for the Material Decline upon Contact with the Europeans of Greenlanders and other Nations Dependant on Hunting), in which he argues that the eradication of the spiritual elite, the *angakkut*, was a significant factor in the general social decline because it also meant the eradication of the Greenlandic authorities, order, and discipline that had kept society in place (1862, 95). Since the decline is a result of changing social structures, Rink argues, the improvement must be sought in the same way (107). He argues that

> distinctions must be made among the natives, and thereupon let those, with insight and capabilities sustain society and govern the rest, as it was in the old days, and that since the Europeans' power in the country only resides partly in the spiritual authority through the mission, and partly in money, one should deploy these means to confer respect upon *Øvrighed* (native positions of authority).
>
> 110

The way to do this, he argues, is to foster native ministers, or to grant the native catechists as much authority as possible, and let this clergy be the "significant element in a secular authority [*verdslig Øvrighed*[42]]," an authority which should consist of the most capable seal hunters, preferably elected by their countrymen. Rink's initiatives in relation to transmission from the oral tradition to writing are complementary to the view advanced in his article. This promotion of writing intersects with the establishment of colleges to educate Greenlandic catechists, and the development of a Greenlandic spiritual authority. Here we have the germ of the struggle over 'Greenlandic-ness,' which

41 In his use of Asad's insights within his analysis of colonialism in the "New World," David Scott attempts to shift the line of questioning from colonial/anti-colonial issues to an examination of "how colonial power transformed the ground on which accommodation of resistance was possible in the first place, how colonial power reshaped or reorganized the conceptual and institutional conditions of possibility of social action and its understanding" (2004, 119).

42 Note that "On Secular Authority" is one of Luther's main writings, and a significant element in the argument of two spheres of authority and the question of natural law, discussed in chapter three.

would take place in another forty years. However, while that struggle is presented as one between the interests of a single group (the hunters) and the interests of the entire nation of Greenlandic speakers, it nevertheless veils an important point: the language-and-traditions option in fact *privileges* a certain form of labour and masculinity—that of the catechists.[43] The realm of the catechist lays claim to a certain form of masculinity that has its roots in a Western intellectual culture, a feature that is downplayed in the focus on language-and-tradition as a neutral and natural foundation for all Greenlanders.[44]

Furthermore, the classed and racialised labour aspects of the office are equally underexposed. The roots of this struggle are set in Rink's literary hunt and subsequent publications. My point is that the catechist colleges are the institutionalisation of a certain configuration of gender and rationality, which established a masculine signifying universe that reconceptualised Greenlandic society. In these colleges, individuals are formed in the image of rational European men, and it is from within this signifying universe that Greenlandic society is constructed.

Mariekathrine Poppel provides a good example of the strength of this understanding of the hunter in an article dealing with Greenlandic men and the labour market. It begins with the following story about an elderly man from North Greenland:

> He told me his story about how he as a young man came to Nuuk. He was born in the 1940s and grew up in North Greenland, but was orphaned before he became an adult and could marry. When his parents died, he moved in with his married sister. The storyteller was a hunter and had a team of dogs, while the brother-in-law was a fisherman. When the family had to move to Nuuk to fish, he phased out his hunting occupation and came along, because, as he said, he had no other family. When he came to Nuuk, he was employed in the docks, unloading, and this is the point of the story: 'It was so difficult to work, you see. I had never worked before; I was a hunter.'
>
> POPPEL 2005a, 126

As Poppel points out, this passage shows that there is a *perceived* difference between being a hunter and being a wage labourer: "work" means wage labour, and hunting does not fall into this category. This is a precise expression of what

43 Thuesen also notes that it was the catechists' notion of Greenlandic-ness that prevailed because Greenlandic society required different labour groups, and could no longer be sustained via hunting alone (2007, 347).

44 As argued by catechists Henrik and Isak Lund (Wilhjelm 2009, 512–13).

I in the course of this chapter have been designating "the ontological status of the hunter," namely, an abstracted hunter identity disassociated from work.

The argument in this section is that the *representation itself* of 'the real Greenlander' transcends the differences between various groups and as such lays claim to certain understandings of 'Greenlandic nature.' I am not arguing that what is represented as the real Greenlander (i.e. the catechist) is in fact a distortion of what is the real Greenlander is (i.e. the hunter), which would be close to what, for example, Rousseau argues. I am arguing that *both* the catechist *and* the hunter are categories constructed or produced to represent 'Greenlandic-ness.'

This universalising move downplays some characteristics while accentuating others—in a sense constructing something new (Laclau 1990, 38). In Greenland, this 'something new' is the idea of a unified Greenlandic identity that subsumes differences within itself. The claim that the real Greenlander is a seal-hunter excludes the catechists and other non-hunting men from the category of 'real Greenlander,' while the claim that the real Greenlander is one who has a connection to the language, the history, and the land—while seemingly embracing all Greenlanders—is in fact fostered through a privileged access to education and the means to express these sentiments. However, both of these claims come from the catechists. Following Lévi-Strauss, I regard the medium for representation as that of alphabetic writing. In Greenland, the ability to read was firmly connected to the dissemination of Christianity and its demands for unquestionable obedience to absolute truth, which led to the notion that *any* written word was of unquestionable authority. Reading and writing are thus part-and-parcel of the shift in conditions, the transformation of the ground and the reorganisation of conceptual and institutional conditions.[45] Writing changes the possibilities of social action.

When Heinrich Rink established the press and the newspaper, and put out the call for oral traditions to preserve them in a written form, he set in motion the material means for a different way of representing Greenlandic society. This coincided with the institutionalisation of the education of the catechists, thus paving the way for an intellectual elite that appropriated the power to represent. The sense of self that is generated through writing demarcates that which is 'out there' as 'nature,' a category of estrangement. This has profound repercussions for the following debates on identity and nationalism, where educated Greenlanders come to speak on behalf of their fellow Greenlanders. This representation, as well as its gendered, racial, and class aspects, is the focus of the final chapter.

---

45 See the quotation from Scott (2004, 119) in note 41 above.

CHAPTER 6

Rewritten Pasts and Scripts for the Future

Heart of Light

The much-acclaimed film *Heart of Light* emphasises the disastrous social outcomes in Greenland of pro-Danish politics from the 1950s and 1960s. These years, commencing with the inclusion of Greenland within *Rigsfællesskabet* (Danish Commonwealth) in 1953, are some of the most intense, challenging, and disillusioning years of Greenlandic colonial history. There were many discussions and much disagreement in Greenland leading up to the change in political status. The highly influential politician Frederik Lynge (grandfather of Greenlandic novelist Hans Anton Lynge, who co-authored the script for *Heart of Light*) was, along with his cousin Augo Lynge, among those politicians who were in favour of modernising Greenland and having it join the Danish Commonwealth.[1]

However, the questions concerning to what extent Greenland was to undergo industrialisation and modernisation, how rapidly, and at what costs, seem to have been the cause for some disagreement, with Frederik Lynge taking the more hesitant approach (DIIS 2007, 431). One of the main reasons behind the desire of elite Greenlanders to enter the Danish Commonwealth was to improve the quality of life and obtain equality between Danes and Greenlanders—especially in wages, where the difference was 25%. Since early colonial times, there had been two wage-systems in operation, one for Greenlanders and one for Danes. In 1958, educated Greenlanders who had lived in Denmark for more than 10 years could be paid the same wage in Greenland as Danes. However, a new law based on place of birth, the so-called *fødestedskriterium,* was introduced in 1964 with the support of the Greenlandic Council. The new measure cemented wage inequality and made it impossible

1 A recent book dealing with the years before and after the Second World War, and entry into the Commonwealth, is *Eske Brun og det moderne Grønlands tilblivelse* (Eske Brun and the Genesis of Modern Greenland) by Jens Heinrich (2012), published under the auspices of the Greenlandic government. The book is a published version of Heinrich's PhD dissertation in history from *Ilisimatusarfik* (University of Greenland). In it, Heinrich argues that the push for industrialisation in the early twentieth century came from Greenlanders themselves in a desire to develop their country. While I don't disagree, I would want to add the word "elite" to "Greenlanders." Indeed, one of the primary actors Heinrich emphasises is Augo Lynge, whom I also discuss in this chapter.

for anyone born in Greenland to be paid Danish wages in Greenland. This law was repealed only in 1990 (Olsen 2005, 72). Wage equality between Danes and Greenlanders, let alone general equality, never occurred within the Commonwealth, and this became one of the primary reasons for the Greenlandic demand for home-rule and, later, self-government. In 1953, however, when Greenland entered *Rigsfællesskabet*, there was an expectation of equality. It is worthwhile to consider *who* had these expectations. As Greenlandic journalist Jørgen Fleischer notes:

> [W]hen the country—after the constitutional change—was incorporated into the Danish kingdom as a province with equal rights, and all Greenlanders became Danish citizens, one had envisioned that the differential treatment finally was over. But that did not happen.
>
> 1999, 209

Note that the phrase "one had envisioned" retains the impersonal expression of the Danish text (*havde man forestillet sig*). Who does this *one* represent? Does it speak on behalf of men, women, and children, families in the towns and the impoverished settlements? Does it include those whose lungs were decomposing from tuberculosis in turf- and stone-houses, and their families? Those who had to beg for bread at the doorstep of the Danish Inspector to stave off starvation for another day, or the fishermen forced to sell their catch at just five per cent of the retail price? Or does it mainly speak on behalf of the 'upper social stratum,' the Greenlanders with Danish ancestors who for decades had been living, eating, and acting like Danes and working in the colonial administration?

Regardless of who had these expectations, the ongoing practices of inequality between Danes and Greenlanders in Greenland soon put them to rest, as this quotation from Knud Hertling, former Minister of Greenland in the Danish Parliament, illustrates:

> Augo Lynge's speech in the country council [the prelude to the Greenlandic Parliament] in 1952 and Frederik Lynge's speech at the [Danish] Parliament's opening in 1953, coupled with declarations in the UN on the equality of all humans etc., made us, who at this time were part of Greenland's hopeful youth, believe that complete equality was possible—also as far as equal pay for the same labour went. Now we had become Danish citizens, real Danes. We cried 'hooray' over these big and powerful words. They gave us an expectation of something good, something big and true. Only ten or eleven years later would we

> realise that we were only spectators at the beginning of the impossible equality.
>
> 1999, 266

This political context concerning Greenland's future provides an important backdrop for *Heart of Light* since these debates are cast as the "colonial footage" in the film. They are staged as the past of which the lead character, Rasmus, is a product, and the reason for his present state of distress. However, they also point to the position of novelist Hans Anton Lynge within the genealogy of modern Greenlandic history as a member of the cultural elite.[2]

---

2 I am presupposing that Lynge had a significant impact on the manuscript. Cultural theorist Erik Gant, however, considers the inclusion of Lynge as part of a usual practice of attaching a prominent Greenlandic cultural figure at an early stage of production to give it a stamp of authenticity (2005, 226). Thisted critiques Gant for making such a presumption without attempting to relate the view on social development and Greenlandic identity in *Heart of Light* to the rest of Lynge's writing (2006a, 76n6). Gant's critique of the film focuses primarily, though not exclusively, on the extensive media attention that accompanied the opening night (25 January 1998). This attention was primarily due to the fact that the film was marketed as the first Greenlandic feature film. The background to such a marketing strategy is the long history of Danish films and novels about Greenland, but now, as Erik Gant sardonically says, "we are so advanced that we can represent ourselves" (2005, 237). In an article devoted to the staging of the film's premiere, Gant argues that the film is not Greenlandic in itself; it becomes so through reference to the many Danish films which precede it, especially *Tukuma* (1984), which features the same actor, Rasmus Lyberth, playing a character named Rasmus, but in a role supporting a Danish leading character who comes to Greenland and thus encounters Rasmus as an other (2000, 131). In *Heart of Light*, a Greenlandic character is now in the lead role and has to play his own role as well as that of the other, while at the same time the other, the different and the incomprehensible, has been displaced onto the event of the film itself and the hype surrounding it. Thus, according to Gant, the cultural difference that was central in *Tukuma* cannot be present in *Heart of Light* because it is a Greenlandic film which has room only for Greenlandic cultural schizophrenia. Instead, the cultural difference is, in all its strangeness, made part of the marketing and presentation of the film, and cast as well-known tropes of reason and emotion. Gant then presents us with multiple references to Greenlandic emotions in the publicity surrounding the film, reviews, and interviews. Gant's point is that even in reviews it was never only a film; it was as much about the reactions of the audience, their sobs, their pain and anguish, their joy and redemption. The Greenlandic event is the uncovering of this emotionality (2000, 133), which is heavily supported by director Jacob Grønlykke's comments on his own rationality and reliance on reason rather than the emotions of Greenlanders (2000, 131). In effect, this displacement functions to keep the Greenlander in the supporting role (2000, 132). The film is therefore a "Greenlandified" result of what the director perceives to be Greenlandic reality, a mixture of every-day life and its dismal reality, and the mythical, ancient—and yet present–universe (2000, 132).

As argued in chapter five, the hunter identity is vital as the other through which the cultural elite maintains an identity as upper-class Greenlanders. It is the material foundation that ensures their wages, *and* serves an atavistic function that secures connections to the past. Therefore, the maintenance of the hunter identity becomes a necessary part of the elite's identity production. This is why it is Rasmus's destiny to be rewritten as a hunter: Greenlandic society needs hunters like him who can function like a cultural reservoir.[3] He is, in a sense, subjected to the intended conduct—as Asad (1992) puts it, "conscripted," or in this case, literally scripted—to a defined role. *Heart of Light* does not just invoke the whole debate over 'Greenlandic-ness' from several generations earlier, and its discussions about whether it was the hunter lifestyle or the language, land, and tradition which constitute the essential core of Greenlandic nature; it also attempts to resolve the debate in the same manner, using the Greenlandic language to connect the hunter identity with the land and the tradition, to regain, or more precisely, *produce* a collective Greenlandic, or rather Inuit, identity.

The aim of this final chapter is to trace the effect of writing and the ontological status of the hunter in a more contemporary setting, namely, *Heart of Light,* in order to problematise this process in a broader global context. As mentioned in the Introduction, *Heart of Light* was marketed as the first Greenlandic movie ever made in Greenland with Greenlandic actors speaking Greenlandic, and a Greenlandic playwright as one of the two scriptwriters. At the same time, the film advocates a reconfiguration of the colonial past and constructs a desired society based on pre-colonial culture and a pan-Inuit identity. My focus is therefore on how the national Greenlandic and the supranational Inuit identities interact, and how the global context frames indigenous people and certain understandings of 'authenticity.'

I have chosen *Heart of Light* because the conditions of its production rest on class differences, racial politics, and educational opportunities cemented by colonialism.[4] In *Heart of Light*, the hunter remains framed by the discourses of

3 Rud, Thomsen, Kleist Pedersen, and Rygaard point out that this image is in harmony with the Danish ideal image of the Greenlander. My argument is that this is an ideal image produced and endorsed by the Greenlandic elite.

4 The idea of "conditions of production" is borrowed from cultural theortist Anne Cranny-Francis's (1992) enquiry into the engendered conditions of production in her study into gender and texts. Cranny-Francis's analysis is explicitly focused on the difference in conditions between men and women, and indicates how class and race may be included in this line of questioning. For example, Cranny-Francis considers access to materials and training, which also includes discursive access, i.e. gendered rules and expectations in textual production that is most often a patriarchal discourse.

the catechist colleges and their production of the ontological status of the hunter. My analysis of *Heart of Light* therefore follows on from the previous chapters of this study. Furthermore, the indigenous identity politics advocated in the film gives rise to a discussion of the hunter and authentic indigenous identity in a global setting: As I have argued throughout this work, if governmentality can be seen as a way of theorising agency as limited or conditioned by a colonial power structure, then the definitions of indigenous authenticity which extend from colonial discourse can also be analysed as particular strategies of subjectification.

The chapter is structured as follows: In the first section, I present the main storyline and situate the film within the arguments I have been presenting. I then analyse the film as a bridge between national identity and global identity politics by employing a qualified version of national allegory developed by literary theorist Fredric Jameson. Subsequently, I proceed to analyse the larger global setting of indigenous identity politics, drawing on some examples from the Australian context. In the previous five chapters I have been concerned with tracing the conditions established by the colonial administration within which Greenlanders could operate. From very early on, it was a particular segment of the Greenlandic population that was given the ability and the tools to define and represent Greenlandic-ness. The aim of this chapter is to explore continuities between the colonial conditions of past representations of Greenlanders and contemporary *global* discourses of indigeneity. My focus remains on the ontological status of the hunter as colonial discourse, but placed in a larger setting, namely, within the 'cult of authenticity' and the demands for 'authentic identities' imposed on indigenous peoples.[5]

The Colonial Conditions of *Heart of Light*

Heart of Light is about reclaiming the past. In the course of his spectacular journey through the ice desert of northern West Greenland, Rasmus is

5 In her 2006 book *Regulating Aversion: Tolerance in the Age of Identity and Empire*, Wendy Brown analyses "tolerance" as a political discourse and practice of governmentality that constructs and positions subjects and cultures in various ways. It emerged with renewed energy in the 1980s as multiculturalism began to challenge notions of belonging and citizenship. This approach to tolerance dismantles the understanding of tolerance as a benign universal, and focuses instead on its practice of normativity. While Brown's topic and approach is much broader than what I am working with in this chapter, our outcomes and objectives are similar. I would like to thank Deane Galbraith for this reference.

confronted with people from his own past and mythological characters of his people's past. He ultimately recovers his Inuit self, a self that had been buried by childhood traumas generated by his father's compliant politics towards Denmark, which included his attempts to turn Rasmus into a Danish boy.

The film operates with three chronological discourses: the 'present,' the 'colonial' and the 'ancestral.' These intertwine in the course of the movie, but each is granted different values. While the movie begins with the colonial past, thus paving the way for a present riddled with unemployment and substance abuse, it is the ancestral past purged of colonialism that is the way out.[6] These discourses are spatialised in the spaces of Ilulissat (present), the ice (ancestral), and Qullissat (colonial). The narrative functions to combine them in a way that allows them to comment on each other. At the beginning of the film, Ilulissat (Jakobshavn) is a place of unemployment, alcoholism, murder, suicide, and utter disillusionment. After Rasmus's trip, it becomes the site of reconciliation, pride, and self-sufficiency. But this transition requires the trip to the icescape. The visit to the abandoned site of Qullissat gives us an intertext of colonial spatial and social politics that functions as a representation of

6 In their thorough and incisive analysis of the film, Jette Rygaard and Birgit Kleist Pedersen directly address the question about the role of contemporary Greenland. They note how the "'present" (ca. 1994) Greenland is characterised by desolation, alcohol-abuse, unemployment, and a high suicide rate (2003, 177). The only solution to this dysfunctional contemporary Greenland is a reclamation of the ancestral past. So what does this mean for the present? Broaching the question requires first that this particular context be broadened. The work of Rygaard and Pedersen is part of a larger project on Greenlandic youth and film, and *Heart of Light* was one of several films screened for five groups of 15-to-19-year-olds to analyse their reaction. The film was also shown to a group of students at *Ilisimatusarfik* (University of Greenland) with the same intent. As explained in the Introduction, even though the film was praised by audiences and critics alike, younger Greenlanders did not recognise this 'authentic' Greenland (2003, 176). Rygaard and Pedersen point to the fact that both parts of the film (i.e. modern Greenland and the solution to the crisis of modern Greenland) draw on the past. The dysfunctional society is rooted in what I have called "the colonial past" and the solution is found in "the ancestral past." Both parts of the film point to the past and leave us with a host of questions concerning the present. We are never told how Rasmus's life turns out from here, whether he can live up to his newfound identity, whether he can help fulfil his son Simon's wish to study in Fairbanks, and whether he ever drinks again—all pertinent and urgent questions for the younger generation. They simply could not see any points of identification between the film and their own lives, neither in the 'present' nor in the 'past.' Rygaard and Pedersen conclude: "If the present is unbearable and virtually hopeless, and the solution to be found in a bygone past, which is postulated in the middle of a dense urban environment, then where does this leave the growing generation?" (2003, 178).

the colonial ordering of Ilulissat. We understand this because of the colonial politics, brought to our attention at the beginning of the film, that explain how the settlement of Qulissat was depopulated and resettled in Ilulissat.[7] The ice, however, with its population of figures and tropes from Greenlandic cultural traditions that Rasmus comes to embrace step by step, is the location or source of two overlapping shifts: first, the ice itself moves from being a place of danger to function as the source for the imagining of a new and alternative Ilulissat; the second shift involves Ilulissat itself, shifting from a place of cultural barrenness to one of abundance.

We first meet Rasmus in the present as an unemployed alcoholic living in a one-bedroom house in the neighbourhood that housed the population that was forcibly removed from Qullissat. By various means (a rifle, the 'colonial footage,' and a vision) we understand that he was actually born into the Greenlandic bourgeoisie,[8] with the only explanation for his social decline being his belated rebellion against his father's pro-Danish politics. After Rasmus's journey into the icescape, he recovers his ancestral identity and rises from the ashes as a hunter. All of these roles (social outcast, bourgeois, and hunter) construct Rasmus as a very ambiguous and social *bricolage*. At first glance, his central function seems to be to unite all of these social roles in one character, providing both the bourgeoisie and the underclass with a point of identification in the film, with the hunter ultimately transcending the chasm between the classes. However, a closer look at Rasmus's 'present' identity reveals that he is defined through hunting as a *present* ideal, one that he is failing to meet.

Rasmus the non-hunter neglects his hunting equipment. His failings as a father to his sons, Niisi and Simon, are intertwined with his failings as a hunter. He cannot provide food for Simon's birthday. Even in a hunting scene that he imagines, and narrates to Marie near the start of the movie, a bear snatches his game and he must return home empty-handed. Rasmus's lack of status, pride, and manliness seems to be connected with his inadequate hunting abilities

7 Qulissat was a town built around a coal mine in 1924. In 1972, the Danish state decided to close the mine and the town, which had a population of 1400. The resettlement and dispersion that followed led to high unemployment and social insecurity, and fostered significant resentment towards the Danish state and the Greenlandic Council, which supported the closure (Olsen 2005, 198).

8 Rasmus's father may be understood as a representative of the ruling class: he was a politician in favour of rapid industrialisation and, as such, would have been part of the cultural elite in an upper-middle-class family. His black-and-white suit and tie certainly signify an upper-class affiliation.

and equipment. This is supported by a significant but undeveloped point in most analyses, namely, the victims of the shooting. Rasmus's older son, Niisi, shoots Nuka and Karina, and then turns the rifle on himself. The two people killed by Niisi had mocked the hunting abilities of the father and son.[9] All interpretations of the film state that he shoots wildly all over and ends up killing these two (Gant 2005, 242; K. Pedersen and Sørensen 1999; Rygaard and Pedersen 2003, 166; see also Thisted 2003, 32). This may have been the case in the actual event that inspired the film: A 19-year-old Greenlandic man fires a semi-automatic rifle at a 1990 New Year's party in Narsaq, Southern Greenland, randomly killing seven people (Gant 2005, 236). This is also the scenario depicted in the manuscript (Grønlykke and Lynge 1997, 59).[10] However, in the film itself the shooting seems quite focused and only two shots are heard, one killing Nuka and the other Karina. The shooting is thus represented less as a random killing spree and more as Niisi's attempt to restore his father's honour, which ultimately happens when Rasmus returns as a *piniartorsuaq* (great hunter). This relationship between the non-hunter and the hunter is further examined in the section on national allegory.

Imagining the Inuit Community

> There probably still exists in most settlements one or more old men or women who shorten the winter nights for their fellows in the settlement by telling stories (legends); but they become fewer and fewer—and not least for that reason is it conceivable that Greenlanders themselves at some point in time will look to *The Danish Collection of Folklore* to draw their old ancestor's history and famous deeds from these sources of our knowledge.
>
> RASMUSSEN 1921, 7

---

9 Nuka had a number of times mockingly addressed Niisi as *piniartorsuaq* (great hunter), and this is Nuka's last word before Niisi shoots him. In Karina's first appearance on screen, she comments on Rasmus's hunting after Niisi turns up at her dorm room to fetch his younger brother Simon so that Rasmus and his two sons can all go hunting. Simon does not want to go, and he is certain that the plans will fall through, as usual, and that Rasmus is probably drinking at that very moment. The exchange between Niisi and Simon is in Greenlandic, which Karina understands, and she says, smiling and in Danish: "Are you going hunting now? Didn't he hunt enough yesterday?" Presumably, she is referring to Rasmus's jailing after he drunkenly shoots up the neighbourhood the previous day. Niisi gets very aggressive and shakes Karina, yelling at her to stay out of it.

10 The manuscript was published the same year the film was released. In some cases, the film departs from the printed manuscript.

As argued in chapters four and five, writing is an important part in the construction of the ontological status of the hunter and the subjectivity of the catechist. In this sub-section, I explore the very central place of writing in the film and what it enables. This will serve as an important lens through which *Heart of Light* may be framed as a national allegory, in that writing provides a crucial link to Inuit identity.

At a key moment in the film, Rasmus finds a note in the bottom of the food bag his wife, Marie, had packed for him. Marie has written the following poem on the note:

> I will visit
> Unknown woman
> Search out hidden things
> Behind the man
> Let the boot-thong hang loose
> Seek thou under man
> And under woman!
> Smooth out the wrinkled cheeks
> Smooth wrinkles out
>
> I walked on the ice of the sea
> Seal were blowing at the blowholes
> Wondering I heard
> The song of the sea
> And the great sighing of the new-formed ice
> Go, then, go!
> Strength of soul brings health
> To the place of feasting.

This poem leads Rasmus to 'remember' that one of the ways to hunt seal is to wait by the blowhole. Excited, he runs off and catches a seal with which he can feed himself and his dogs, with and leave a chunk of meat for his spiritual counsellor, Qivittoq.[11] This victory constitutes his first constructive act in the storyline, and seems to strengthen him to move on, northbound. Not only does

11 A *qivittoq* is someone who has consciously turned his/her back on society for reasons such as jealousy, shame or anger. In common lore, it was thought that the *qivittoq* gained supernatural powers from nature, such as flying through the air (Thisted 2004a, 136). In *Heart of Light*, Qivittoq possesses the knowledge that will lead Rasmus towards an understanding of his past, so he may be defined as a spiritual counsellor (Rygaard and Pedersen 2003, 176).

the poem thus fulfil an important role in the storyline of the film, it also constitutes one of two trans-Arctic references, the other being the surviving son Simon's desire to study in Fairbanks, Alaska. Simon thus represents a generation that is seen as more internationally and practically oriented, strengthening tribal ties, and not bogged down in the counterproductive mire of Denmark-Greenland relations so characteristic of his father's generation (Gant 2005, 241).

While the circumpolar orientation of Simon has been noted in various analyses of the film (Gant 2005, 241; Rygaard and Pedersen 2003, 165), the Inuit provenance of the poem, as well as its significance as an identity resource, has gone unnoticed. The poem is actually a song from Bathurst Inlet, and is one of a number of songs in the Inuit material collected on the fifth Thule expedition (1921–1924), which covered territory from Greenland to Siberia (Rasmussen 1999, 264). The trip was undertaken by Knud Rasmussen and a team that included Peter Freuchen, ethnographer Kai Birket-Smith, archaeologist Therkel Mathiassen and, most importantly, their seven indigenous helpers: Iggianguaq and his wife, Anarulunguaq; her cousin, Miteq; Arqioq and his wife, Anaranguaq; and Nasaitordluarsuk and his wife, Aqatsaq (Cole 1999, xxi).[12] As Thisted notes, the aim of the expedition was to prove the linguistic and cultural connections between the Eskimo tribes of the Arctic and thus place Greenlandic culture within a larger cultural unit (2009, 243). This particular song was one of several performed for Rasmussen by the people of Bathurst Inlet (1999, 257–267), and he has classified it as one of the Spirit Songs.

The focus on the common Arctic identity as the source of a non-Danish identity is not irrelevant, especially when considered in relation to a specific political event in the year preceding the release of the film: the establishment of the Arctic Council in 1996. This Canadian initiative to establish a council to function as an umbrella organisation for collaboration in the Arctic had been under way since 1992 (Thomsen 2006, 296). The council is a strengthening of the ties between Arctic communities and their indigenous peoples, and is an extension of the ties and Arctic politics that were consolidated with the

12 At the April 2012 opening of the Greenlandic film festival *Greenlandic Eyes* in Berlin, the Greenlandic performance artist Makka Kleist told the story of how the sacred gift of celebration was given to humans. Kleist introduced the story by noting that it was 5000 years old, written down by Knud Rasmussen on the fifth Thule exhibition, and known all over Inuit land. There is no longer a tension between oral and written transmission; they coincide in almost perfect harmony. However, is it known all over Inuit land because it was written down by Knud Rasmussen?

establishment of the Inuit Circumpolar Conference (ICC) in the late 1970s (Thomsen 2006, 200). The council was established as a

> high level intergovernmental forum to provide a means for promoting cooperation, coordination and interaction among the Arctic States, with the involvement of the Arctic Indigenous communities and other Arctic inhabitants on common Arctic issues, in particular issues of sustainable development and environmental protection in the Arctic.
>
> Arctic Council 1996

So the struggles of Rasmus, who moves from denying what he thought to be his not-quite-Danishness to discovering a pan-Inuit identity of which he is actually a part, would resonate strongly with the increasing consolidation of a circumpolar Inuit identity forged in the Arctic Council in those years.

Heart of Light presumes and advocates a pan-Inuit identity that is emphasised in Simon's desire to study in Fairbanks and, I would argue, in this song, which constitutes the only piece of (alphabetic) writing in the film. It also constitutes a significant turning point for Rasmus's journey. In the film, the pan-Inuit identity as a source for Greenlandic Inuit identity is thus transmitted in writing. Furthermore, this tradition is handed down via Knud Rasmussen's fifth Thule expedition, on which he collected this material. When Rasmus reads the song, we hear Marie's voice speaking the words, but this does not erase the fact that the song is transmitted to Rasmus in writing. That *writing* should set in motion the series of events leading to Rasmus's recovery of his Greenlandic self seems oddly out of place in a film that identifies colonial history as the source of all decline.

Nevertheless, as I have argued in chapter four, writing is crucial for the construction or representation of the Greenlander as a hunter. And the necessity of writing as a way of conserving what otherwise would have been lost, as presumed in the epigraph from Rasmussen, is, in a sense, assumed in the film. The note is what reminds Rasmus of the ways of the ancestors—just as Rasmussen hoped his collection would do for the Greenlanders.[13] To some extent, writing displaces the oral and becomes a crucial feature of recording,

---

13 The epigraph is taken from the foreword to the publication of the legends from West Greenland, and thus does not explicitly refer to the publications from the fifth Thule expedition. That preservation of Inuit material also was part of the motivation for the fifth Thule expedition is argued in Thisted's article on the narratives of that Thule expedition (2009, esp. 243).

and thus transmitting, this ethnographic material, which we see carried out in *Heart of Light*.[14]

And so, in *Heart of Light*, the hunter—once again written by the elite—is scripted into a web of intertextual allusions, which primarily refer to Rasmussen. This is not only evident in the use of the Bathurst Inlet song but also upon Rasmus's return: he is dressed from head to toe in furs and skins, not the 'European' clothes he wore going out. This, as Rygaard and Pedersen point out, echoes the early footage from Thule where Rasmussen is clad in fur (2003, 177).

Knud Rasmussen, however, was *not* a hunter. He was a celebrated Arctic explorer, born in Greenland in 1879. His maternal grandmother was Greenlandic, and he himself spoke Greenlandic fluently. Peter Gundel (whom we met in the previous chapter), characterises Rasmussen as a Danish *præstesøn* (minister's son) from Greenland (Gundel and Tølbøll 2004, 27) and stated the following after having met him: "Once, my difficult blood caught a closer glimpse of his mind and from there obtained knowledge of his sense [of importance] as a descendant of the 'Danish-Greenlandic people' who will never become hunters/capturers (Danish: *fanger*) of my primitive nation-heart." Picking up the argument from my previous chapter, this characterisation of Rasmussen is also a class issue. Rasmussen's family was part of the Danish-Greenlandic elite, and Greenlanders such as Peter Gundel regarded Rasmussen as Danish (Thisted 2004b, 120). But Knud Rasmussen was also a celebrity, an important man. When Gundel is summoned to enter Rasmussen's cabin to the surprise of all spectators, Gundel notes, "*I conquered the hero* and watched by all, including those on land, I was led into a room and was there a couple of minutes, perhaps around 10–15 mins" (Gundel and Tølbøll 2004, 251; emphasis in original). Gundel says they departed as "friends," which Gundel places in quotation marks, indicating that they were not really friends. As Thisted comments, the visit with Rasmussen on board the ship takes place like any Greenlander's visit to the grand houses (2004b, 122). There is thus a notable class difference between Gundel and Rasmussen that cannot be *reduced* to their Danish heritage, but cannot be understood apart from it, either. Furthermore, it is also necessary to analyse what Rasmussen symbolised. As one of the most pre-eminent Arctic explorers of his time, he was regarded as the chief spokesperson for indigenous people, and as a promoter of the positive rather than primitive image of the peoples of nature.

14 Pedersen notes the discursive production of an "authentic ethnic theatre" by the Tuukkaq Theatre troupe, which drew upon Rasmussen's material (which Kleist refers to as Danish) and was directed and managed by the Norwegian Reidar Nillson (1997, 164–166).

As discussed above, Rasmussen was also attempting to conserve indigenous culture before it disappeared, and he was much enamoured of the Darwinian theory of evolution, which he propagated through a series of articles in Danish and Greenlandic. In these articles, he makes the following contested remark: "[T]he future life of all peoples of nature is solely dependent on the development of its possibilities under new circumstances: the way forward must proceed over the corpse of their own race" (1920, 19). According to Thisted, the focus of the statement is less on the destruction of the old race than it is on the emergence of the new: "Through centuries the Eskimos have mixed blood with the Europeans and they have learned and acquired the European culture" (2006b, 135). The Greenlandic people are no longer Eskimos but reborn as a new people through new blood and new culture.[15] However, as Thisted notes, Rasmussen also expresses praise in the same article for the untouched Thule as the real country of the Inuit, thus retaining a romantic view of the old hunting culture alongside his evolutionary ideas. Nevertheless, it is the romantic and nostalgic view of the Eskimo and the hunting culture that has survived and is popularly regarded as Rasmussen's main contribution (2006b, 139).

Nationalising and Allegorising Greenland: National Allegory and the Global Community

National Allegory: First Take

Rasmus's struggles with himself and his past may be seen as representing the journey of a nation: Greenland coming to terms with its colonial past and present. This feature is central to what literary critic Fredric Jameson has defined as national allegory (1991). He offers the following definition: "The story of the private individual destiny is always an allegory of the embattled situation of the public Third-World culture and society" (1991, 86). "Third World" covers cultures that are neither independent nor autonomous but "locked in a life-and-death struggle with First-World cultural imperialism" (1991, 85). According to Jameson, the distinction between First- and Third-World

15 Finn Lynge argued in an early article that 'Greenland' is a synthesis of Eskimo and Danish culture: "Greenlanders today are neither Eskimos nor Danes. For more than two centuries, the Eskimos and the Danes have mingled with each other, and the present population is conscious of having left its Eskimo past behind without, however, becoming Danes, in the usual sense of the word. A new people has arisen: the Greenlanders, bilingual and of double ethnic heritage, and culturally with a past, which reaches back to both the world of the Eskimos as well as the world of the Danish-Norwegian colonisers and settlers (1970, 71)."

literatures is important because First-World literature maintains a distinction or split between private and public, a distinction that is not maintained by Third-World literature. Hence, the private and the public (nationalism and the experiences of colonialism and imperialism) in Third-World novels must necessarily be intertwined.

It must be emphasised that Jameson's understanding of the "Third World" is more complex than what can be briefly related here. These distinctions between private and public are conditioned by the economic inequality occasioned by cultural capitalism rather than some perceived backwardness inherent in the "Third World" and its literature, as I discuss later. Elsewhere, Jameson argues that major changes in global economics, politics, and culture came from the "Third World" only to become appropriated and claimed as "First-World" initiatives (1984, 182–83).

In the present context, I apply Jameson's national allegory to discuss a film from what is now known as the 'Fourth World,' the collective term for disenfranchised indigenous peoples living across national boundaries. This is not the context in which Jameson developed his theory; nonetheless, the application of national allegory within a 'Fourth-World' context will help illustrate some of the problems in Jameson's work to which Ahmad points in his critique. I return to Ahmad and Jameson in the sub-section *National Allegory: Second Take* below, but briefly point out here that it concerns the contemporary *perception* of indigenous people by non-indigenous communities, as well as the *representation* of indigenous people *by* indigenous people. While the latter issue has been substantially treated throughout this book, the former has not. They are not, however, unrelated, as I aim to show in this chapter.

Were we to see Rasmus as a symbol of Greenland, we could ask: with what kind of image of Greenland does the film present us? A Greenland that, unsure of its identity and contaminated by Danish influences that caused it to lose its way, has to cut through several hundred years of colonial history to find its pure state in its Inuit past and dispel its colonial history to make way for a future based on Greenlandic spiritual and material resources. This provokes the question: is the film attempting to erase the conditions of its own production? I would answer "yes." However, the attempt to erase the colonial past points to a different set of problems about the future. This is a complex argument that will unfold gradually.

To begin with, and to recapitulate what was explained in the first section of the present chapter, Rasmus represents both the bourgeoisie and the underclass; he then emerges as the hunter, transcending the chasm between the classes. The hunter is understood as the unifying figure around which they all can gather and reunite according to ancestral customs of reconciliation.

However, there is one figure missing in this gathering: Rasmus the non-hunter, who through the ancestral discourse has shed the "non-" in "non-hunter" to become a hunter. At the same time, this means that Rasmus the alcoholic has been written out of cinematic existence. Rasmus the alcoholic is not only the result of colonialism but also poses a problem to be solved. The hunter is seen as the answer.[16] In the film, the problem as well as its solution is seen as a masculine issue. I shall explore this issue of abject masculinity further because this is the narrative that the film urges us to pursue. If one follows this dominant narrative, then the conditions of the film's production are suspended. It is this narrative and its agenda that I want to question in my own analysis, as I will argue in the rest of the chapter, after outlining the film's presentation of abject masculinity.

Abject Masculinity

After the funeral of the shooting victims, Rasmus lies on the sofa. Marie hits him, sobbing, and wails: "What kind of man are you?" Within the narrative of the film, the answer must be: not much of one. If Rasmus as a failed hunter is tantamount to a failure as a man, the film does not leave much room for diverse models of masculinity in contemporary Greenland, which is the brunt of the critique of Pedersen and Rygaard noted above. The bumbling alcoholic is not an unknown figure in contemporary Greenlandic society. As a figure, he is indicative of a range of social issues in post/colonised societies and dysfunctional assertions of masculinity, most commonly domestic violence and substance abuse.[17]

---

16 The same applies to the more recent film *Inuk*, also known as *Le Voyage d'Inuk* (2012) by Mike Magidson. See promotional material here http://www.inuk-film.com/.

17 See Brendan Hokowhitu's entry on indigenous and First-Nation masculinities in the *International Encyclopaedia of Men and Masculinities* (2007). In this article, Hokowhitu discusses important issues such as: the Western construction of indigenous masculinities as fixed, traditional, and patriarchal; the educational system's role in assimilation to colonising masculinities and the cultural rupture this occasioned; the inequality between indigenous men and their colonisers; and, the social problems arising from dysfunctional assertions of masculinity. The brevity and general nature of Hokowhitu's entry is very telling of the *International Encyclopaedia of Men and Masculinities* project as a whole: Considerable space is devoted to histories of masculinities in various countries, while indigenous and First Nation masculinities are brought together in a single article, thereby giving low priority to the specific nature of various populations.

As noted in chapter one, sociologist Mariekathrine Poppel draws on the work of Connell to establish hunting as the hegemonic masculinity that then becomes threatened under colonialism.[18] In particular, following the marginalisation of Greenlandic men, Poppel identifies the rapid industrialisation of the 1950s and 1960s and the importing of Danish seasonal labour as reasons for the extensive social problems faced by Greenland today (Poppel 2005b). Her argument corresponds to the narrative structure of *Heart of Light*. This notion that non-white men have been and continue to be emasculated through processes of racism, colonialism, and imperialism is known as "the emasculation thesis," and was most commonly developed in black masculinity studies. The earliest proponent of this thesis is Franz Fanon, but Robert Staples (1982) and David Marriott (2000) also promulgate the same argument. As Tim Edwards argues in his study on masculinity, one of the problems with this thesis is the insistence on systemic emasculation as the root of all violence and social ills—in other words, violence, sexism, and homophobia are regarded as systemic and hence beyond the responsibility of the individual man (2006, 66). Indeed, anthropologist Bo Wagner Sørensen notes in an article on the representation of violence and Greenlandic men that this tends to present men's violence as a reflection of their vulnerable position in society (2001), thus denying them social agency and positioning them as victims of social change.

Poppel works with the emasculation thesis, and draws on Connell as the main theorist. This combination consequently generates an *under*developed notion of systemic violence and a corresponding emphasis on visible violence.[19] I seek to complicate the notion of violence and use it to discuss Poppel and Sørensen's analyses of violence via a brief reading of Rasmus's character. Although Rasmus does not exhibit physical violence, unlike, for example, Jake 'The Muss' Heke in Lee Tamahori's 1994 film *Once Were Warriors*, he nevertheless displays self-destructive and erratic behaviour, warranting a closer look at violence in order to situate the emasculation thesis within a more complex structure.

---

18 Both Mike Donaldson (1993) and Charlotte Hooper (2001) point to Connell's structuralism as being problematic, and indeed I argue that this structuralism impedes any suggestion of external influences or challenges to Connell's concept of masculinity, which inevitably reproduces his own cultural conditions. Precisely for that reason, I find Connell's approach less useful in theorising the systemic inequalities generated by colonial power and its consequences for local gender formations.

19 It is worth remembering that Tim Edwards's critique of studies working with the emasculation thesis was directed more at the underdeveloped nature of most of the analyses, and their lack of theorisation (2006, 70).

In his study on violence, Žižek distinguishes between subjective violence and two forms of objective violence. Subjective violence is directly visible violence (crime, conflict, unrest), while objective violence is subdivided into symbolic violence, "embodied in language and its forms" (2008, 1), and systemic violence. Žižek (2) argues that subjective and objective violence cannot be perceived from the same standpoint because subjective violence is always seen in relation to a "non-violent zero-level" as an aberration to the peaceful and normal state of things, while objective violence is inherent to the peaceful and normal state of things and is, as such, invisible. This parallax is the result of neoliberal mystification, which obstructs the immediate insight into the systemic and symbolic violence inherent in the status quo. As Ellen Meiksins Wood (1995, 256) points out in a different context, "the cult of civil society also tends to reproduce the mystifications of liberalism, disguising the coercions of civil society and obscuring the ways in which state oppression itself is rooted in the exploitative and coercive relations of civil society."

To apply this to the case at hand: when both Sørensen and Poppel take domestic violence as their point of departure, they focus on subjective violence. Poppel construes the marginalisation of men and domestic violence as a consequence of rapid industrialisation and growth. Sørensen, however, rejects this master narrative of a transition from traditional to modern society that usually governs analyses of domestic violence, and instead advocates an approach that takes individual agency into account (2001, 1994). While Sørensen emphasises individual agency as the point of departure, Poppel emphasises external reasons for domestic violence. Although Sørensen does not therefore venture outside subjective violence, Poppel does—to some extent. Poppel (2005b) points to the profound cultural invasion of Christianity and its introduction of new ideals of masculinity, as well as the symbolic violence enacted by the catechists in the shaming of violent men. She interprets violence as an integral part of the pre-colonial habitus, which became unacceptable in colonial Christian culture, and thus today manifests itself as domestic violence.

Although I find Sørensen's point concerning the master narrative of transition well taken, I find his emphasis on the individual to be problematic because it places subjective violence in the foreground and thus veils symbolic and systemic violence. As I argued above, the Danish colonial administration set a powerful dynamic in motion that led to a variety of social manifestations in terms of race and class. In the course of the present study, I have suggested that the project of masculinising the catechist inevitably produces an other, which is evident in *Heart of Light* as the emasculated abject—the social underclass. In the film, this particular understanding of masculinity is ousted from the limited number of acceptable ways of being a man. Therefore, privileged masculinities, such as that of Frederik Berthelsen, cannot be constructed without abject masculinity, like that of Peter Gundel. These masculinities in turn build on preconceived notions of race and intellect, generating profound social differences, which I have labelled "class."

Consequently, I find the separation of subjective violence from systemic violence just as one-sided and fruitless as the individual separated from the social. Instead, we must ask: what does the individual enactment of violence say about objective violence? How are the two related?[20] If, as critics of the emasculation thesis claim, the focus on systemic violence negates individual responsibility, then why cannot the same be said for the reverse, namely that the focus on the individual is in danger of eliding systemic violence and its discursive formations? This is where the governmentality thesis, especially its accentuation of the encounter between technologies of self and technologies of domination, is useful; it simultaneously pays attention to the individual and to systemic conditions. And so *Heart of Light* relies on a relatively unsophisticated version of the emasculation thesis via colonial footage and repeated references to Denmark-Greenland issues, causing us to focus on systemic violence to the detriment of individual agency. A return to Jameson's national allegory will enable us to refocus and consider Rasmus as an allegory for Greenland.

Before returning to Jameson and national allegory, I must make one more point concerning gender so as to use it to discuss the broader global context of the film. If we read Rasmus as representing Greenlandic society through the concept of national allegory, we need to briefly address the problem of men representing the social—not an unfamiliar trope in feminist theory. In her analysis of the body politic and representation, Moira Gatens (1996, 21) draws attention to "metonymical representation of a complex body by a privileged part of that body." The body politic is a masculine body politic, which in early contract theory is used to construct a unity (1996, 23). However, are we looking at the same construction as the one we encounter in the social-contract theories of Hobbes and Locke, and which Gatens (1996, 25; see also Pateman 1988) calls a male fantasy—the masculine body politic? Not quite. Gatens (1996, 23) notes that the inclusive nature of the body politic is exclusive, and that it excludes not only women, as Carol Pateman notes, but also indigenous people, children and the working class.

Here Charles Mills's supplement to Pateman's *Sexual Contract* becomes pertinent in that Mills draws attention to the colonial context as well as the social

20 I thank Elaine Kelly for pressing me on this point in developing the argument on abject masculinity.

consequences of these contract theories (1997). As an indigenous man, Rasmus is hardly in a privileged position within Western society; indeed, the first third of the film goes to great pains to show how dysfunctional Rasmus really is. The vindicated Rasmus who returns, and around whom society 'falls into place,' can very well be seen as a masculinist fantasy. In the film, the masculinist fantasy is a contrast to the disenfranchised indigenous man within a westernised and modern urban Greenland. The fantasy thus reinstates the Greenlandic man in the transformed social space. This imaginary space is transformed from one that sought to exclude him to one where he is once again in control. In order to imagine this as possible, it is necessary to rewrite colonial history, because, within that colonial history, he has been written out or imprisoned in the 'state of nature.' In *Heart of Light*, he returns to the icescape, the 'proper' or Greenlandic imagining of that space. The identity of the hunter is here emphasised as a primary (or to use the term of Poppel and Connell, "hegemonic") mode of masculinity. Visions and spiritual counsellors are a perfectly acceptable part of this mode of masculinity, and in fact serve as connections to the past and as reservoirs of strength and wisdom, rather than being indicative of superstition and folly.[21]

National Allegory: Second Take

This possibility of the emergence of the Greenlandic/Inuit man-as-hunter at the end of the twentieth century is worth probing further because it seemingly signals a change in the conditions for indigenous people and their place in a larger global order. I do this by addressing the following questions: What is the connection between the national emphasis on the film (its Greenlandic actors, language, location, etc.) and the circumpolar context towards which the film gestures? And what does this say about indigenous people and representation on the global scene? I engage with the first question in this section, and take up the latter question in the final subsection.

Returning to Jameson, one may, following Ahmad (1992), critique the sweeping scope of Jameson's interpretation, as well as the equally sweeping term 'Third World'.[22] As Ahmad points out, Jameson's argument is governed by the

---

21 In contrast, consider the way of life envisioned in Augo Lynge's 1931 science fiction novel *300 Years After*, which envisions Greenlandic society as one of abundant commodities, rich furnishings and clothing, and a bourgeois lifestyle in which the hunter is stigmatised as quaint and tied to a superstitious worldview and life in abject poverty. Incidentally, Augo Lynge was also very influenced by Knud Rasmussen's views on race (Thisted 2006b, 140; Thorleifsen 1991).

22 Jameson's article, Ahmad's response, and Jameson's response to Ahmad were originally published in the journal *Social Text*, vols. 15 and 17, in 1986 and 1987.

desire to outline a "theory of the cognitive aesthetics of Third World literature" (Jameson 1991, 104n26, quoted in Ahmad 1992, 95), which accounts in part for these generalisations. These generalisations in turn *create* a Third World that denies the heterogeneity of its societies, its colonial histories and its class formations (Ahmad 1992, 104). It is baffling that Jameson does not even consider the conditions of the productions of the texts, and to what extent the allegories enforce a representation upon the rest of the nation. Ahmad makes the very valid point that if the 'Third World' is "constituted by the experience of colonialism and imperialism," then capitalist economic relations have to varying extents been implemented in these social formations, thus shaping these societies in its own economic image (1992, 107). This means that if one takes seriously the fact that the Third World is constituted by the experience of colonialism and imperialism, one must also take into account the profound restructuring of society generated by capitalism, thus making it difficult to imagine how these societies should also be socially undisturbed by the movements of capitalism, in particular its distinction between public and private.

Jameson is describing (and thereby constructing) a Third World that is heavily affected by capitalism, yet unshaped by it. At the very least, argues Ahmad (1992, 107), capitalism's distinction between public and private would be experienced among the urban intelligentsia, who are the producers of the texts, and thus are "caught in the world of capitalist commodities." Not only is Jameson's Third World already shaped by capitalism, but the literature he analyses is produced by the class *constituted* by capitalist development within the social formations. To use von Braun's terms, Ahmad criticises Jameson for assuming a matter untouched by *logos*, which is impossible, given the practices of colonialism and, of course, capitalism.

Ahmad's point may be illustrated by what Michael Hardt and Antonio Negri call the *production of locality* (2000). They argue that the dichotomy between the local, understood as preserving heterogeneity and difference, and the global, which "entails homogenisation and undifferentiated identity," is a false dichotomy (2000, 44) constructed from an assumption that the local is primary and natural, and simply 'was' before globalisation, against which it must be protected. However, Hardt and Negri maintain that *both* globalisation and localisation should be understood as "a *regime* of the production of identity and difference, or really of homogenization and heterogenization" (2000, 45; emphasis in original). The local—or rather the-local-as-natural—is a (very marketable) product of the global, a point with which von Braun would agree.

This is a very important point with significant implications for ideas of 'authenticity,' to which I return in the next section. But it also has repercussions for the discussion of 'First World,' 'Third World' and 'Fourth World.' As anthropologist Renato Rosaldo points out:

> The view of an authentic culture as an autonomous internally coherent universe no longer seems tenable in a postcolonial world. Neither 'we' nor 'they' are as self-contained and homogenous as we/they once appeared. All of us inhabit an interdependent late 20th-century world, which is at once marked by borrowing and lending across porous cultural boundaries, and saturated with inequality, power and domination.
>
> 1988, 87

The untenable positioning of autonomous and authentic societies reinforces Ahmad's point, namely, that capitalism has penetrated so deeply into the structures of 'Third-World' societies that making a distinction between 'First' and 'Third' worlds is virtually meaningless. I will advance the same argument in relation to 'Fourth-World' societies. Note, also, that I say *virtually* meaningless, for the ideological power of such labelling is still forceful.

If these 'World' labels have little to do with economic and cultural distinctions, and are rather ideological labels, then what does this mean for the concept of national allegory? National allegory becomes a way of *pronouncing* an identity or a feature in relation to a text. In determining the Lu Xun short story from China "Diary of a Madman" as a national allegory, Jameson simultaneously declares it a 'Third-World' text, and with this declaration follows a host of assumptions of economic development and authentic culture. Hence, Jameson identifies a feature in a text that indicates it is partially enveloped by capitalism but still retains a foothold outside of it.

We must also consider whether an author is evoking certain genres in order to frame the text in a certain way. For example, in her discussion of the 'Greenlandic nature' of the novel *Qoorqa* (1971) by Greenlandic author Ole Brandt, Thisted argues that Greenlandic authors experiment with the hierarchies of writing and orality, and employ the conventions and characteristics of oral traditions within their novels (2002, 118).[23] In such a case of conscious framing, *Heart of Light* may be seen as *claiming* an identity through a text, which brings us back to the ontological status of the hunter and the national allegory at the basic level, as explored in "National Allegory: First Take" above.

---

23 The context of Thisted's article is a discussion with linguist Karen Langgård about the nature of Greenlandic literature and to what extent this 'nature' requires a specific literary theory (see Langgård 1996; Thisted 2002).

This is where the question of *who* produces the text becomes important: it is the intelligentsia that produces representations of its nations or peoples *as though* a struggle against capitalism and global politics *were still possible.* However, the reason Jameson looks towards Third-World literature is that this literature represents struggles *within* capitalism; that is, the struggle between the national and the international, a struggle that has ceased to take place in the literature of the 'First World' (to stay with Jameson's terminology). In Jameson's own words, "national allegory should be understood as a formal attempt to bridge the increasing gap between the existential data of everyday life within a given nation-state and the structural tendency of monopoly capital to develop on a worldwide, essentially transnational scale" (1979, 94). This quotation is cited from *Fables of Aggression,* in which Jameson analyses Wyndham Lewis's *Tarr* from 1918, written at a time when the conditions for national allegory in European literature were still prevalent (see Boer 1997, 99). These conditions no longer apply; nor, I suggest, are they valid in relation to contemporary 'Fourth-World' texts and films.

Jameson's key 'Third-World' texts are from the early – and mid-twentieth century, and are therefore situated within an emerging global order, thus lending some plausibility to the idea of a conceivable struggle between nationalism and internationalism. *Heart of Light,* on the other hand, is produced in 1997 at a much more advanced stage of global capitalism, and is already a subdued and authenticated (according to Western standards) representation of indigeneity, namely, a product of what Deborah Root (1996, 73–74) calls "cannibal culture." The struggle that the film expresses as its primary struggle is the one against the colonial force. This is the level of the Danish-Greenlandic schism that Rasmus and his generation represent. However, this situation is to *some* extent resolved because the film was produced nearly 20 years after implementation of Greenlandic home rule in 1979. The reaction of the younger generation of Greenlanders, who did not find the issues of the film pertinent to their own situation, indicates as much.[24] The younger generation, represented by Rasmus's son, Simon, are instead urged to orient themselves towards the pan-Inuit identity symbolised by the hunter. This image of the Inuit resonates with the contemporary circumpolar politics and its regional focus.[25] Nevertheless, I have also argued that the hunter in colonial discourse has been

24 See note 6 and the Introduction.

25 This relationship between the national (Kalaallit Nunaat/Greenland) and the regional (Inuit) is also implied in the following quotation from the President of ICC-Greenland, Aqqaluk Lynge: "Our ancestors have lived in these vast regions for thousands of years, adapting to one of the most severe climates of the planet, living off the resources that

ontologised, and abstracted into a true Greenlandic identity, in other words as *an authenticated representation of indigeneity*.[26] What this entails, as well as the implications for indigenous communities, is the focus of this last section.

Indigenised Politics

An Australian Context

> White Australia uses Aboriginal imagery and native fauna and flora to promote tourism and other industries. These things belong to the Black Fella. However, an underlying assumption that arises out of this use of our imagery is that there has been a conciliation process through which an equitable partnership between Black Australians and White Australians has been created. Patently, blatantly, gratingly, this is not true. Never, ever has the White Fella sat down and talked with us about all of the things they now call their own (they even call us *their* Aborigines—as if we are their chattels). It is true, however, that they have talked to and at us on many, many occasions. But only on relatively minor matters like Native Title.
>
> BELL 2002; emphasis in original.

I begin with Australia because I want to explore the production and appropriation of indigeneity by (Western) consumers which Kamilaroi artist Richard Bell forcefully describes in the above quote. Australia is a suitable way into this discussion because of the discrepancy between the eager appropriation of Indigenous spirituality over against the political reality and material conditions of many indigenous Australians.[27] Bain Attwood (1996, xxvi) speaks of commodified images of Aboriginality, such as Uluru, Kakadu, and the "Power of the Land: Masterpieces of Aboriginal Art" exhibition, which have seized upon a segment of Aboriginal culture that can be appropriated into a discourse of Aboriginality, a discourse with little connection to the material conditions

---

nature could supply. Although we have been divided by political boundaries, we share the same vision through the Inuit Circumpolar Council" (http://www.inuit.org/index.php?id=134 accessed 13 April 2010).

26 Erik Gant also notes how hunting has been constructed as the indigenous marker of Greenlanders (1996, 187).

27 This is a burning issue in the work of a number of artists in Australia, including Waanyi artist Gordon Hookey (2006) and Richard Bell (2002).

of indigenous Australians. These various commodified images represent Aboriginality as a thing of the past, a representation which resonates well within the tourist industry (Attwood 1996, xxvii).[28] Indigenous Australians are thus constructed as having "deep and abiding links with the land," requirements that are also necessary to claim Native Title over a given area in Australia.

The *Native Title Act* was implemented on 1 January 1994, and constitutes the recognition in Australian law that some Indigenous people continue to hold rights to their land and waters that come from their traditional laws and customs. Two things are important for the present task in assessing 'authentic indigeneity.'[29] First, it is important to keep the actors in mind: who is granting what to whom? Second, it is significant to note what construction of indigeneity is produced, and what is required to claim Native Title. Turning to the second issue first, here is what the *Native title claimant applications: A guide to understanding the requirements of the registration test*[30] states:

> The High Court has said that laws and customs are only 'traditional' when they can be shown to be based in the laws and customs of the Indigenous society that had native title when the British first asserted sovereignty over the claim area.
>
> The court also said that this society must have continuously existed from the date of sovereignty until the present day, with the body of laws and customs of that society having been acknowledged and observed and traditionally passed on from generation to generation through to the current claim group without any substantial interruption.
>
> National Native Title Tribunal 2004, 28

28 Note the incredible attention paid at Circular Quay, Sydney, to Aboriginal performers dressed in loin cloths, painted in ochre, and playing the didgeridoo and other instruments. These performers are part of an indigenous intitiative that has as its goal to promote Aboriginal culture. The performance of indigeneity on Circular Quay helps raise money for this endeavour.

29 For discussions of authentic indigeneity, see Jeffrey Sissons, *First Peoples: Indigenous Cultures and their Futures* (2005) and Francesca Merlan, "Beyond Tradition" (2006).

30 Accessed 17 April 2010 online at http://www.nntt.gov.au/Publications-And-Research/Publications/Documents/Booklets/Native%20title%20claimant%20applications%20April%202008.pdf.
This link is no longer valid; the document is now available at http://www.nntt.gov.au/News-and-Communications/Publications/Documents/Booklets/Native%20title%20claimant%20applications%20April%202008.pdf accessed 9 April 2012.

As Bell sardonically points out:

> The NTA [*Native Title Act*] specifically requires Aboriginal People to prove that Native Title exists (in the claimed area) by means of song, dance, storytelling, etc. We have to prove that we are related to the birds, the animals, the insects, the microbes, the Earth, the Wind and fire. This is an extremely difficult task even for the Aboriginal People with minimal 'White' contact.
>
> 2002

In order to claim Native Title and land rights, Indigenous Australians therefore have to exhibit a kind of primordial aboriginality that corresponds to a set of parameters established by anthropologists, for example.[31]

The first issue mentioned above, that of agents, is explored by cultural and legal theorist Maria Giannacopoulos (2007). The point of departure in her article is the overturning of the *terra nullius* doctrine in the Mabo judgement,[32] and Giannacopoulos moves from there to discuss the nature, jurisdiction, and enactment of Australian law in relation to indigenous dispossession of land and non-British immigrants. Giannacopoulos outlines the construction of Australian law as it is staged in the Mabo judgement, and reveals how it *produces* the colonizers as non-immigrants and produces a law that is ethnically-neutral and has no jurisdictional limits:

> In this decision [Mabo] the judges are able to 'recognise' a form of native title since they have also just 'decided' to overturn the doctrine of *terra nullius*. So while they have ostensibly removed from law this much criticized doctrine, what remains firmly in place is their position of judgment. By virtue of having the power to judge, determine and decide, the judges can rule on the questions *before* the law while denying what came historically *before* white law, in fact they are able to rule precisely *because* of the denial of what came *before*. Their position of judgement

31 Evidence for this "connection to country" is affidavits, anthropological reports, and historical reports (National Native Title Tribunal 2004, 29).

32 The Mabo judgement relates to the Australian High Court judgement in "Mabo v. Queensland," a case that took ten years and resulted in a ruling in favour of Eddie Mabo. This meant that Murray Islanders held Native Title to land in the Torres Strait, thus overturning the principle of *terra nullius*, 'no man's land.' Following this ruling, the *Native Title Act* was approved by Parliament in December 1993 and was implemented on 1 January 1994.

> can generate new laws, e.g., (Mabo acts in common law terms as a fresh judgement) but the position occupied by the judges in order to make this decision, functions to *keep* an overarching white, non-ethnic, non-immigrant universalized notion of law firmly entrenched.
>
> 2007, 3; emphasis in original

Due to the denial of what came "before white law" (that is, native ownership), the judges are able to "overturn *terra nullius*," and "recognise" Native Title. It is thus only by adhering to the colonising principle of *terra nullius* that the judges can decide to overturn it. This places the judges in a position outside the law, and functions to keep the law firmly universalised. Hence, the positions of white and black, as well as the position of the universal law, are "firmly entrenched."

I now turn to these discursive constructions of indigeneity and position of judgement in relation to the International Whaling Commission (IWC) regulations for "aboriginal subsistence whaling." It should be noted that the issues raised in what follows should be regarded as highlighting the need for further research, not as conclusive analyses. The conclusions that follow are thus extensions of my examination of constructions of hunting and subjectivities rather than detailed analyses of international bodies and their structures or charters in their own right.

Aboriginal Subsistence Whaling

"In several parts of the world native peoples are dependent on whale products for survival."[33] This is the heading on the International Whaling Commission's website for the subsection on aboriginal subsistence whaling and, it seems, the logic behind the special status allotted to certain countries. Two images accompany this heading: The first depicts five men, dressed in anoraks, in a small boat with paddles, and ice and snow in the foreground. The second image is not completely clear but appears to depict a whale hauled up on the ice. The important point here is that both images present a *commonly acknowledged context* for aboriginal subsistence whaling as the Arctic—despite the fact that one of the communities to have been granted whaling rights is the Bequia community of the Caribbean. The image of the men in the boat also carries undertones of indigenous 'local' practice, with the small boat and seemingly ceremonial dress. This certainly does not reflect the contemporary practice of harpoon cannons, penthrite grenades, and rifles used to hunt whales in the Arctic. The "Report of the Workshop on Whale Killing Methods and Associated Welfare Issues" from the

33 http://www.iwcoffice.org/conservation/aboriginal.htm, accessed 18 April 2010.

Annual Report of the IWC 2003[34] indicates that the larger whaling communities (Greenland and Alaska) use grenades and harpoon cannons because these kill the whale more quickly.[35] The smaller communities, such as the Makah community in the USA and the Bequia community in Saint Vincent and the Grenadines, use 'traditional' methods, supplemented by dart guns or high-calibre rifles to comply with international conventions requiring humane deaths to the whales.[36]

The Aboriginal Subsistence Whaling (ASW) permit is granted to only a number of communities, as follows:

> Under current IWC regulations, aboriginal subsistence whaling is permitted for Denmark (Greenland, fin and minke whales), the Russian Federation (Siberia, gray and bowhead whales), St Vincent and the Grenadines (Bequia, humpback whales) and the USA (Alaska, bowhead and gray whales). It is the responsibility of national governments to provide the Commission with evidence of the cultural and subsistence needs of their people. The Scientific Committee provides scientific advice on safe catch limits for such stocks.[37]

So when did Aboriginal Subsistence Whaling begin and, given the heated debates on whaling, what notion of 'Aboriginal' is implied in this permit?

The first document to decide on action in relation to whaling is the "Convention for the Regulation of Whaling" signed in Geneva under the auspices of the League of Nations on 24 September 1931. The killing of a number of whale species was prohibited, with article 3 providing the important exception:

> The present convention does not apply to aborigines dwelling on the coast of the territories of the high contracting parties provided that:
> 1. They only use canoes, pirogues or other exclusively native craft propelled by oars or sails;
> 2. They do not carry firearms;
> 3. They are not in the employment of persons other than aborigines;
> 4. They are not under contract to deliver the products of their whaling to any third person (Convention 1931, 169).

34 The "Report of the Workshop on Whale Killing Methods and Associated Welfare Issues" is available at http://iwc.int/index.php?cID=2654&cType=document, accessed 19 April 2012.

35 Much of current whale-killing technology, especially the penthrite grenade, was developed in Norway and Japan (Workshop report, 88–89).

36 http://www.makah.com/whalingrecent.html, accessed 19 April 2010.

37 http://www.iwcoffice.org/conservation/aboriginal.htm, accessed on 17th April 2010.

The "high contracting parties" that signed the document included Albania, Denmark, Germany, USA, Belgium, Colombia, Great Britain (including Ireland and the Dominions beyond the Seas), Spain, Finland, France, Greece, Italy, Mexico, Norway, the Netherlands, Poland, Romania, Switzerland, Czechoslovakia, Turkey, and Yugoslavia. Any of these countries having aborigines dwelling on the coast of their territories will not be included in the prohibition if the above conditions are met. In this particular document, the superiority of the granting body is clear. The League of Nations stated the conditions, and thus "graciously" granted permission for the continuance of this cultural practice if it remained within the designated parameters. The colonial context of the first document is carried over into the wording of the IWC statement, with the rights being granted to Denmark rather than Greenland.

Over the years, the various adaptations and amendments to this treaty have maintained the distinction between Aboriginal Subsistence Whaling and commercial whaling (WSPA 2008, 4).[38] The definition of "subsistence" in the IWC context has been much debated (without reaching any formal agreement), but the definition of aborigines is left standing as self-evident. This is perceived as a significant problem by the World Society for the Protection of Animals (WSPA), which bemoans the lack of "any internationally agreed definition based on cultural or anthropological parameters" (WSPA 2008, 4).

I do agree that the lack of a definition for "aborigine" is a problem. But while the WSPA is aggrieved by the plasticity of the term, I am more concerned with its colonial history. If the first mention of "aborigine" in the context of whaling politics is in the Geneva document of 1931, then the term is deployed in a context of racial discrimination and segregation, with undertones of a 'primordial nature' and 'savagery.' This is an excellent example of what Attwood (1996) and Johannes Fabian (2002) call "the denial of coevalness," where the anthropological object is denied the same place in space and time as the anthropological subject. The 'aborigine' is thus outside, or beyond, 'our' time and space. This is also, in a sense, what the WSPA protests: the IWC's use of the term implies a notion of authenticity which the WSPA does not believe the Greenlanders have. Put another way, it seems that the WSPA is confident that should an anthropological or cultural definition of 'aborigine' ever be agreed upon, Greenlanders would fall outside it.

This issue brings us back to the matter of authenticity. The source of anger for the WSPA is what it calls "the myth of Greenlandic subsistence whaling," which it claims is false because Greenlandic whaling is, in fact, commercial.

38 The report is available online at http://www.wspa-usa.org/Images/ExplodingMyths_tcm21-3402.pdf.

This is "exposed" in a 2008 pamphlet entitled *Exploding Myths: An Exposé of the Commercial Elements of Greenlandic Aboriginal Subsistence Whaling.* The key problem for the WSPA, it would appear, is the nature of 'subsistence' as opposed to 'commercial.' In the pamphlet, ten key findings are presented to prove that Greenlandic whaling is commercial. A key finding is that "approximately a quarter of the total volume of whale products available from Greenlandic hunts have been purchased, processed and sold for onward retail sale by the privately owned company Arctic Green Food" (WSPA 2008, 3).[39]

In other words, whale meat is sold in supermarkets in Greenland. According to the WSPA, this violates not only the subsistence/commercial distinction, but also the aboriginal/non-aboriginal distinction, since even "foreign nationals" may purchase whale meat in the supermarket (WSPA 2008, 3). Another finding is that "[h]unters generally prefer to sell their products at local markets, where the best prices of 30–40 DKK/kg (US $6.30–$8.40/kg) are paid. Once these markets are saturated, the hunters have the option of selling their goods to Arctic Green Food for around 20 DKK/kg (US $4.20/kg)" (WSPA 2008, 3).

These are highly contentious and explosive political issues,[40] but I am concerned here with the idea of aboriginality expressed in the conceptions of 'local' and 'subsistence' at work in this pamphlet. The WSPA seems to rely on 'the ontological status of the hunter' visualised in Rasmus in *Heart of Light* and the 'kinship networks' to which he *should* belong. According to the pamphlet he should not be dressed in GORE-TEX® and rubber boots, he should not be using a speedboat or a Winchester rifle, a Kongsberg 50mm harpoon cannon, and penthrite grenades. Furthermore, any idea of making a profit from hunting is seen as a commercial and thus 'non-aboriginal' feature, which is clear in the following quotation by anthropologist Mark Nutall that appears in the pamphlet: "Put simply, commercial whaling is intensive, large-scale, and potentially unsustainable if mismanaged. Commercial whaling also aims to maximize profits. Subsistence whaling, on the other hand, is considered to be small-scale, sustainable and aimed at satisfying local needs. Furthermore, there is no profit incentive that drives subsistence whaling—it is inextricably linked to and underpins the culture and economy of aboriginal peoples" (cited in WSPA 2008, 16). This is also part of a larger colonial discourse on

---

39 WSPA notes that at least 114 supermarkets in Greenland carry whale products for retail sale, and that the commercial sale of Arctic Green Food's retail products generates the equivalent of US $1 million annually.

40 For a fascinating study into the emergence of an anti-whaling discourse in the second half of the twentieth century, see Charlotte Epstein's *The Power of Words in International Relations: Birth of an Anti-Whaling Discourse* (2008).

aboriginality, namely, that capitalism, economic gain, and development are fundamentally 'non-indigenous.'[41]

The pamphlet also operates with a naive notion of the local as being outside the global, and thus not marked by concepts like money and profit. However, as noted in the above discussion of *Heart of Light*, Greenlandic society has also been profoundly reshaped by capitalism, which influenced not only hunting patterns but also distribution practices. The colonial shops in Greenland came to replace the old system of bartering with English and Dutch whalers in the course of colonisation, and became the place where hunters would trade their catch for credit instead of distribution and internal exchange. Thus, the subsistence/commercial distinction as understood by the WSPA was already untenable 200 years ago.

In response to a 2007 advertisement by the WSPA in the Danish newspaper *Information*, the North Atlantic Group[42] submitted the following petition to the Environmental Department in the Danish Parliament:

> We want the same principles to operate in the usage of all the ocean's resources, whether we are talking about herring, cod, tuna, seals or whales. If the populations can sustain hunting, they should be used to feed people. We are opposed to sacred sea cows—especially when enforced upon us by others, who do not suffer the slightest consequences, either culturally or financially. *We would rather catch the whales commercially, in the same way we catch shrimps and halibut, than being reduced to cultural weirdos, who most graciously are allowed to slaughter a couple of sacred cows, while we are being suffocated by dubious manipulators on the animal welfare market.*[43] We are perfectly aware that renewed,

---

41 This discourse is not limited to Greenland. See Eve Darian-Smith's (2002, 2004) work on Native American casinos. For indigenous development in Australia see, e.g., Banerjee (2004) and Banerjee and Tedmanson (2010), and for a discussion of the Ngai Tahu tribe in Aotearoa New Zealand, see Sissons (2005, 152–153). See also the article in the *Sydney Morning Herald* "Green Activism 'Keeping Aborigines in Poverty,'" where Marcia Langton, an indigenous academic, argues that "the environmental movement has emerged as 'one of the most difficult of all the obstacles hindering Aboriginal economic development'" http://www.smh.com.au/national/green-activism-keeping-aborigines-in-poverty-20121123-29yz2.html#ixzz2DPV09EpA, accessed 27 November 2012.

42 The North Atlantic group was an independent coalition within the four elected members of the Danish Parliament from Greenland and the Faroe Islands working for full independence from Denmark. It was founded in 2001, and dissolved after the Danish federal election of September 2011.

43 This particular quote is printed in the WSPA pamphlet in a different translation which reads: "We would rather catch the whales commercially, like we catch shrimps and

> internationally controlled commercial whaling can have an impact on our quotas – we certainly do not need WSPA to attempt to lecture us and belittle us as though we were colonial children—since this would make our hunting into a normal industry, which is highly preferable to this ethnic charity.
>
> JOHANSEN, HOYDAL AND ROSSEN 2007

Here it is apparent that the North Atlantic Group is reacting strongly not only to what they see as paternalistic measures forced on them by others, but also the implication that they are ignorant of sustainable and responsible hunting practices. The IWC's Scientific Committee provides advice on safe catch limits for such stocks, and permits are granted on this basis. The North Atlantic Group sees as demeaning that the Greenlanders themselves should be perceived as unable to take stock, and instead must be allotted quotas by a third party on account of their aboriginal status. Instead, they want the right to develop whale hunting as a sustainable industry without having to defend the sale of whale meat in supermarkets.

The clashes between Greenlandic hunters and the WSPA are indicative of a larger set of problems framed by colonial discourse.[44] Whereas hunting as a practice has continued through and beyond colonisation, it has been overshadowed by a parallel construction: the ontological status of the hunter, which arose as part of internal Greenlandic identity politics and colonial discourse. While the ontological status of the hunter governs Aboriginal Subsistence Whaling rights, the North Atlantic Group advocates *repossession,* understood in Jeffrey Sissons's sense as "less a recovery of the past than a return of things or people to indigenous agency" (2005, 143) and a reclaiming of "the ability to be diversely authentic in a rejection of the racism and essentialism that characterized settler regimes of identification" (2005, 148).

As we see in *Heart of Light*, the ontological status of the hunter has taken on a stereotypical function as the authentic Greenlandic identity that controls or even overrides representations of indigeneity at national levels, a process I have traced in the preceding three chapters of the present study. However, this stereotype is also evident in the notions of aboriginality in the IWC's Aboriginal Subsistence Whaling rights, as well as the WSPA's expectations of

---

halibut, than being reduced to cultural weirdos, who most gratefully are allowed to slaughter a couple of sacred cows, while we are being manipulated by the animal welfare market" (WSPA 2008, 16).

44 See also the disturbing chapter on the Makah whale hunt in Ter Ellingson's *The Myth of the Noble Savage*, which analyses the 'Noble Savage' rhetoric deployed in the political debates surrounding this whale hunt in 1999 (2001, 359–372).

indigenous identity, and fits into global ideas of indigeneity as being 'primordial' and, in a sense 'sacred' to Western identity—that is, above and beyond change. Within this image, ideas of development and indigenous profit-making seem offensive and directly anti-aboriginal. However, that these representations are being challenged may be gleaned not only from the North Atlantic Group but also the reactions of the younger generation to *Heart of Light*. This is, however, not only a struggle between indigenous people and the 'West;' it is also very much a struggle within the indigenous communities themselves.

Conclusion

Returning to *Kolonihavnen* in Nuuk, we have now traversed the church, the catechist college, the Inspector's printing press, and the meat market. What then is the connection between Frederik Berthelsen and contemporary international whaling policies?

Beginning from the end, I have taken the *Native Title Act* in Australia and the Aboriginal Subsistence Whaling Rights of the International Whaling Commission as my points of departure to analyse the concept of indigeneity inherent in contemporary policies. I argue that these processes reinforce cultural stereotypes of indigenous people, and contain indigenous people in a primordial compartment within a larger global order. The increasing UN-affiliated networks that pertain to the rights of indigenous people play a part in this global construction.[1] I do not deny the importance these networks have had for empowering indigenous people. Instead, I point to their 'soft underbelly,' how these non-governmental organisations also foster and contain a certain perception of indigeneity that is, potentially, just as stereotypical as that of 'the noble savage.' While my analysis has been positioned in relation to the IWC's policies, similar questions could be directed at, for example, the 2007 UN Declaration on the Rights of Indigenous Peoples.[2] These questions concern what Sissons calls "oppressive authenticity," which "requires that the distinctions between 'native' and 'settler' be continuously reproduced, although always in new guises" (2005, 39).

Such a representation of indigeneity is manifested as an ideal identity in the Greenlandic film *Heart of Light*, in which the hunter is portrayed as the solution to a masculine identity crisis generated by colonialism. The film resolves the struggle against colonialism in the lead character's transition from a dysfunctional local Greenlandic alcoholic to an Inuit hunter. However, I argue that this cinematic production and its understanding of indigeneity rest on particular class conditions that can be traced back to the colonial past, and which the film attempts to erase, or at the very least, obscure.

---

1 Hardt and Negri define non-governmental organisations as one of empire's powers of intervention precisely because of their non-affiliation with the structures of the state (2000, 312).

2 See the incredibly provocative article by Adam Kuper (2003), in which he points to some of the problems in defining indigenous communities, and how the UN resorted to archaic anthropological essentialisms to define what is indigenous (nomads or hunters; in harmony with nature) about indigenous people. Indeed, Kuper claims that "native" and "indigenous" are merely euphemisms for "primitive." While Kuper's article has caused much offense (see the discussion and references in Barnard 2006), he nevertheless raises important issues.

The crucial figure is the 'man of nature,' or the 'ontological status of the hunter' as produced by colonialism. Whereas most previous studies emphasise that the colonial powers fostered the image of Greenlanders as part of nature, I stress that the Greenlandic catechists simultaneously (i) produced themselves as individual subjects, abstracted and detached from (ii) what became constructed as nature, to which their fellow-Greenlanders belonged. I thus shift the role of the colonisers to one of setting coordinates within which the various groups of Greenlanders could operate. The way in which such a production could take place, I argue, is through writing as a gendered governmental technique. I suggest that the transformation of the oral tradition enabled it to function as a mirror, objectifying Greenlanders as hunters and nature. The catechists played a central role in this process by recording and copying the material that at the same time subjectified them as producers of nature. This process was intensified by their employed positions, which required constant journal writing, prompting them to regard their surroundings from the perspective of the observer. In this context, the figure of the hunter is of particular interest because it became central not only in the construction of the catechist identity but also during the Greenlandic identity debates of the early twentieth century.

The catechists, primarily men of 'mixed' background, were handpicked by the missionaries. In the mid-nineteenth century, this practice became institutionalised with the establishment of the catechist colleges, when formal education took shape. Frederik Berthelsen was one of the first men to be singled out and favouritised by the missionary in charge, before this became standard practice. My analysis of the dynamics between the missionary and his catechists in chapter one indicates not only the web of mastery in which missionary Hveyssel and Frederik Berthelsen are caught, but also the emergence of a Greenlandic elite self, which was more drawn to the lifestyle of the Danes than to the Greenlandic hunting lifestyle.

What holds this narrative together is the matter of subjectification, which is a crucial undercurrent of the present work and discussed in chapters two and three. As noted in chapter six, I have avoided using postcolonial terminology to analyse the situation in Greenland because, following Ahmad, I do not regard it as attentive to social stratification. Postcolonial theory does not sufficiently examine the non-subject, the merely represented, and the abject,[3] but rests on a celebration of the hybrid as the ambivalent subject-position of postcolonial discourse, and an erasure of its own conditions of emergence, as was the case

3 Some uses of 'the subaltern' could come close, but the use of the term within postcolonial discourse is so obscure that it mystifies more than explains.

with *Heart of Light*. Instead I have chosen Michel Foucault's theory of subjectification, *governmentality*, to analyse the dialectic between the individual and the social structure, because in such an analysis it becomes clear who is subjectified, how, and why. The social structure under scrutiny in this book has been the Danish colonial administration of Greenland, which set the parameters for the construction of subjects and their complementary objects. The main ideology of the colonial administration was, as argued in chapter three, Lutheranism. By regarding Lutheranism as an ideology, I emphasise its social dimensions and realm of influence, following Foucault's notion of pastoral power as that which exceeds the institutional confinement of the church and extends into ways of governing and constituting subjects. The particular Protestant inflection that I identified in the Lutheran pastorate was that of catechism, which subordinates the individual within a hierarchical social structure. The technologies of self become the means by which individuals shape themselves within the designated framework. In this case, I have identified writing as a fruitful way of tracing not only how elite individuals made sense of themselves and their surroundings within the new framework of the Lutheran social structure implemented by colonialism, but also how they produce abstractions of Greenlandic identity.

In his introduction to the chapter on Danish colonialism in *A Historical Companion to Postcolonial Literatures: Continental Europe and its Empires*, cultural theorist Lars Jensen (2008, 62) remarks on the scarcity of English-language material dealing with postcolonial Denmark, as well as the existing Danish material, which "suffers from a lack of attention to the power paradigm which the Danish state spread over its possessions." While I do not claim that the present work is a postcolonial analysis of Denmark, I have nevertheless paid detailed attention to Danish state power and the implementation of this power on one of its "possessions." My approach to this issue arises from a personal dissatisfaction with the general academic trend of simplifying and edifying narratives of mission and Lutheranism in Greenland. The logic of these mission narratives colludes neatly with commonplace narratives of secularisation that separate the missionaries from the colonisers, thereby not only constructing a 'pure' notion of Evangelical-Lutheran Protestantism, but also ignoring its cultural influence and invasive understandings of gender, class, and society.

My task has therefore involved the problematisation and complication of these compartmentalising narratives by way of a critical appropriation of a number of theoretical concepts, including Foucault's concept of governmentality as a particular subjectification practice. I have analysed the colonial administration's Lutheran subjectification practice on a segment of the Greenlandic population, namely men from 'mixed' families. I have then traced the subjectification of these men as catechists, which involved the process of an ontologisation of the hunter, abstracted from the every-day practice of hunting. Utilising such concrete analyses in the course of the colonial history of Greenland and Denmark, I have shown how the missionaries implemented their own ideological systems. Beginning with the informal racialised missionary politics of the eighteenth century teased out from the reports to the missionary college on the Habakuk movement, I traced how these informal policies became institutionalised in the educational practices of the nineteenth century, and resulted in the fragmentation and governmentalisation of the Greenlandic people in the twentieth century.

My aim with this analysis was threefold. First, I set to troubling the distinction between colonial powers and missionaries by showing that the idealisation of the hunter was quite reliant on technologies of self—in this particular case, writing—which, as a colonial instrument of power, was firmly connected to scripture. The relations between writing and the production of truth, alphabetised Greenlandic and representation, and the abstracted self and nature, are all contingent on the bible as scripture containing the absolute truth. I am not asserting that 'the hunter' is really a Christian figure; instead, I argue that the hunter is an abstraction of ideal identity that grew out of a representational practice connected to Western writing practices. Writing carried an absolute authority due to its connection to scripture as well as the power structures it enabled through controlled access to education and training.

A second basic aim of the study was to show the extent of cultural invasion enacted within Greenlandic society. To do so, I traced the gradual institutionalisation of the catechist, paying attention to the racial and social politics that paved the way for this particular group to become part of the Greenlandic ruling class. Through this emphasis, I problematised synchronic approaches to ideas of race, and placed them within a political and administrative structure at a much earlier stage in the colonial system. I argued that the Danish colonial administration implemented ideas of race and class that influenced and structured society in certain ways, developing distinctions and alliances that continue to shape present-day Greenland.

Finally, I have emphasised the hunter as a product of colonial ideologies of race and explored the subjectification process of the catechist. I showed particular interest in how the missionaries fostered a rational, controlled masculinity, which simultaneously set the catechists outside Greenlandic nature even as they were producing it. This meant tracing the strategies of implementing a Lutheran ideal of rationality over against Greenlandic 'folly', Lutheran Protestant Christianity over against Greenlandic superstition, Protestant civilisation over against Greenlandic nature, and writing over against orality. While there are multiple examples of Greenlandic subversions of these imposed hierarchies, it was not been my intention to point to such deconstructions: I paid close attention to the binary logic of the colonisers to show how they effectively intervened into Greenlandic society, segregated the population, implemented governing and disciplining strategies, and fostered a ruling class that proceeded to construct society from preconceived ideals of 'nature' and 'civilisation.' I chose to focus on the ontological status of the hunter as an overarching figure, not only in Greenlandic identity politics but also in contemporary global politics. Such a perspective disclosed how indigenous self-representation was discursively constrained and conditioned by colonial categories of representation, and how these power structures continue to haunt indigenous politics in Greenland.

My attempt to complicate the colonial web of power by emphasising the role of the emerging Greenlandic ruling class should not be seen as an attempt to exonerate the Danish colonial administration: my focus on cultural practices such as writing was deployed to emphasise the fact that Danish cultural interventions in Greenland were, as Nicholas Dirks puts it, "not antidotes to the brutality of domination but extensions of it. Representation in the colonial context was violent; classification a totalizing form of control" (1992, 5). The Danish colonial administration fundamentally reconfigured Greenlandic society and its power structures. It implemented means of surveillance and control that were constantly refined to match the social situation. It exploited, humiliated, and belittled Greenlanders. In sum, I sought to show the insidiousness and pervasiveness of Danish enactments of power, the class differences it established, and the mess it left behind. As stated in my Introduction, my intent has been to draw attention to the processes of colonial construction in an attempt to unravel it. I have attempted the task of tracing the complex process of colonial governmentality founded upon colonial politics, social inequality, racial prejudice, and patriarchal privilege, well aware that this can only ever be a beginning.

Bibliography

Primary References

All primary references are from Rigsarkivet (*Danish National Archives*).

Missionskollegiet og Direktionen for Vajsenhuset: Indkomne sager den grønlandske mission vedk. 1786–88, folder 1786, no. 14: Hveyssel's report to the Missionary Department, 7 September 1786.

Missionskollegiet og Direktionen for Vajsenhuset: Indkomne sager den grønlandske mission vedk. 1786–88, folder 1786, no. 14: Merchant Lund's account from 1785–86.

Missionskollegiet og Direktionen for Vajsenhuset: Indkomne sager den grønlandske mission vedk. 1786–88, folder 1788, no. 15: Hveyssel's report to the Missionary Department, 30 June 1788.

Missionskollegiet og Direktionen for Vajsenhuset: Indkomne sager den grønlandske mission vedk. 1789–91, folder 1789, no. 23: Hveyssel's report to the Missionary Department, 14 August 1789.

Missionskollegiet og Direktionen for Vajsenhuset: Indkomne sager den grønlandske mission vedk. 1789–91, folder 1789, no. 29: Report from Andreas Ginge to the Missionary department, 27 August 1789.

Missionskollegiet og Direktionen for Vajsenhuset: Indkomne sager den grønlandske mission vedk. 1789–91, folder 1789: Otho Fabricius's report on Kolonien Sukkertoppen to the Missionary Department, 12 June 1790.

Missionskollegiet og Direktionen for Vajsenhuset: Indkomne sager den grønlandske mission vedk. 1789–91, folder 1790, no. 23: Hveyssel's report to the Missionary Department, 30 June 1790.

Missionskollegiet og Direktionen for Vajsenhuset: Indkomne sager den grønlandske mission vedk. 1788–91, folder 1791, no. 13: Hveyssel's report to the Missionary Department, 23 July 1791.

Missionskollegiet og Direktionen for Vajsenhuset: Indkomne sager den grønlandske mission vedk. 1788–91, folder 1791, no. 24: Hveyssel's letter to the Missionary Department, 15 August 1791.

Secondary References

Agamben, Giorgio. 1998 [1995]. *Homo Sacer: Sovereign Power and Bare Life.* Translated by D. Heller-Roazen. Stanford, CA: Stanford University Press.

Ahmad, Aijaz. 1992. *In Theory: Classes, Nations, Literatures.* London: Verso.

——. 1992. "Jameson's Rhetoric of Otherness and the 'National Allegory'." In his *In Theory: Classes, Nations, Literatures,* 90–122. London: Verso.

Althusser, Louis. 1997 [1951]. "On Conjugal Obscenity." In *The Spectre of Hegel: Early Writings.* Edited with an Introduction by François Matheron. Translated by G.M. Goshgarian, 231–240. London: Verso.

Anderson, Benedict. 2006 [1983]. *Imagined Communities Reflections on the Origin and Spread of Nationalism,* rev. ed. London & New York: Verso.

Annett, Kevin D. 2001. "Hidden From History: The Canadian Holocaust—The Untold Story of the Genocide of Aboriginal Peoples by Church and State in Canada—A Summary of an Ongoing, Independent Inquiry into Canadian Native 'Residential Schools' and their Legacy." The Truth Commission into Genocide in Canada.

Arias, Arturo. 2009. "Anti-Colonial Struggle in Latin-America from the Conquista to the Present" In *A Historical Companion to Postcolonial Literatures: Continental Europe and its Empires.* Edited by P.K. Poddar, L. Jensen, and R.S. Patke, 522–526. Edinburgh: Edinburgh University Press.

Arnfred, Signe. 1991. "Kvinder, mænd, arbejde og seksualitet i den grønlandske moderniseringsprocess." In *Kvinder i Grønland – sammen og hver for sig.* Edited by Lise Lennert, 82–125. Nuuk: Atuakkiorfik.

Aron. 1999. *Således skriver jeg, Aron. Samlede fortællinger og illustrationer af Aron fra Kangeq.* Edited by K. Thisted. Nuuk: Atuakkiorfik.

Asad, Talal. 1992. "Conscripts of Western Civilisation." In *Dialectical Anthropology: Essays in Honour of Stanley Diamond.* Vol. 1, *Civilisation in Crisis.* Edited by C. Gailey, 333–351. Gainesville: University Press of Florida.

Attwood, Bain, ed. 1996. Introduction. In *In the Age of Mabo: History, Aborigines and Australia,* vii-xxxvii. Sydney: Allen & Unwin.

Bærenholdt, Jørgen Ole. 2007. *Coping with Distances: Producing Nordic Atlantic Societies.* Oxford: Berghahn Books.

Banerjee, Subhabrata. 2004. "Indigenous Incorporated or Indigenous Recolonised? A Comment." *Current Anthropology* 45 (2): 224–225.

Banerjee, Subhabrata, and Deirdre Tedmanson. 2010. "Grass Burning under our Feet: Indigenous Enterprise Development in a Political Economy of Whiteness." *Management Learning* 41 (2): 147–165.

Barnard, Alan. 2006. "Kalahari Revisionism, Vienna and the 'Indigenous Peoples' Debate." *Social Anthropology* 14 (1): 1–16.

Beinssen-Hesse, Silke, and Kate Rigby. 1996. *Out of the Shadows: Contemporary German Feminism.* Melbourne: Melbourne University Press.

Bernauer, James, and Jeremy Carrette, eds. 2004. *Michel Foucault and Theology: The Politics of Religious Experience.* Farnham: Ashgate.

Beverley, John. 2009. "Colonial Baroque." In *A Historical Companion to Postcolonial Literature: Continental Europe and its Empires*. Edited by L. Jensen, P.K. Poddar, and R.S. Patke, 536–545. Edinburgh: Edinburgh University Press.

Blake, Lynn A. 1999. "Pastoral Power, Governmentality and Cultures of Order in Nineteenth-Century British Colombia." *Transactions of the Institute of British Geographers* 24 (1): 79–93.

Blanco, John D. 2009. *Frontier Constitutions: Christianity and Colonial Empire in the Nineteenth-Century Philippines*. Berkeley: University of California Press.

Bloch, Ernst 1987 [1961]. *Natural Law and Human Dignity.* Translated by D.J. Schmidt. Cambridge, MA: MIT Press.

Boer, Roland. 1996. *Jameson and Jeroboam* (*Society of Biblical Literature Semeia Studies*). Atlanta: Scholars Press.

——. 1997. "National Allegory in the Hebrew Bible." *Journal for the Study of the Old Testament* 74:95–116.

——. 2007. *Criticism of Heaven: On Marxism and Theology*. Leiden: Brill.

Bredsdorff, Thomas. 2003. *Den brogede oplysning. Om følelsernes fornuft og fornuftens følelse i 1700 tallets nordiske litteratur*. København: Gyldendal.

Breinholt Larsen, Finn. 1997. "Scoresbysund: A Hunting Community in East Greenland." In *The Anthropology of Community-Based Whaling in Greenland: A Collection of Papers Submitted to the International Whaling Commission.* Edited by Marc G. Stevenson, Andrew Madsen and E.L. Maloney, 103–125. Edmonton: Canadian Circumpolar Institute, University of Alberta.

Brown, Wendy. 2006. *Regulating Aversion: Tolerance in the Age of Identity and Empire*. Princeton, NJ: Princeton University Press.

Brydon, Diana. 1989. "Commonwealth or Common Poverty?" In *After Europe: Critical Theory and Post-Colonial Writing.* Edited by S. Slemon and H. Tiffin, 1–16. Sydney: Dangaroo Press.

Buch-Hansen, Gitte. 2007. "It is the Spirit that Makes Alive (John 6:63). A Stoic Understanding of Pneuma in John." PhD diss., Copenhagen University.

Burchell, Graham, Colin Gordon, and Peter Miller, eds. 1991. *The Foucault Effect*. Chicago: University of Chicago Press.

Burrus, Virginia. 2004. *The Sex Lives of Saints: An Erotics of Ancient Hagiography.* Philadelphia: University of Pennsylvania Press.

Carter, J. Kameron. 2008. *Race: A Theological Account.* Oxford: Oxford University Press.

Castelli, Elizabeth A. 1991. *Imitating Paul: A Discourse of Power*. Louisville, KY: Westminster/John Knox.

——. 2004. *Martyrdom and Memory: Early Christian Culture Making*. New York: Columbia University Press.

Chow, Rey. 1993. *Writing Diaspora: Tactics of Intervention in Contemporary Cultural Studies*. Bloomington: Indiana University Press.

Christensen, Magnus. 2007. "Kirke og statsdannelse 1536–1660." *Den jyske historiker* 116:76–92.

Chrulew, Matthew. 2011. "Foucault and the Genealogy of Christianity." PhD diss., Monash University.

Clark, Elizabeth A. 1999. *Reading Renunciation: Asceticism and Scripture in Early Christianity*. Princeton, NJ: Princeton University Press.

——. 2004. *History, Theory, Text: Historians and the Linguistic Turn*. Cambridge, MA: Harvard University Press.

Cohn, Bernard S. 1996. *Colonialism and its Forms of Knowledge: The British in India*. Princeton, NJ: Princeton University Press.

Cole, T. 1999. Introduction. In *Across Arctic America:. Narrative of the Fifth Thule Expedition,* xi–xxxviii. Fairbanks: University of Alaska Press.

Collins, James, and Richard K. Blot. 2003. *Literacy and Literacies: Texts, Power and Identity*. Cambridge: Cambridge University Press.

Comaroff, Jean, and John Comaroff. 1991. *Christianity, Colonialism and Consciousness in South Africa*. Vol. 1 of *Of Revelation and Revolution*. Chicago/London: University of Chicago Press.

——. 1997. *The Dialectics of Modernity on a South African Frontier*. Vol. 2 of *Of Revelation and Revolution*. Chicago/London: University of Chicago Press.

Connell, Robert/RaewynW. 1993. "The Big Picture: Masculinities in Recent World History." *Theory and Society* 22 (5): 597–623.

——. 2005. *Masculinities*. 2nd ed. Oxford: Blackwell.

Cranny-Francis, Anne. 1992. *Engendered Fictions: Analysing Gender in the Production and Reception of Texts*. Sydney: New South Wales University Press.

Cross, F.L., and E.A. Livingstone, eds. 2005. *The Oxford Dictionary of the Christian Church*. 3rd ed. Oxford: Oxford University Press.

Dahl, Jens. 1986. *Arktisk Selvstyre*. København: Akademisk Forlag.

——. 2000. *Saqqaq: An Inuit Hunting Community in the Modern World*. Toronto: University of Toronto Press.

Darian-Smith, Eve. 2002. "Savage Capitalists: Law and Politics Surrounding Indian Casino Operations in California." *Studies in Law, Politics, and Society* 26:109–137.

——. 2004. *New Capitalists: Law, Politics, and Identity Surrounding Casino Gaming on Native American Land*. Belmont, CA: Thomson/Wadsworth.

Dean, Mitchell. 1999. *Governmentality: Power and Rule in Modern Society*. London: Sage Publications.

Derrida, Jacques 1998 [1967]. *Of Grammatology*. Translated by G.C. Spivak. Baltimore, MD: Johns Hopkins University Press.

DIIS (Dansk Institut for Internationale Studier). 2007. *Afvikling af Grønlands kolonistatus 1945–54. En historisk udregning.* Copenhagen: DIIS.

Dirks, Nicholas B., ed. 1992. Introduction. In *Colonialism and Culture*, 1–25. Ann Arbor, MI: University of Michigan Press.

Dirlik, Arif. 1994. "The Postcolonial Aura: Third World Criticism in the Age of Global Capitalism." *Critical Inquiry* 20 (2): 328–356.

Donaldson, M. 1993. "What is Hegemonic Masculinity?" *Theory and Society* 22 (5): 643–657.

Duedahl, Poul. 2003. "Dansk raceantropologi i Grønland." *Historisk Tidsskrift* 103:335–358.

Dupré, Louis. 1993. *Passage to Modernity: An Essay in the Hermeneutics of Nature and Culture.* New Haven, CT: Yale University Press.

——. 2004. *The Enlightenment and the Intellectual Foundations of Modern Culture.* New Haven/London: Yale University Press.

Dyer, Richard. 1997. *White.* London: Routledge.

Edwards, Tim. 2006. *Cultures of Masculinity.* London: Routledge.

Egede, Hans. 1745. *A Description of Greenland.* London: C. Hitch.

——. 1925. *Relationer fra Grønland 1721–36.* Edited by L. Bobé. *Meddelser om Grønland.* København: Bianco Lunos bogtrykkeri.

Egede, Paul. 1766. *Testamente Nutak eller Det Nye Testamente oversat i det Grønlandske sprog, med Forklaringer, Paralleler og udförlige Summarier.* Kiøbenhavn: Trykt paa Missionens bekostning af Gerhard Giese Salikath.

——. 1788. *Efterretninger om Grønland uddragne af en journal holden fra 1721 til 1788 af Paul Egede.* Edited by M. Lidegaard. *Det Grønlandske Selskabs skrifter 29.* København: Det Grønlandske Selskab.

Egede, Paul, and Niels Egede. 1939. *Continuation af Hans Egedes relationer fra Grønland.* Edited by H. Ostermann Vol. 120, *Meddelelser om Grønland.* København: C.A. Reitzels Forlag.

Ellingson, Ter. 2001. *The Myth of the Noble Savage.* Berkeley: University of California Press.

Epstein, Charlotte. 2008. *The Power of Words in International Relations: Birth of an Anti-Whaling Discourse.* Cambridge, MA: MIT Press.

Fabian,Johannes. 2002 [1983]. *Time and the Other: How Anthropology Makes its Object.* New York: Columbia University Press.

Fatum, Lone. 1982. "Forsagelse og heksejagt. Kvindespejlinger fra diskriminationens historie." *Kvindestudier* 6 (Kvindens naturer): 39–87.

Felbøl, Britta. 1983. *Grønlandske kvinder i en brydningstid*, Social Studies & Geography, Roskilde Universitetscenter, Roskilde.

Fetscher, Iring. 1985. "Class Consciousness." In *A Dictionary of Marxist Thought.* Edited by T. Bottomore, 79–81. Oxford: Blackwell.

Fienup-Riordan, Ann. 1995. *Freeze Frame: Alaska Eskimos in the Movies.* Singapore: University of Washington Press.

Fleischer, Jørgen. 1999. "Dagligliv i kolonitiden, Hjemmestyre, partier." In *Inuit, kultur og samfund-en grundbog i eskimologi.* Edited by J. Lorentzen, E.L. Jensen, and H.C. Gulløv, 205–214. Århus: Systime.

Foucault, Michel. 1996 [1978]. "What is Critique?" In *What is Enlightenment? Eighteenth-Century Answers and Twentieth-Century Questions.* Edited by J. Schmidt, 382–398. Berkeley/Los Angeles: University of California Press.

——. 1998 [1976]. *The Will to Knowledge: The History of Sexuality.* Vol. 1. Translated by R. Hurley. London: Penguin Books.

——. 2000a. "Technologies of the Self." In *Ethics: The Essential Works of Foucault 1954–1984.* Edited by P. Rabinow, 223–351. London: Penguin Books.

——. 2000b. "On the Genealogy of Ethics." In *Ethics: The Essential Works of Foucault 1954–1984.* Edited by P. Rabinow, 253–280. London: Penguin.

——. 2000c. "The Subject and Power." In *Power: The Essential Works of Foucault, 1954–1984.* Edited by J.D. Faubion, 326–348. London: Penguin.

——. 2000d. "Governmentality." In *Power: The Essential Works of Foucault 1954–1984.* Edited by P. Rabinow, 201–222. London: Penguin.

——. 2000e. "Self Writing." In *Ethics: The Essential Works of Foucault 1954–1984.* Edited by P. Rabinow, 207–222. London: Penguin.

——. 2002. "Truth and Power." In *Power: The Essential Works of Michel Foucault, 1954–1984.* Edited by J.D. Faubion, 111–133. London: Penguin.

——. 2007. *Security, Territory, and Population. Lectures at the Collège de France* 1977–1978. Edited by Michael Senellart. Translated by Graham Burchell. New York: Palgrave Macmillan.

——. 2008. *The Birth of Biopolitics: Lectures at the Collège de France, 1978–1979.* Edited by Michael Senellart. Translated by Graham Burchell New York: Palgrave Macmillan.

Frandsen, Niels. 1999. "Lært at læse – og hvad så?" *Grønlandsk kultur og samfundsforskning* 1998/99: 201–215.

Gad, Finn. 1969. *Grønlands historie, vol. 2, 1700–1782.* København: Nyt Nordisk Forlag.

——. 1974. *Fire detailkomplekser i Grønlands historie 1782–1808.* København: Nyt Nordisk Forlag Arnold Busck.

——. 1976. *Grønlands historie.* Vol.3, *1782–1808.* København: Nyt Nordisk Forlag.

Gagnier, Regenia. 1991. *Subjectivities: A History of Self-Representation in Britain, 1832–1920.* Oxford: Oxford University Press.

Gant, Erik. 1996. "Den excentriske eskimo." *Tidsskriftet Grønland* 1996 (6): 169–193.

——. 2000. "Grønland som begivenhed." In *Grønlandsk kultur – og samfundsforskning 98/99*, 125–134. Nuuk: Atuagkat.

——. 2005. Eskimotid. Analyser af filmiske fremstillinger af eskimoer med udgangspunkt i postkolonialistisk teori og med særlig vægtning af danske grønlandsfilm, Ph.D diss., Institut for Æstetiske Fag, Afdeling for Æstetik og Kultur – Tværæstetiske Studier, Aarhus University, Århus, Denmark.

Gatens, Moira. 1996. *Imaginary Bodies: Ethics, Power, and Corporeality*. London: Routledge.

Gessain, Robert. 1970 [1969]. *Ammassalik. Den påtvungne civilisation.* Translated by J. Juhl-Jensen. København: Rhodos. Original edition, Ammassalik.

Giannacopoulos, Maria. 2007. "Nomos Basileus: The Reign of Law in a World of Violence." *ACRAWSA e-journal* 3 (1): 1–12.

Gierke, Otto 1957. *Natural Law and the Theory of Society 1500 to 1800.* Translated by Ernest Barker Boston: Beacon Press.

——. 1987. *Political Theories of the Middle Age*. Cambridge: Cambridge University Press.

Glahn, Henric Christopher. 1921. *Dagbøger for årene 1763–64, 1766–67*. Edited by H. Ostermann. *Det Grønlandske selskabs skrifter IV*. København: Det Grønlandske Selskab.

Glebe-Møller, Jens. 2010. "Protestantisme og magt. Sammenblanding af regimenterne." *Kritik* 195: *Protestantisme og politik*: 21–25

Goldberg, David Theo. 1993. *Racist Culture: Philosophy and the Politics of Meaning.* Oxford: Blackwell.

——. 2002. *The Racial State*. Oxford: Blackwell.

Golder, Ben. 2007. "Foucault and the Genealogy of Pastoral Power." *Radical Philosophy Review* 10/2: 157–176.

Goodman, Dena. 2005. "L'Ortografe des Dames: Gender and Language in the Old Regime." In *Women, Gender, and Enlightenment.* Edited by S. Knott. & B. Taylor. Palgrave Macmillan. Original edition, French Historical Studies 25 (Spring 2002): 195–223.

Goody, Jack, ed. 1968. Introduction. In *Literacy in Traditional Societies*. Cambridge: Cambridge University Press.

——. 2000. *The Power of the Written Tradition*. Washington DC: Smithsonian Institution Press.

Gordon, Colin. 1991. "Governmental Rationality: An Introduction." In *The Foucault Effect: Studies in Governmentality.* Edited by G. Burchell, C. Gordon, and P. Miller, 1–51. Chicago: University of Chicago Press.

Gorski, Philip S. 2003. *The Disciplinary Revolution: Calvinism and the Rise of the State in Early Modern Europe.* Chicago: University of Chicago Press.

Grau, Marion. 2011. *Rethinking Mission in the Postcolony: Salvation, Society and Subversion.* London: Continuum Press.

Gray, Marion W. 2000. *Productive Men, Reproductive Women: The Agrarian Household and the Emergence of Separate Spheres during the German Enlightenment*. New York: Berghahn Books.

Grønlykke, Jacob, and Hans Anton Lynge. 1997. *Qaamarngup uummataa/Lysets hjerte. Filmiliassamut najoqqutassiaq/Filmmanuskript*. Nuuk: Atuakkiorfik.

Gundel, Peter, and Gudrun Tølbøll, ed. 2004. *Jeg danser af glæde. Peter Gundel. Dagbogsbreve 1923–1930*. København: Det Grønlandske Selskab.

Hackel, Steven W., and Hilary E. Wyss. 2010. "Print Culture and the Power of Native Literacy in California and New England Missions." In *Native Americans, Christianity, and the Reshaping of the American Religious Landscape*. Edited by Joel W. Martin and Mark A. Nicholas, 201–221. Chapel Hill: University of North Carolina Press.

Hannah, Matthew G. 2000. *Governmentality and the Mastery of Territory in Nineteenth-Century America*. Cambridge: Cambridge University Press.

Hardt, Michael, and Antonio Negri. 2000. *Empire*. Cambridge, MA: Harvard University Press.

Heinrich, Jens. 2012. *Eske Brun og det moderne Grønlands tilblivelse* Nuuk: Atuagkat.

Hermansen, Karsten. 2005. *Kirken, kongen og enevælden*. Odense: Syddansk Universitetsforlag.

Hertling, Knud. 1999. "Udvikling – på danske forudsætninger." In *Kalaallit Nunaat. Gyldendals bog om Grønland*. Edited by B. Gynther and A. Møller, 259–266. København: Gyldendalske Boghandel Nordisk Forlag.

Himmelweit, Susan. 1985. "Exploitation." In *A Dictionary of Marxist Thought*. Edited by T. Bottomore. Oxford: Blackwell.

Høiris, Ole. 1982. "Heinrich Johannes Rinks teoretiske ideer." *Tidsskriftet Grønland* 1982 (1): 28–34.

——. 1983. "Grønlænderne i dansk antropologi før 2. Verdenskrig." *Tidsskriftet Grønland* 1983 (1): 30–46.

——. 1986. *Antropologien i Danmark. Museal etnografi og etnologi 1860–1960*. København: Nationalmuseet.

Hokowhitu, Brendan. 2007. "Indigenous and First Nation Masculinities." In *International Encyclopaedia of Men and Masculinities*, 331–334. London: Routledge.

Hookey, Gordon. 2006. "Terrorism and Terraism." *Borderlands e-journal* 5(1).

Hooper, Charlotte. 2001. *Manly States: Masculinities, International Relations, and Gender Politics*. New York: Columbia University Press.

Huggan, Graham. 2001. *The Postcolonial Exotic: Marketing the Margins*. London: Routledge.

Hull, Isabel V. 1997. *Sexuality, State, and Civil Society in Germany, 1700–1815*. New York: Cornell University Press.

Hunter, Ian. 1994. *Rethinking the School: Subjectivity, Bureaucracy, Criticism*. New York: St Martin's Press.

——. 1998. "Uncivil Society: Liberal Government and the Deconfessionalisation of Politics." In *Governing Australia: Studies in Contemporary Rationalities of Government.* Edited by Mitchell Dean and Barry Hindess, 242–264. Cambridge: Cambridge University Press.

——. 2001. "Christian Thomasius' Attack on Protestant Scholasticism." *ANZHES* 30/1.

Ingesman, Per. 2010. "Skriften, Loven og Sværdet. Mosaisk lovs indflydelse på dansk retsudvikling efter reformationen." *Kritik* 195: *Protestantisme og politik*: 12–20.

James, Roberta. 1997. "Rousseau's Knot: The Entanglement of Liberal Democracy and Racism." In *Race Matters: Indigenous Australians and 'Our' Society.* Edited by G.A.M. Cowlishaw and Barry Morris, 53–75. Canberra: Indigenous Studies Press.

Jameson, Fredric. 1979. *Fables of Aggression: Wyndham Lewis, the Modernist as Fascist.* Berkeley: University of California Press.

——. 1984. "Periodizing the 60s." In *The 60s without Apology.* Edited by S. Sayres, 178–209. Minneapolis: University of Minnesota Press.

——. 1991. "Third-World Literature in the Era of Multinational Capitalism." *Pretexts: Studies in Writing and Culture* 3 (1–2): 82–104.

Jennings, Eric. 2004. *Vichy in the Tropics: Petain's National Revolution in Madagascar, Guadeloupe, and Indochina, 1940–44.* Stanford, CA: Stanford University Press.

Jennings, Willie James. 2010. *The Christian Imagination: Theology and the Origins of Race.* New Haven, CT: Yale University Press.

Jensen, Karsten Sejr. 1980. Trolddom i Danmark 1500–1588, MA thesis, Copenhagen University.

Jensen, Lars. 2008. "Denmark and its Colonies: Introduction." In *A Historical Companion to Postcolonial Literatures—Continental Europe and its Empires.* Edited by P.K. Poddar, R.S. Patke, and L. Jensen, 59–62. Edinburgh: Edinburgh University Press.

Juschka, Darlene M. 2009. *Political Bodies/Body Politic: The Semiotics of Gender.* London: Equinox.

Karlsen, Mads Peter. 2008. "Pastoralmagt – om velfærdssamfundets kristne arv." København: Anis.

Kipp, Rita Smith. 1990. *The Early Years of a Dutch Colonial Mission: The Karo Field.* Ann Arbour: University of Michigan Press.

Kjærgaard, Katrine. 2009. Grønland som en del af den bibelske fortælling: Studier i billeder og forestillinger 1721–2008. PhD diss., Ilisimatusarfik/Grønlands Universitet/University of Greenland.

Kjærgård, Mona-Lene. 1982. Den grønlandske kvinde: En sammenlignende analyse af grønlandske kvinders placering i udviklingen af Grønland med kvinders placering i udviklingslandene generelt, Political Science, Aarhus University, Århus, Denmark.

Kleivan, Inge. 1986. "The Virgin Mary of Tasiussaq: A Case of Feminism." *Arctic Anthropology* 23 (1–2): 221–238.

——. 1995. Efterskrift. In *Livet på de yderste øer. Beretninger af den grønlandske fanger Johannes, kaldet Ungaaralak.* Edited by F. Nielsen, 95–119. Nuuk: Atuakkiorfik.

——. 1999. "Habakuk og andre profeter i Vestgrønland." In *Inuit, kultur og samfund. En grundbog i Eskimologi.* Edited by J. Lorentzen, E.L. Jensen, and H.C. Gulløv, 49–54. Århus: Forlaget Systime.

Kleivan, Inge, and Birgitte Sonne. 1985. *Eskimos, Greenland and Canada (Iconography of Religions Section 8—Arctic Peoples).* Leiden: Brill.

Koch, Hal, and Bjørn Kornerup, eds. 1951. *Den danske kirkes historie.* 8 vols. Vol. 5. København: Gyldendalske Boghandel Nordisk Forlag.

Koefoed, Nina Javette. 2008. *Besovede kvindfolk og ukærlige barnefædre. Køn, ret og sædelighed i 1700-tallets Danmark.* København: Museum Tusculanums Forlag.

Kreutzmann, Jens. 1997. *Jens Kreutzmann: Fortællinger og akvareller.* Edited by K. Thisted. Nuuk: Atuakkiorfik.

Kuper, Adam. 2003. "The Return of the Native." *Current Anthropology* 44(3): 389–395.

Lackey, Michael. 2009. "Foucault, Secularization Theory, and the Theological Origins of Totalitarianism." In *Foucault's Legacy.* Edited by C.G. Prado, 124–145. London/New York: Continuum.

Laclau, Ernesto. 1990. *New Reflections on the Revolution of Our Time.* London: Verso.

Laclau, Ernesto, and Chantal Mouffe. 2001 [1985]. *Hegemony and Socialist Strategy: Towards a Radical Democratic Politics.* London: Verso.

Langgård, Karen. 1996. "Does Greenlandic Literature Call for a Specific Greenlandic Literary Theory." *Cultural and Social Research in Greenland 95/96: Essays in Honour of Robert Petersen*: 158–170.

——. 1998. "An Examination of Greenlandic Awareness of Ethnicity and National Self-Consciousness through Texts Produced by Greenlanders 1860s-1920s." *Etudes/Inuit/Studies* 22 (1): 83–107.

——. 1999a. "Fishermen are Weaklings: Perceptions of Fishermen in *Atuagalliuttit* before the First World War." In *From Sealing to Fishing: Social and Economic Change in Greenland, 1850–1940.* Edited by O. Marquardt, P. Holm, and D.J. Starkey, 40–61. Esbjerg: Fiskeri – og Søfartsmuseet.

——. 1999b. "Vestgrønlænderes syn på østgrønlændere gennem tiden." *Grønlandsk kultur og samfundsforskning* 98/99: 175–200.

——. 2000. "Natursynet i den grønlandske litteratur." In *Nordisk litteratur og mentalitet.* Edited by M. Marnersdóttir and J. Cramer, 299–308. Torshavn: Faroe University Press.

——. 2004. "Ordinationsritualer i Grønland – set diakront ud fra en postkolonial synsvinkel." *Kirkehistoriske Samlinger* 2004: 71–108.

——. 2008a. "Race and Ethnicity, Greenland." In *A Historical Companion to Postcolonial Literatures – Continental Europe and its Empires.* Edited by P.K. Poddar, R.S. Patke, and L. Jensen, 92–95. Edinburgh: Edinburgh University Press.

Lauridsen,Thomas Kring, and Kaspar Lytthans. 1983. Det grønlandske kald. MA thesis, Institut for Etnologi og Antropologi, Københavns Universitet, København.

Lévi-Strauss, Claude. 1989 [1955]. *Tristes Tropiques*. Translated by J.A.D. Weightman *Picador Classics*. London: Pan Books.

Lidegaard, Mads. 1986. "Profeterne i Evighedsfjorden." *Tidsskriftet Grønland* 34 (6–7): 177–244.

——. 1993. *Grønlændernes kristning*. Nuuk: Atuakkiorfik.

Lloyd, Genevieve. 1993 [1984]. *The Man of Reason: 'Male' and 'Female' in Western Philosophy*. Minneapolis: University of Minnesota Press.

Lynge, Finn. 1970. "Mission og kirke i det yderste nord. Et forsøg på analyse og vurdering." *Tidsskriftet Grønland, 1970*(3): 65–79.

——. 2006. "Tro og udsyn." In *Grønland i Verdenssamfundet. Udvikling og forandring af normer og praksis*. Edited by Hanne Petersen, 95–116. Nuuk: Atuagkat.

MacCormack, Carol, and Marilyn Strathern, eds. 1980. *Nature, Culture and Gender*. Cambridge: Cambridge University Press.

Mamdani, Mahmood. 1996. *Citizen and Subject: Contemporary Africa and the Legacy of Late Colonialism*. Princeton, NJ: Princeton University Press.

Manniche, Jens Christian. 2002. Sprogbeherskelse og Herskersprog – om sprog og kolonialisme i Grønland i 1800-tallet. Århus: Historisk Institut, Aarhus Universitet.

Marchal, Joseph A. 2008. *The Politics of Heaven: Women, Gender, and Empire in the Study of Paul*. Minneapolis, MN: Fortress Press.

Marquardt, Ole. 1998. "Lønarbejdere som overklasse – om den grønlandske arbejderklasse i 1800-tallet." *Arbejderhistorie* 1998 (2):1–14.

——. 1999. "An Introduction to Colonial Greenland's Economic History." In *From Sealing to Fishing: Social and Economic Change in Greenland 1850–1940*. Edited by O. Marquardt, P. Holm, and D.J. Starkey, 7–17. Esbjerg: Fiskeri – og Søfartsmuseet.

——. 2000. "Reservation, Westernization or Annihilation: A Comparison of US Indian Policy and Danish Eskimo Policy in the 19th Century." Edited by I. Sigurdsson and J. Skaptáson 68–80. *Aspects of Arctic and Subarctic History: Proceedings from the International Congress on the History of the Arctic and Subarctic Region*. Reykjavik.

Marriott, David. 2000. *On Black Men*. Edinburgh: Edinburgh University Press.

MartinJoel W., and Mark A. Nicholas, eds. 2010. *Native Americans, Christianity, and the Reshaping of the American Religious Landscape*. Chapel Hill: University of North Carolina Press.

Marx, Karl. 1979. *The Eighteenth Brumaire of Louis Bonaparte*. In *Karl Marx & Frederick Engels Collected Works*. Vol. 11, 99–197. Moscow: Progress Publishers.

McClintock, Anne. 1995. *Imperial Leather: Race, Gender and Sexuality in the Colonial Conquest*. New York/London: Routledge.

Meiksins Wood, Ellen. 1995. *Democracy Against Capitalism: Renewing Historical Materialism*. Cambridge: Cambridge University Press.

Merlan, Francesca. 2006. "Beyond Tradition." *The Asia Pacific Journal of Anthropology* 7 (1): 85–104.

Milloy, John S. 1999. *A National Crime: The Canadian Government and the Residential School System, 1879 to 1986*. Winnipeg: University of Manitoba Press.

Mills, Charles W. 1997. *The Racial Contract*. Ithaca, NY: Cornell University Press.

Moi, Toril. 2002 [1986]. *Sexual/Textual Politics*. 2nd ed. *New Accents*. London: Routledge.

Møller, Poul B., and Susanne Dybbroe. 1981. Om betingelserne for Grønlands kolonisering, MA thesis, Institut for forhistorisk arkæologi, middelalder-arkæologi, etnografi og socialantropologi, Aarhus, Århus.

Moore, Stephen D. 1996. *God's Gym*. London/New York: Routledge.

——. 2001. *God's Beauty Parlor and other Queer Spaces in and around the Bible*. Stanford, CA: Stanford University Press.

Moore-Gilbert, Bart. 1997. *Postcolonial Theory: Contexts, Practices, Politics*. London: Verso.

Moreton-Robinson, Aileen. 2003. "I Still Call Australia Home: Indigenous Belonging and Place in a White Postcolonizing Society." In *Uprootings/Regroundings: Questions of Home and Migration*. Edited by Sara Ahmed, Claudia Castañeda, Anne Marie Fortier, and Mimi Sheller, 23–40. Oxford: Berg.

——, ed. 2004. *Whitening Race*. Canberra: Aboriginal Studies Press.

——, ed. 2007. *Sovereign Subjects: Indigenous Sovereignty Matters*. Sydney: Allen & Unwin.

Moxnes, Halvor, Jostein Børtnes, and Dag Øistein Endsjø, eds. 2002. *Naturlig sex? Seksualitet og kjønn i den kristne antikken*. Oslo: Gyldendal Akademisk.

Nuttall, Mark. 1992. *Arctic Homeland: Kinship, Community and Development in Northwest Greenland*. Toronto: University of Toronto Press.

O'Hanlon, Rosalind, and David Washbrook. 1992. "After Orientalism: Culture, Criticism, and Politics in the Third World." *Comparative Studies in Society and History* 34/1: 141–167.

Olden-Jørgensen, Sebastian. 2001. "Historien om et ritual. De danske kongekroninger fra Christian III (1537) til Christian IV (1596)." *Transfiguration. Nordisk tidsskrift for kunst og kristendom* 3 (1): 83–99.

Olrik, Jørgen. 1923. "Oversætterens indledning" In *Fejekost. Til at udfeje den gamle Surdejg eller de i de danske Lande tiloversblevne og her for Dagen bragte Levninger af saavel Hedenskab som Papisme*. København: Det Schønbergske Forlag.

Olsen, Tupaarnaq Rosing. 2005. *I skyggen af kajakkerne. Grønlands politiske historie 1939–79*. Nuuk: Atuagkat.

Ong, Walter J. 1982. *Orality and Literacy: The Technologizing of the Word*. London: Routledge.

Ostermann, H. 1921. *Den grønlandske missions og kirkes historie*. København.

——, ed. 1939. *Poul og Niels Egede: Continuation af Hans Egedes Relationer fra Grønland samt Niels Egedes Beskrivelse over Grønland, Meddelser om Grønland 120*. København: Kommissionen for Videnskabelige Undersøgelser i Grønland, C.A. Reitzels Forlag.

——. 1945. *Danske i Grønland i det 18. Aarhundrede*. København: C.A. Reitzels.

Paine, Robert, ed. 1971. *Patrons and Brokers in the East Arctic*. St. John's: Institute of Social and Economic Research, Memorial University of Newfoundland.

Pateman, Carole. 1988. *The Sexual Contract*. Stanford, CA: Stanford University Press.

Pedersen, Birgit Kleist. 1997. "Den ædle vilde som projekt. Synet på forfædrene i den grønlandske litteratur i perioden 1970–1990." *Grønlandsk kultur og samfundsforskning* 97:153–173.

Pedersen, Johannes 1951. "Pietismens tid. 1699–1746." In *Den Danske kirkes historie*. Edited by H.K. and B. Kornerup, 11–229. København: Gyldendalske Boghandel Nordisk Forlag.

Peikoff, Tannis. 2002. Anglican Missionaries and Governing the Self: An Encounter with Aboriginal Peoples in Western Canada, 1820–1865. PhD diss., University of Manitoba.

Pestana, Carla Gardina. 2009. *Protestant Empire: Religion and the Making of the British Atlantic World*. Philadelphia: University of Pennsylvania Press.

Petersen, Robert. 1974. "Some Considerations Concerning the Greenlandic Longhouse." *Folk* 16–17 (1974/1975): 171–188.

——. 1990. "On the Material Element in the Supernatural Aspect of the Former Greenlandic Religion." *Temenos* 26:95–103.

——. 1996. "Body and Soul in Ancient Greenlandic Religion." In *Shamanism and Northern Ecology*. Edited by J. Pentikäinen. Berlin/New York: Mouton de Gruyter.

——. 2003. *Settlements, Kinship and Hunting Grounds in Traditional Greenland: A Comparative Study of Local Experiences from Upernavik and Ammassalik*, (*Meddelelser om Grønland*). Copenhagen: Danish Polar Centre.

Peterson, Jacqueline, and Jennifer S.H. Brown, eds. 1985. *The New Peoples: Being and Becoming Métis in North America, Manitoba Studies in Native History*. Winnipeg: The University of Manitoba Press.

Petterson, Christina. 2007. "Kap farvel til Umanarssuaq": Bibel – og menneskesyn i Paul Egedes fortale til oversættelsen af det Ny Testamente til grønlandsk. *Dansk Teologisk Tidsskrift* 70/1: 103–115.

——. 2008. "En engleskare stor." Kirken og dens menighed i Grønland', Religion, 2008/4: 44–52

——. 2009. "Habakuk og Maria Magdalena – nu også i kønshistorisk belysning." *Grønlandsk kultur og samfundsforskning* 2008–9: 14–29.

——. 2012a. "En konge i sin faders sted. Bibel og konge i den danske enevælde." In *Bibelske Genskrivninger*. Edited by Mogens Müller and Jesper Høgenhaven, 413–434. Copenhagen: Museum Tusculanums Forlag.

——. 2012b. "Configuring the Language to Convert the Pagans: Translation and Conversion in Greenland." In *Ideology, Culture, and Translation*. Edited by S. Elliott and R. Boer Atlanta: Society of Biblical Literature.

Plumwood, Val. 1993. *Feminism and the Mastery of Nature*. London: Routledge.

Pontoppidan, Erik. 1923 [1736]. *Fejekost. Til at udfeje den gamle Surdejg eller de i de danske Lande tiloversblevne og her for Dagen bragte Levninger af saavel Hedenskab som Papisme*. Translated by J. Olrik. København: Det Schønbergske Forlag.

Poppel, Mariekathrine. 2005a. "Barrierer for grønlandske mænd på arbejdsmarkedet." In *Arbejdsmarkedet i Grønland. Fortid – nutid og fremtid.* Edited by A.V. Carlsen, 125–140. Nuuk: Ilisimatusarfik.

——, ed. 2005b. "Køn og vold under kulturelle forandringer i det koloniale Grønland." In *Suiaassuseq persuttaasarnerlu/Køn og vold i Grønland* Nuuk: Atuagkat., 176–194.

Porter, Eric. 1981. The Anglican Church and Native Education: Residential Schools and Assimilation. PhD diss., University of Toronto.

Pratt, Angela M. 2003. Indigenous sovereignty–never ceded": sovereignty, nationhood and whiteness in Australia. PhD diss., University of Wollongong. Available on http://treatyrepublic.net/content/indigenous-sovereignty-never-ceded-sovereignty-nationhood-and-whiteness-australia accessed 19th April 2012.

Pugliese, Joseph. 1994. "Embodied Economies of Colonialism and Desire in Hegel's Empire of Reason." *Social Semiotics* 4 (1–2): 163–183.

Rafael, Vicente L. 1993 [1988]. *Contracting Colonialism: Translation and Christian Conversion in Tagalog Society under early Spanish Rule*. Paperback ed. Durham/London: Duke University Press.

Randell-Moon, Holly. 2008. A Broad Church: Representations of Religion, Race and National Identity under the Howard Government. PhD diss., Macquarie University, Sydney.

Rasmussen, Hans-Erik. 1982. "Socio-symboler og etno-politiske symboler i Grønland eksempler fra 1930–40'erne samt fra perioden ca. 1976–1982" In *Nordisk Etnografmøde*. København, 20.-22. oktober 1982.

——. 1983. Social endogami og symbolbrug i Vestgrønland analyse af nogle strukturelle karakteristika ved reproduktion af dele af den koloniale samfundsformation, samt bidrag til en analyse af nogle former for brug af visuelle symboler blandt kvinder i det vestgrønlandske øvre sociale lag, MA thesis, Institut for Eskimologi, Københavns Universitet, Copenhagen.

——. 1986a. "Genealogier og social stratifikation: eksempler fra Grønland." *Fortid og nutid* XXXIII (2): 81–164.

——. 1986b. "Some Aspects of the Reproduction of the West Greenlandic Upper Social Stratum, 1750–1950." *Arctic Anthropology* 23 (1–2): 137–150.

——. 1986c. "Ændringer i husholdsstruktur og genealogiske relationer, Fiskenæsset, Vestgrønland ca. 1834–1911 case study." Stockholm, juni 1986.

——. 1987. "On Socio-genealogies in South West Greenland, 1750–1950: Some Explanatory Sketches." University of Tromsø, Norway, May 31 to June 2, 1987.

Rasmussen, Knud. 1920. Tanker om Grønlændere i Fortid og Fremtid. Indledning. *Danmarksposten* Januar: 17–20.

——. 1921. *Myter og Sagn fra Grønland vol 2*. København: Gyldendalske Boghandel Nordisk forlag.

——. 1999. *Across Arctic America: Narrative of the Fifth Thule Expedition*. Fairbanks: University of Alaska Press.

Reinhartz, Adele. 1999. "'And the Word was Begotten': Divine Epigenesis in the Gospel of John. *Semeia* 85: God the Father in the Gospel of John: 83–103.

Richarz, Irmintraut. 1991. *Oikos, Haus und Haushalt: Ursprung und Geschichte der Haushaltsökonomik*. Göttingen: Vandenhoeck & Ruprecht.

Richter, Lise. 2009. Da der var vilde mennesker i Zoo. *Information*.

Rink, Hinrich Johannes. 1862. Om Aarsagen til Grønlændernes og lignende, af Jagt levende, Nationers materielle Tilbagegang ved Berøringen med Europæerne. Dansk Månedsskrift 2/Ekstrahæfte: 85–110.

——. 1974 [1877]. *Danish Greenland, its People and Products*. Montreal: McGill-Queens University Press.

Robert, Dana L., ed. 2003. *Converting Colonialism: Visions and Realities in Mission History, 1706–1914*. Grand Rapids, MI: Wm. B. Eerdmans Publishing.

Robert-Lamblin, Joëlle. 1986. *Ammassalik, East Greenland: End or Persistence of an Isolate? Anthropological and Demographical Study on Change, Meddelelser om Grønland, Man & Society 10*. Copenhagen: Danish Polar Centre.

Rønsager, Mette. 2006. Imellem læger og landsmænd. Den vestgrønlandske jordemoderinstitution 1820–1920, PhD diss., Afdeling for Eskimologi og Arktiske Studier, Institut for Tværkulturelle og Regionale Studier, Københavns Universitet, København.

Root, Deborah. 1996. *Cannibal Culture: Art, Appropriation, and the Commodification of Difference*. Boulder, CO: Westview Press.

Rosaldo, Michelle Zimbalist, Louise Lamphere, and Joan Bamberger, eds. 1974. *Woman, Culture and Society*. Stanford, CA: Stanford University Press.

Rosaldo, Renato. 1988. "Ideology, Place, and People without Culture." *Cultural Anthropology* 3 (1): 77–87.

Rose, Nikolas. 1999 [1989]. *Governing the Soul: The Shaping of the Private Self.* London: Free Association Books.

Rose, Peter W. 1992. *Sons of the Gods, Children of Earth: Ideology and Literary Form in Ancient Greece*. Ithaca, NY: Cornell University Press.

Rud, Søren. 2006. "Erobringen af Grønland: opdagelsesrejser, etnologi og forstanderskab i attenhundredetallet." *Historisk Tidsskrift* 106 (2): 488–520.

——. 2007. "Foucaults governmentality-begreb og studiet af kolonialisme." *Den jyske historiker* 116: 182–193.

Rygaard, Jette, and Birgit Kleist Pedersen. 2003. "Lysets hjerte – en rejse til fortiden eller uddrivelsen af historien." *Kosmorama* 232 (Film fra Nord): 153–180.

Schrøder, Urban. 1959. "Enevældens første aar 1670–1700." In *Den danske kirkes historie.* Edited by H.K. and B. Kornerup, 380–443. København: Nordiske Forlag.

Schwarz Lausten, Martin. 1987. *Danmarks kirkehistorie.* København: Gyldendal.

Scott, David 1995. "Colonial Governmentality." *Social Text* 43 (Autumn, 1995): 191–220.

——. 2004. *Conscripts of Modernity.* Durham: Duke University Press.

Scott, Joan W. 1986. "Gender: A Useful Category of Historical Analysis." American Historical Review 91 (5:) 1053–75.

Seiding, Inge Høst, and Peter A. Toft 2011. "Koloniale identiteter: Ægteskaber, fællesskaber og forbrug i Diskobugten i første halvdel af det 19. århundrede." In *Fra vild til verdensborger. Grønlandsk identitet fra kolonitiden til nutidens globalitet.* Edited by Ole Højris and Ole Marquardt, 273–315. Århus: Aarhus Universitetsforlag 2011.

Seiding, Inge Høst. 2012. Married to the Daughters of the Country: Intermarriage and Intimacy in Northwest Greenland ca. 1750 to 1850. PhD diss., *Ilisimatusarfik* (University of Greenland), Nuuk.

Shiach, Morag. 1991. *Helene Cixous: A Politics of Writing.* London: Routledge.

Singh, Yii-Jan. 2007. "Semen, Philosophy, and Paul." *Journal of Philosophy and Scripture* 4 (2): 32–45.

Sissons, Jeffrey. 2005. *First Peoples: Indigenous Cultures and Their Futures.* London: Reaktion Books.

Smith, Jonathan Z. 1990. *Drudgery Divine: On the Comparison of early Christianities and the Religions of late Antiquity,* Jordan Lectures in Comparative Religion 14. London: School of Oriental and African Studies, University of London.

Smith, Linda Tuhiwai. 1999. *Decolonizing Methodologies: Research and Indigenous Peoples.* Dunedin, New Zealand: University of Otago Press.

Söderberg, Staffan. 1974. *Profetens roll i religionsmötet. Iakttagelser från religionsmötets Västgrönland.* Lund, Sweden: Studentlitteratur.

Sonne, Birgitte. 1983. "Blodhævnens ideologi og virkelighed i Grønland før og under missionens påvirkninger." *Chaos* 3:51–63.

——. 1986. "Toornaarsuk, an Historical Proteus." *Arctic Anthropology* 23 (1–2): 199–219.

——. 1999. "Myter og sagn." In *Inuit, kultur og samfund. En grundbog i eskimologi.* Edited by J. Lorentzen, E.L. Jensen and H.C. Gulløv, 20_32. Århus: Systime.

——. 2000. "Heaven Negotiated: The Realms of Death in early Colonial West Greenland." *Etudes Inuit* 24 (2): 65–87.

Sørensen, Axel Kjær. 1983. *Danmark-Grønland i det 20. århundrede – En historisk oversigt*. København: Nyt Nordisk Forlag Arnold Busch.

Sørensen, Bo Wagner. 1991. "Sigende tavshed. Køn og etnicitet i Nuuk. Grønland." *Tidsskriftet Antropologi* 24: 41–58.

——. 1994. "Jagten på den indre grønlænder : køn, kultur og identitet." *Kvinder, køn og forskning* 3 (2): 53–68.

——. 1994. *Magt eller afmagt? : køn, følelser og vold i Grønland*. København: Akademisk forlag.

——. 1997. "Contested Culture: Trifles of Importance." In *Braving the Cold. Continuity and Change in Arctic Clothing*. Edited by C. Buys and J. Oosten 169–187. Leiden: Research School CNWS, School of Asian, African, and Amerindian Studies.

——. 2001. "'Men in Transition': The Representation of Men's Violence Against Women in Greenland." *Violence Against Women* 7 (7): 826–847.

——. 2003. Sød musik eller mislyd i Grønlands hovedstad? *Magasinet Humaniora*, 8–11.

Staples, Robert. 1982. *Black Masculinity: The Black Man's Role in American Society*. San Francisco: Black Scholar's Press.

Stenbæk, Jørgen. 1983. "Religion og politik i den unge danske enevælde." *Religionsvidenskabeligt Tidsskrift* 3: 51–63.

Stoler, Ann Laura. 1995. *Race and the Education of Desire*. Durham, NC: Duke University Press.

——. 2002. *Carnal Knowledge and Imperial Power: Race and the Intimate in Colonial Rule*. Berkeley/Los Angeles: University of California Press.

——. 2009. *Along the Archival Grain: Epistemic Anxieties and Colonial Common Sense*. Princeton, NJ: Princeton University Press.

Stratton, Kimberly B. 2007. *Naming the Witch: Magic, Ideology and Stereotype in the Ancient World*. New York: Columbia University Press.

Sveistrup, P.P. 1943. *Det Almindelige Handelskompagni 1747–1774 med særligt henblik paa dets virksomhed i Grønland*. Vol. 9, *Meddelelser om Grønland*. København: Kommissionen for Videnskabelige Undersøgelser i Grønland, C.A. Reitzels Forlag.

Taylor, Charles. 1989. *Sources of the Self: The Making of the Modern Identity*. Cambridge, MA: Harvard University Press.

Thisted, Kirsten. 1990. "Nationalfølelse og skriftsprog – et studie i de første grønlandske romaner. *Danske studier*" 85 (8/1): 109–129.

——. 1993. Som perler på en snor, fortællestrukturer i grønlandsk fortælletradition, med særligt henblik på forholdet mellem de originale og de udgivne versioner, PhD diss., Eskimologi/Arctic Studies, Copenhagen University, København.

——. 1994. "Om udforskningen af den grønlandske fortælletradition – en forelæsning." *Grønlandsk kultur og samfundsforskning* 1994: 200–221.

——. 1996. "Republication of Greenlandic Tales Collected in the Nineteenth Century." *Grønlandsk kultur og samfundsforskning* 1996: *Cultural and social research in Greenland 95/96. Essays in Honour of Robert Petersen*: 253–264.

——. 1997a. "Dengang i de ikke rigtigt gamle dage" Grønlandsk fortælletradition som kilde til 1700 tallets kulturmøde.' In *Digternes Paryk. Studier i 1700 tallet.* Edited by M. Alenius, 73–86. København: Museum Tusculanums Forlag.

——. 1997b. Introduktion. In *Jens Kreutzmann. Fortællinger og akvareller.* Edited by K. Thisted, 7–49. Nuuk: Atuakkiorfik.

——. 2002. "Teoretiske indfaldsvinkler til grønlandsk litteratur." *Grønlandsk kultur og samfundsforskning* 2002: 107–126.

——. 2003. "Danske grønlandsfiktioner: om billedet af Grønland i dansk litteratur." *Kosmorama* nr. 232: *Film fra Nord*, 32–67

——. 2004a. "Hvem går qivittoq?" Kampen om et litterært symbol eller relationen Danmark – Grønland i postkolonial belysning. *TijdSchrift voor Skandinavistiek* 25 (2): 133–159.

——. 2004b. "Peter Gundel, Dagbogsbreve til læge Jørgen Hvam." *Tidsskriftet Grønland* 2004 (3–4): 81–128.

——. 2006a. "Eskimoeksotisme – et kritisk essay om repræsentationsanalyse." In *Jagten på det eksotiske* (*KULT 3*). Edited by L.B. Christiansen, 61–77. Roskilde: Institut for Kultur og Identitet, RUC.

——. 2006b. "Over deres egen races lig" Om Knud Rasmussens syn på kulturmødet og slægtskabet mellem grønlændere og danskere. *Tidsskriftet Antropologi* 50:131–147.

——. 2009. "Knud Rasmussen." In *Grønland – en refleksiv udfordring.* Edited by O. Høiris, 239–280. Århus: Aarhus Universitetsforlag.

——. 2011. "Nationbuilding – nationbranding. Identitetspositioner og tilhørsforhold under det selvstyrede Grønland." In *Fra vild til verdensborger. Grønlandsk identitet fra kolonitiden til nutidens globalitet.* Edited by Ole Højris and Ole Marquardt, 597–637. Århus: Aarhus Universitetsforlag.

Thomas, Nicholas. 1994. *Colonialism's Culture: Anthropology, Travel and Government.* Cambridge: Polity Press.

Thomsen, Hanne. 1998. "Ægte grønlændere og nye grønlændere — om forskellige opfattelser af grønlandskhed." *Den jyske historiker* 81:21–56.

Thomsen, Marianne Lykke. 2006. "Hvorfor Arktisk Råd? — Et grønlandsk perspektiv." In *Grønland i verdenssamfundet.* Edited by H. Petersen, 199–213. Nuuk: Atuagkat.

Thorleifsen, Daniel. 1991. Politikeren Augo Lynge : Augo Lynges ide om ligestilling mellem danske og grønlændere ca. 1930–1950, MA thesis, Aarhus University, Århus, Denmark.

——. 1999. "The Prelude to Greenland's Commercial Fishery." In *From Sealing to Fishing: Social and Economic Change in Greenland, 1850–1940.* Edited by O. Marquardt, P. Holm, and D.J. Starkey, 62–83. Esbjerg: Fiskeri – og søfartsmuseet.

Thuesen, Søren. 1988. *Fremad, opad. Kampen for en moderne grønlandsk identitet.* København: Rhodos.

——. 2007. *Fremmed blandt landsmænd. Grønlandske kateketer i kolonitiden.* Nuuk: Atuagkat.

Troeltsch, Ernst. 1992 [1912; English orig. 1931]. *The Social Teaching of the Christian Churches.* Vol. 2. Translated by O. Wyon [orig. ed. 1931]. Louisville, KY: Westminster John Knox Press.

Tróndheim, Gitte. 2004. "Kinship in Contemporary Urban Settings." In *Dynamics and Shifting Perspectives: Arctic Societies and Research, Proceedings of the First IPSSAS Seminar, Nuuk 2002.* Edited by M. Therrien, 85–98. Nuuk: Ilisimatusarfik.

——. 2010. Slægtskab og køn i grønlandske bysamfund: Følelser af forbundethed. PhD diss., Ilisimatusarfik, Ilimmarfik-instituttet, Nuuk 2010.

van der Veer, Peter. 2001. *Imperial Encounters: Religion and Modernity in India and Britain.* Princeton, NJ: Princeton University Press.

van Toorn, Penny. 2006. *Writing Never Arrives Naked: Early Aboriginal Cultures of Writing in Australia.* Canberra: Aboriginal Studies Press.

Viemose, Jørgen. 1976. *Dansk kolonipolitik i Grønland.* København: Demos.

Viswanathan, Gauri. 1989. *Masks of Conquest: Literary Study and British Rule in India.* New York: Colombia University Press.

——. 1998. *Outside the Fold: Conversion, Modernity, and Belief.* Oxford/New York: Oxford University Press.

von Braun, Christina. 2001. *Versuch über den Schwindel. Religion, Schrift, Bild, Geschlecht.* Zürich: Pendo Verlag.

——. 2009 [1985]. *NICHT ICH. Logik – Lüge – Libido.* Berlin: Aufbau.

Waucaush, Chad M. 2009. Becoming Christian, Remaining Ojibwe: The Emergence of Native American Protestant Christianity in the Great Lakes, 1820–1900. PhD diss., Michigan State University.

Wallace, Peter G. 2004. *The Long European Reformation.* In the series *European History in Perspective.* Edited by J. Black. Hampshire/New York: Palgrave Macmillan.

Weber, Max 1996 [1930]. *The Protestant Ethic and the Spirit of Capitalism.* London: Routledge.

Webster, Anthony K. 2006. "Keeping the Word: On Orality and Literacy (with a Sideways Glance at Navajo)." *Oral Tradition* 21 (2): 296–324.

Weihe, Hans-Jørgen Wallin. 1999. Social Work and Missionary Work as Part of the Power Game: A Discussion through two Examples; Hans Egede Missionary in Greenland 1721–1736 and the Norwegian Saami Mission in Finnmark; The Period of Establishment of Missions and Social Services 1888–1900. PhD diss., School of Social Work, Lund, Sweden.

Weisner, Merry E. 1998. *Gender, Church and State in Early Modern Germany.* London: Longman.

White, Owen. 1999. *Children of the French Empire: Miscegenation and Colonial Society in French West Africa, 1895–1960*. Oxford: Oxford University Press.

Wilhjelm, Henrik. 1997. *De store opdragere. Grønlands seminarer i det 19. århundrede*. København: Det Grønlandske Selskab.

——. 2001. *"af tilbøielighed er jeg grønlandsk" Om Samuel Kleinschmidts liv og værk*. Vol. XXXIV, *Det Grønlandske selskabs skrifter*. København: Det Grønlandske Selskab.

——. 2005. Menneske (inuk) og kristen så? *Dansk Teologisk Tidsskrift* 68 årg. (2005/1): 1–20.

——. 2008. *De Nye Grønlændere, Det Grønlandske selskabs skrifter XL*. København: Det Grønlandske Selskab.

Williamson, Karla Jessen. 2006. Inuit Post-colonial Gender Relations in Greenland. PhD diss., University of Aberdeen, Scotland.

Witte, John. Jr. 2002. *Law and Protestantism: The Legal Teachings of the Lutheran Reformation*. Cambridge: Cambridge University Press.

——. 2006. *God's Joust, God's Justice: Law and Religion in the Western Tradition*. Grand Rapids, MI: William B. Eerdmans Publishing.

Young, Robert J.C. 1995. *Colonial Desire: Hybridity in Theory, Culture and Race*. London: Routledge.

Žižek, Slavoj. 2001. *On Belief*. London: Routledge.

——. 2008. *Violence. Six Sideways Reflections*. New York: Picador.

Web References

Arctic-Council. 1996. Declaration on the Establishment of the Arctic Council, accessed 2 February 2009. http://arctic-council.org/filearchive/Declaration%20on%20the%20Establishment%20of%20the%20Arctic%20Council-1. pdf.

Bell, Richard. 2002. Bell's Theorem. *Aboriginal Art – It's a White Thing!* accessed 8 March 2010. http://www.kooriweb.org/bell/theorum.html.

Heinrich, Jens 2010. http://www.ilisimatusarfik.gl/Portals/0/Ekstern/Generelt/Dokumenter/Jens%20Heinrich%20Eske%20Brun%20og%20det%20moderne%20Gr%C3%B8nlands%20tilblivelse.pdfInternational Whaling Commission. *Aboriginal Subsistence Whaling*, accessed 18 April 2010. http://www.iwcoffice.org/conservation/aboriginal.htm.

International Whaling Commission. *Workshop Report*, accessed 18 April 2010. http://iwcoffice.org/_documents/meetings/workshop2003.pdf.

International Whaling Commission. *Progress Report*, accessed 19 April 2010. http://iwcoffice.org/_documents/sci_com/2002progreports/SC-54-ProgRep%20StVincent.pdf.

Inuit Circumpolar Council (ICC). *ICC Greenland: Message from the President of ICC-Greenland*, accessed 13 April 2010. http://www.inuit.org/index.php?id=134.

Johansen, Lars-Emil, Høgni Hoydal, and Sofia Rossen. 2007. *WSPA MISBRUGER GRØNLAND*, Copenhagen: Folketinget, accessed 19 April 2010. http://www.dnag.dk/Default.aspx?SectionId=323.

Makah. *Recent Whaling*, accessed 18 April 2010. http://www.makah.com/whalingrecent.html.

National Native Title Tribunal, *Native Title Claimant Applications Guide*, accessed 17 April 2010. http://www.nntt.gov.au/Publications-And-Research/Publications/Documents/Booklets/Native%20title%20claimant%20applications%20April%202008.pdf.

WSPA. 2008. *Exploding Myths. An exposè of the commercial elements of Greenlandic Aboriginal Subsistence Whaling*, accessed 13 April 2010. http://www.wspa-usa.org/Images/ExplodingMyths_tcm21-3402.pdf.

Index